The Works of Shonda Rhimes

SCREEN STORYTELLERS

Series Editor: Anna Weinstein

THE WORKS OF SHONDA RHIMES

Edited by Anna Weinstein

BLOOMSBURY ACADEMIC
NEW YORK • LONDON • OXFORD • NEW DELHI • SYDNEY

BLOOMSBURY ACADEMIC
Bloomsbury Publishing Inc
1385 Broadway, New York, NY 10018, USA
50 Bedford Square, London, WC1B 3DP, UK
29 Earlsfort Terrace, Dublin 2, Ireland

BLOOMSBURY, BLOOMSBURY ACADEMIC and the Diana logo are trademarks of Bloomsbury Publishing Plc

First published in the United States of America 2024

Editors © Anna Weinstein, 2024

Each chapter © of Contributors, 2024

For legal purposes the Acknowledgments on p. xiii constitute an extension of this copyright page.

Cover design: Eleanor Rose
Cover photograph: Simone Ashley and Jonathan Bailey in *Bridgerton*, Series 3, Episode 1, 2024 © Liam Daniel / Netflix
Credit: Collection Christophel / ArenaPAL www.arenapal.com

All rights reserved. No part of this publication may be reproduced or transmitted in any form or by any means, electronic or mechanical, including photocopying, recording, or any information storage or retrieval system, without prior permission in writing from the publishers.

Bloomsbury Publishing Inc does not have any control over, or responsibility for, any third-party websites referred to or in this book. All internet addresses given in this book were correct at the time of going to press. The author and publisher regret any inconvenience caused if addresses have changed or sites have ceased to exist but can accept no responsibility for any such changes.

A catalog record for this book is available from the Library of Congress.

ISBN: HB: 978-1-5013-9966-4
PB: 978-1-5013-9970-1
ePDF: 978-1-5013-9968-8
eBook: 978-1-5013-9967-1

Series: Screen Storytellers

Typeset by Deanta Global Publishing Services, Chennai, India

To find out more about our authors and books visit www.bloomsbury.com and sign up for our newsletters.

CONTENTS

Preface: The Influence of Screenwriters · viii
Acknowledgments · xiii

INTRODUCTION: THE INFLUENCE OF SHONDA RHIMES · 1
Anna Weinstein

Part I
HOW SHE WORKS
Creating Television Series

Chapter 1
SCANDAL AS A NEW SERIES MODEL · 21
   William Rabkin

Chapter 2
THE ART OF DEVELOPING "HUMANISTIC" FEMALE CHARACTERS · 33
   Rosanne Welch

Chapter 3
CRAFTING THE PILOT: SOMEONE ARRIVES · 42
   Rani Deighe Crowe

Part II
SIGNIFICANT WORKS
Normalizing Diverse Representation

Chapter 4
COLOR-AWARE CASTING · 53
   Chriss Williams

Chapter 5
BLACK MATERNAL BODIES ON THE SCREEN: SHONDALAND AND THE NEW REPRESENTATIONAL PARADIGM OF BLACK MOTHERHOOD · 65
   Zsuzsanna Lénárt-Muszka

Chapter 6
REWORKING THE "MONSTROUS MOTHER" FOR THE MODERN ERA   77
Louise Coopey

Chapter 7
RESPECTABILITY IN SHONDALAND: VILLAINOUS QUEERINGS   86
Sébastien Mignot

Chapter 8
FROM FAMILY SHAME TO DOCTOR'S PRIDE: SHIFTING TRANS NARRATIVES ON *GREY'S ANATOMY*   98
Kara Raphaeli

Chapter 9
RESTORATIVE VERSUS RETRIBUTIVE JUSTICE: THEMES FROM *HOW TO GET AWAY WITH MURDER*   110
Sara Correia-Hopkins and Cate Correia-Hopkins

Chapter 10
HIDDEN FANTASTIC MODALITIES OF SHONDA RHIMES'S PROCEDURAL DRAMAS   120
Ida Yoshinaga

Chapter 11
BRIDGERTON: THE PROGRESSIVE PERIOD PASTICHE   133
Shelley Anne Galpin

Chapter 12
BRIDGERTON'S QUEER ETHOS   145
Anthony Guy Patricia

Part III
RECENT WORKS
Building Shondaland

Chapter 13
ENSEMBLE STORYTELLING IN *HOW TO GET AWAY WITH MURDER*   157
E. Deidre Pribram

Chapter 14
STREAMING SHONDALAND: SHONDA RHIMES AND
NETFLIX—FROM *BRIDGERTON* AND BEYOND   168
    Sheri Chinen Biesen

Chapter 15
HEY, PELOTON! SAY YES!   177
    Stephanie O'Brien

List of Contributors   187
Bibliography   191
Index   200

Preface

The Influence of Screenwriters

According to a 2018 research report released by the Lyda Hill Foundation and the Geena Davis Institute on Gender in Media, two characters in Shonda Rhimes's television series have been groundbreaking in motivating women and young girls to pursue STEM careers: Meredith Grey (Ellen Pompeo) from *Grey's Anatomy* (2005–) and Addison Montgomery (Kate Walsh) from *Grey's* and its spin-off *Private Practice* (2007–13).[1] But for Dr. Hope Jackson, assistant professor of surgery at the George Washington School of Medicine and Health Sciences, it was another *Grey's* character that inspired her career: Miranda Bailey (Chandra Wilson). "[she] was one of the first women of color I'd ever seen in the surgical field—and not just on TV."[2] Jackson served as a medical advisor on *Grey's* after completing medical school and three years of residency, working closely with veteran Shondaland writer-producer Zoanne Clack, who is also a medical doctor. "In the real world, women of color make up less than half of all medical school graduates; of that number, only 7.9 percent are black women," Jackson said. "So *Grey's* will always be more than just a television show that I watch or worked on . . . It is and will always be a powerful reminder of the importance of representation and the positive impact it can have."[3]

The precise impact of Shonda Rhimes's television series, and those produced by Shondaland, is difficult to quantify. But there are several datasets from research studies reported by Geena Davis's institute, among others,[4] that are important to consider in determining how Rhimes's work has influenced television in the past two decades. Though she has said she wrote *Grey's* "with no character descriptions, no clue as to what anyone should look like"[5]—except Bailey, who she initially pictured as a "tiny blonde with curls"[6]—and her goal in casting the *Grey's* pilot was to hire the best actors, Rhimes changed course with her third series, *Scandal* (2012–18), intentionally creating a show centered on a Black woman. The character of Olivia Pope (Kerry Washington) is inspired by real-life DC crisis manager Judy Smith, and in reimagining Smith's occupation for a fictional character leading a television series,[7] Rhimes not only created the first network drama in thirty-eight years to feature a Black woman;[8] she also positioned this character in an elite career with immense power.

There were few representations of Black women in film and television before the 1990s,[9] and a study of Black female characters in screen stories released between 1997 and 2006 found that 60 percent were depicted as service workers.[10] As of 2019, according to research from Davis's institute, Black women characters in film and television now have careers that are predominately "high status" and these characters make up "14 percent of prominent characters on prime-time television shows and 6 percent of prominent characters in popular films." While these numbers may not sound high, in fact the representation of Black women in film now "mirrors the US population, and their representation in television is even better."[11]

If there is any ever question whether screenwriters and their work can have an impact, one only needs to look to Shonda Rhimes as a source of inspiration.

The Screen Storytellers Series

The Screen Storytellers book series is motivated by my desire to bring much-deserved attention to screenwriters who have developed films and television shows of significant aesthetic or cultural achievement, critical acclaim, or commercial success, and to offer close readings of the films and series from the perspective of story, screenwriting craft, audience reception, and cultural impact. Designed for students, professors, and enthusiastic consumers of film and television, the books in this series will include chapters that are both accessible and critically rigorous.

This volume, *The Works of Shonda Rhimes*, is the first in what I hope will be an enduring study of contemporary and historically significant screenwriters' works, each book exploring films and television series written or created by one writer. I expect that over time we will include volumes on some of the most widely celebrated screenwriters whose work is regularly taught at the university level; however, a primary goal for this series is to critically examine important films and television series created by screenwriters whose work is commonly left out of course syllabi, including writers of color, international writers, LGBTQ+ writers, and women writers, as well as male writers whose films and series are rarely studied in screenwriting classrooms.

Most often when we study cinema we reflect on the directors' choices since directors have traditionally been considered the "authors" of film. With the rise of television in recent years and the notoriety of many writers bringing stories to the small screen, audiences are becoming more aware of the significance of the writer in the process of screen storytelling. The influx of television series and the major networks expanding to now include Netflix, Amazon, Hulu, Apple TV+, and other streaming platforms has transformed not only the film and television industry but also the ways in which the authorship of screen stories is acknowledged and referenced. As such, it seemed appropriate to launch this book series with a volume on Shonda Rhimes, whose series have continued to test the boundaries of what audiences will accept (and delight in) in terms of both character representation and story delivery, meanwhile breaking records in viewership, longevity, and fandom.

Each semester, I poll my screenwriting students at the beginning of the term to see what names come to mind when they think of the most important film and television writers of all time. Interestingly, despite the television boom in the past decade, the list always begins with feature film writers. The list of writers that emerge—and I usually scribble the names on the white board as students shout them out—is nearly always comprised of writers who are also directors. Quentin Tarantino, James Cameron, Greta Gerwig, Jordan Peele, Joel and Ethan Coen, Christopher Nolan, Rian Johnson, Edgar Wright, and Nora Ephron are names that make the list just about every semester. I encourage the students to think of screenwriters who do not typically direct their own films, who work (or worked) exclusively as writers or writer-producers. This usually stumps students for a moment until they remember that I'm also looking for television writers. The first name they almost always call out is Shonda Rhimes (hence this book), and then they gain momentum—Ryan Murphy, Amy Sherman-Palladino, J. J. Abrams, Aaron Sorkin, Joss Whedon, David Benioff, the Duffer brothers. And then they begin to peter off. I offer support at this stage, naming films and television shows I'm certain they admire and ask if they know who wrote the screenplays or created the series. "How about *Friends*?" I ask. "Who created that series?" Sometimes they know the answer (David Crane and Marta Kauffman), though not always. And we continue down this road as I offer a list of writers who I think they should know and the names of the films they wrote and series they created. I also offer the names of a handful of films that I suspect they have seen (*Forrest Gump*, *The Insider*, *The Curious Case of Benjamin Button*, *A Star Is Born* [2018], *Dune*, *Killers of the Flower Moon*, for instance) and magically surprise them revealing that they were all written or co-written by the same screenwriter (Eric Roth).

It is probably safe to say that most aspiring screenwriters, whether studying in a college setting or on their own, know more about directors and their films than they do about screenwriters and their screenplays or television creators and their pilots and series. This is not only a missed opportunity; it's detrimental to their learning. In much the same way that it's crucial for aspiring directors to study a filmmaker's canon, it's critical for aspiring writers to study a writer's oeuvre.

It is problematic that only a select few books offer close examinations of screenwriters' bodies of works. Scholars look to William Goldman's books for this type of in-depth study or perhaps to volumes on the works of famed playwrights such as David Mamet or Sam Shepard. William Goldman, Billy Wilder, Joseph Mankiewicz, Paddy Chayefsky, and Preston Sturges are widely known as some of the best screenwriters of all time, and each of these writers has at least one book dedicated to the study of his work.

It is notable that the above list includes only one demography of writers. Despite the fact that the film and television industry has historically minimized participation from BIPOC, LGBTQ+, and women writers (except in the earliest days of the film industry when women were at the forefront of developing the art form), there are a great many ingenious underrepresented writers who have gifted audiences with commercially successful and critically acclaimed films and television series, many of which have also—much like in the case of Shonda Rhimes's shows—had considerable impact on audiences worldwide. Not to mention the countless international writers working outside the Hollywood system who have amassed bevies of films and television series that require careful examination.

Published criticism and interrogation of the craft and cultural impact of screenwriting is not only invaluable to those studying the art form; it also helps to ensure that screenwriters' contributions to global film and television industries are not lost in the archives. My hope is that the Screen Storytellers book series will accomplish both these goals: teaching student scholars about the craft and cultural impact of screenwriting and safeguarding the work of some of our most beloved and noteworthy screenwriters.

Notes

1 Geena Davis Institute on Gender in Media, "Portrayals of Female STEM Characters in TV and Film Haven't Improved in 10 Years," *Geena Davis Institute*, September 25, 2018, https://seejane.org/gender-in-media-news-release/portrayals-of-female-stem-characters-in-tv-and-film-havent-improved-in-10-years/. See also Elisabeth C. McLemore, Sonia Ramamoorthy, Carrie Y. Peterson, and Barbara L. Bass, "Women in Surgery: Bright, Sharp, Brave, and Temperate," *The Permanente Journal*,

54–9, https://www.ncbi.nlm.nih.gov/pmc/articles/PMC3442763/. In 2010, more women applied for surgical residencies in medical school than ever before, 35 percent of all applicants; and there were 41 percent more women entering medical school in 2011 than there were four decades earlier in 1970.
2 Jackson quoted in McKenna Princing, "I Was a Medical Advisor for *Grey's Anatomy*. Here's What I Learned," *Right as Rain, UW Medicine*, October 4, 2017, https://rightasrain.uwmedicine.org/well/stories/i-was-medical-advisor-greys-anatomy-heres-what-i-learned.
3 Ibid.
4 See also the latest research reports from UC San Diego's Center for the Study of Women in Television and Film, USC's Annenberg Inclusion Initiative, and the Writers Guild of America West (WGA).
5 Rhimes quoted in Oprah.com, "Shonda Rhimes Talks to Oprah," https://www.oprah.com/omagazine/oprah-interviews-greys-anatomy-creator-shonda-rhimes_2/all.
6 Ibid.
7 See Shonda Rhimes's MasterClass, "Shonda Rhimes: Writing for Television," MasterClass, segment "Creating Memorable Characters, Part 1," https://www.masterclass.com/classes/shonda-rhimes-teaches-writing-for-television/chapters/creating-memorable-characters-part-1.
8 Teresa Graves was the first Black actress to lead a sixty-minute drama on network television, *Get Christie Love!* (1974–5). See Cary O'Dell, "Why 'Christie Love' Matters," *Library of Congress Blogs*, April 5, 2023, https://blogs.loc.gov/now-see-hear/2023/04/why-christie-love-matters/.
9 Geena Davis Institute on Gender in Media, "Representations of Black Women in Hollywood," *The Geena Davis Institute*, 2021, https://seejane.org/wp-content/uploads/rep-of-black-women-in-hollywood-report.pdf.
10 Nancy Signorielli, "Race and Sex in Prime Time: A Look at Occupations and Occupational Prestige," *Mass Communication and Society* 12 (2009): 332–52.
11 Geena Davis Institute on Gender in Media, "Representations of Black Women in Hollywood."

ACKNOWLEDGMENTS

I'm sure I speak for all the contributors to this volume in first thanking Shonda Rhimes and her collaborators at Shondaland for gifting audiences worldwide with thousands of hours of smart, entertaining, and innovative television in the past two decades. As this book focuses primarily on the television creators and writers, we most often address these individuals in these pages; however, I would like to use this space to also thank the producers, directors, actors, editors, story editors, and all the other creatives who have helped bring Shondaland's stories to the screen.

There is just one name on the cover of this volume, but this collection exists because of the sixteen contributors who generously devoted a combined hundreds of hours to distill their scholarly curiosities and expertise into chapters that I hope will be as transcendent for readers as they have been for me. A very sincere thank-you to Katie Gallof Houck for championing a book series on film and television writers. We first began discussing the concept for the series in 2019, and I will be forever grateful for her initial enthusiasm as well as her patience and support as the series has taken shape over the past few years. Thanks also to Stephanie Grace-Petinos at Bloomsbury for her editorial assistance and to the volume editors who have jumped on board to participate. I am looking forward to seeing these books develop in the years to come.

In large part, this book exists because of support from Kennesaw State University. I am grateful to the Radow College of Humanities and Social Sciences, to my English Department Chair Dr. John Havard, and to my brilliantly engaged colleagues and students whose conversations about film and television inspire me week after week. Dr. Amy Buddie, Jennifer Harb, and Michelle Chatelain in the Office of Undergraduate Research deserve a special mention for their generous support of the Women Writers of Film & Television (WWFTV) digital humanities project, which has in many ways contributed to my work on this book. Thanks also to Dr. Nurudeen Akinyemi and Saundra Rogers in the Center for Africana Studies for supporting WWFTV, as well as the many student scholars who have worked on the project in the past few years. I am also grateful to Dr. Stacy Keltner's support through the Gender and Women's Studies program—and especially our weekly writing sessions, which offered the time and space to work on this volume.

As always, a big thank-you to my family and friends—in this case, in particular, my parents and sister who have joined me virtually in recent months to watch *Grey's* (my parents) and *Private Practice* (my sister). What fun! Meredith may have Cristina, but I have Jody, Rachel, and Connie. My people. And finally, Chris, Abraham, and Gabriel, you have my heart and fill my life in ways that film and television cannot.

INTRODUCTION

The Influence of Shonda Rhimes

Anna Weinstein

In the pilot episode of *Grey's Anatomy* (2005–), Meredith Grey (Ellen Pompeo) and Cristina Yang (Sandra Oh) are established as brilliant and competitive rising stars in Seattle Grace Hospital's surgical residency program. On their first day, Meredith, Cristina, and their fellow interns are charged with determining why a patient, fifteen-year-old Katie, is having life-threatening seizures. "The clock is ticking fast, people," Dr. Derek Shepherd (Patrick Dempsey) tells them. "If we're going to save Katie's life, we have to do it soon." Meredith and Cristina get to work reviewing Katie's case files. Cristina suggests that Katie might have an aneurysm, which Meredith dismisses (no blood on the CT, no headaches), but then while telling Cristina that Katie is a Miss Teen hopeful and her talent is "rhythmic gymnastics," Meredith suddenly realizes something.

CUT TO: Meredith and Cristina running to find Derek. As he busily enters an elevator, Cristina calls out, "Dr. Shepherd, just one moment." Derek waits. "Katie competes in beauty pageants," Cristina says breathlessly. "I know that," he snips, "but we have to save her life anyway." Frantic, Meredith and Cristina share their suspicion—that Katie might have a ruptured aneurysm, a result of a recent fall while practicing for the upcoming pageant.

"Do you know what the chances are a minor fall could burst an aneurysm?" Derek asks rhetorically. "One in a million. Literally." He would know—he's a renowned neurosurgeon. But upon studying Katie's angiogram, Derek discovers that Meredith and Cristina's hypothesis is correct. The case is one in a million.[1]

Looking back at this bold introduction to what would soon become Shonda Rhimes's empire, the "one in a million" discussion is fitting in examining Rhimes as a creative powerhouse in the global television industry. One of the most talked-about women in the history of the medium, journalists and fans have bequeathed her the titles "mogul," "queen," and "legend," to name a few, as well as the National Broadcast Association's designation of her as "one of the greatest storytellers of our time."[2] Off the heels of the publication of her memoir *Year of Yes*, Rhimes gave a TED Talk in which she referred to herself as a "titan."

"I don't tell you this to impress you," she assured her audience.

> I tell you this because I know what you think of when you hear the word *writer*. I tell you this so that all of you out there who work so hard, whether you run a company or a country or a classroom or a store or a home, take me seriously when I talk about working ... I work a lot. Very hard. And I love it.[3]

The moral of her story wasn't in fact that she believed the hype of this titan label. The thesis of her talk had to do with the need to engage in play to find inspiration for work. She had gotten so swept up in the pressures of running a slate of hit television shows in the mid-2010s, she'd lost the "hum" that filled her work with "light and air" and inspired her to strive for greatness. "Work doesn't work without play," she told the roomful of people.[4] Her daughter had asked her to play, and she said "yes." And the more she played with her daughters and her fingers became sticky with bubbles, the more she realized who she was. The hum returned at work—but importantly, it was the hum of life and love. "The more I feel *that* hum," she said, "the more this strange, quivering, uncocooned, awkward, brand new, alive, *non-titan* feels like me."[5]

That was in 2016 while Rhimes was still at ABC, with Shondaland's *Grey's*, *Scandal* (2012–18), and *How to Get Away with Murder* (2014–20)[6] dominating its Thursday night lineup. One year later, Rhimes entered her unprecedented partnership with Netflix, worth at the time an estimated $100 to $150 million, and re-upped in 2021 after the blockbuster success of *Bridgerton*'s (2020–)[7] first season.[8]

Rhimes was born and raised outside Chicago and received her BA from Dartmouth College and her MFA from USC School of Cinema-Television. She began her career writing movies—the critically acclaimed *Introducing Dorothy Dandridge* (1999), which was nominated for eleven Emmys and won five;[9] the mostly dismissed but recently rediscovered *Crossroads* (2002);[10] and the wildly popular *The Princess Diaries 2: Royal Engagement* (2004), which grossed more than $130 million worldwide.[11] On these films, she teamed up with veteran directors Martha Coolidge, Tamra Davis, and Garry Marshall, as well as celebrity actresses and singers Halle Berry, Britney Spears, Anne

Hathaway, and Julie Andrews. An impressive beginning for a career in screenwriting—but still, no indication of what was about to come.

A midseason replacement for ABC in the spring of 2005, *Grey's* was an instant success, the most-watched midseason drama in more than a decade.[12] Rhimes had sold her pilot to the network two years earlier when she was just thirty-three years old. As Sandra Oh said in 2015, "To get anything, any show, past a pilot is a miracle, but to make it ten years is lightning in a bottle. I don't know who rolled the dice at ABC a decade ago on this incredibly talented young woman. But I'm sure they're glad they did."[13] Now in its nineteenth season, *Grey's* was recently renewed for a twentieth. The series has become as much a cultural phenomenon as Rhimes herself an icon. More than five million viewers still tune in each week to watch *Grey's*[14]—down from its height of more than nineteen million viewers during seasons 2 and 3,[15] but still going strong—and the series holds the title of longest-running primetime medical drama on US television.

While *Grey's* has carried on all these years, Shondaland has churned out hit after hit,[16] beginning with ABC's *Private Practice* (2007–13), *Scandal*, *HTGAWM*, and *Station 19* (2018–23), followed by Netflix's *Bridgerton*, *Inventing Anna* (2022), and *Queen Charlotte: A Bridgerton Story* (2023). Fans and critics worldwide marvel at Shondaland's seemingly magical ability to tap into the cross-cultural zeitgeist, delivering stories viewers didn't even know they were craving until they saw the previews. Collectively, Rhimes, her long-standing producing partner Betsy Beers, and the series coming out of Shondaland have been celebrated with awards from the Emmys, Peabody, Producers Guild of America (PGA), Writers Guild of America (WGA), American Film Institute (AFI), NAACP, GLAAD, and others.

Rhimes's success over the past two decades has blazed a trail for women television writers, writers of color, and especially women writers of color. In 2005, Rhimes was one of just a handful of Black women with her own show on US network television. Today, there are more series created by women of color than ever before, accounting for 9.9 percent of all writers developing shows and writing pilots for networks and streamers.[17] Yet still, the statistics are nowhere near approaching parity. In 2022–3, women creators as a whole (including women of color) made up only 23 percent of all creators in broadcast television and 29 percent in streaming shows,[18] and in 2021–2 only 26 percent of all scripted shows were created by BIPOC writers (including both men and women).[19] But with the influx of Black women celebrity actresses, writers, and producers who have created their own shows in the past decade, including Issa Rae, Ava DuVernay, Lena Waithe, Quinta Brunson, Tracy Oliver, Nkechi Okoro Carroll, and Courtney A. Kemp, audiences are aware of the many women of color developing innovative series for network and streamers. In fact, we're now so accustomed to seeing women's names attributed to the credits "created by," "developed by," and "produced by," zoomers (Generation Z) are unlikely to grasp the magnitude of change in the past twenty years and Rhimes's influence on the television shows coming out of Hollywood.

Rhimes's impact on the industry has become known as the "Shonda effect." "...we're all living it,"[20] said Robin Thede, creator and star of HBO's *A Black Lady Sketch Show* (2019–23). Janine Sherman Barrois, creator of *The Kings of Napa* (2022), said of Rhimes,

> She's somebody who did a medical show on a network that made a billion dollars. And then she did it again, and then she did it *again*. There came a point where people looked and said, "Oh my gosh, people of color, Black people, can create global hits, and so we cannot count them out." And then the doors started opening more.[21]

The result of the doors opening to television writers of color, and women writers in particular, is that audiences are gifted opportunities to watch shows centered on characters that look, speak, and behave differently than most of the characters in series released in the first fifty years of the medium. It's not only a matter of representation of race, ethnicity, gender, or sexual identity on screen; it's also about representational *points of view*. Audiences rejoice in seeing reflections of their personal experiences, perspectives, and private struggles—and with the industry widening the playing field to include television creators with diverse backgrounds and life experiences, more viewers begin to recognize themselves in the characters and stories that make it to the screen. In other words, the more inclusive the industry, the wider the reach.[22]

The Women of Grey's Anatomy

With Rhimes's first foray into network television, she strategically conceived of female characters for *Grey's* that embody real women's goals and behaviors. "I wanted to create a world in which you felt as if you were watching very real women," Rhimes told Oprah in 2006. "Most of the women I saw on TV didn't seem like people I actually knew. They felt like ideas of what women are. They never got to be nasty or competitive or hungry or angry. They were often just the loving wife or the nice friend."[23]

Screenwriters understand the relevance of *action* in developing characters for film and television stories. When characters are passive, audiences are less likely to become invested in them and their role in the narrative. By contrast, when characters are active, audiences have opportunities to emotionally engage with the characters' goals and pursuits. Said another way, active characters make interesting characters that viewers can root for. Traditionally in film and television, female characters have not been afforded the same opportunity as their male counterparts to be active participants in the stories. Being "loving" and "nice," as Rhimes described the women she saw on television, is not active; it's supportive—which is exactly how women were so often positioned, in supporting roles. A stereotypical woman character is passive. She does not have agency and is therefore not engaging in a hero's narrative journey; she is merely along for the ride—and most often, that ride is a male hero's journey.

In life (not television), we think of heroes as people who "save lives," and as such, it's easy to consider that Meredith, Cristina, and the other women characters in *Grey's* are heroes because of their chosen careers. But if instead we consider these characters heroes because they, as scholar Jeanine Basinger defines, defy conventional rules, take control of their lives, excel in their work, and form healthy bonds with other women,[24] we can begin to examine how Rhimes constructed these women to have agency in the series. In each episode—beginning with the pilot—the women of *Grey's* are confronted with situations where they must make choices. In addition to being brilliant (which in and of itself would not give them agency), Rhimes positioned them so that they would be forced to choose whether to prioritize their careers over romance or social niceties, among countless other higher-stakes choices. In the pilot, Meredith chooses to shut down any further amorous involvement with Derek, telling him an intimate relationship would be inappropriate. She also chooses to "scrub in" with Derek when she promised the surgery to Cristina. And she boldly demonstrates her knowledge to the chief of surgery, Dr. Richard Webber (James Pickens Jr.), a choice that makes a male colleague, Alex Karev (Justin Chambers), look inept.[25] This three-part string of choices that Meredith makes, which are spaced out over the course of the pilot, is exemplar of all the female leads on the show. Cristina, Izzie (Katherine Heigl), and Miranda Bailey (Chandra Wilson) each have a similar succession of career-prioritizing decisions that they make in the pilot episode (career over romance or politeness).

And this schema for the series pays off episode after episode, season after season, as the women characters strive to advance in their careers while balancing their desire for intimate relationships, marriage, and/or family (children). A now-memed and dramatic example is in season 6, episode 11 ("Blink," written by Debora Cahn), when Cristina offers to trade her boyfriend, trauma surgeon Dr. Owen Hunt (Kevin McKidd), for the opportunity to continue working with cardiothoracic surgeon Dr. Teddy Altman (Kim Raver).[26]

Though Meredith is the title character of the series and her "dark and twisty" interior was inspired by Rhimes's own internal musings (as well as sharing her education at Dartmouth), Rhimes has said it is Cristina she relates to most. As she wrote in *Year of Yes*,

> It's no wonder I leaned into Cristina.... Let her do and think and live in ways that voiced my dreams. She did not want to get married. She had a genius that she chased. She loved her work. I gave her a strident desire to not have children because while I adore children, I wanted to watch her fight that feminist battle and win.[27]

Rhimes wrote that she and Sandra Oh created Cristina together as the series progressed: "A piece of my soul and a piece of Sandra's soul wound around each other and placed on television."[28] But she initially had to battle for Oh to get the role of Cristina, and this fight for a Canadian Korean actress to play the character that effectively became Rhimes's avatar on the small screen wound up being the turning point in her transition from writer-creator to showrunner.[29]

But before the casting stage, while the script was still in development, Rhimes received pushback from the network on her introduction to Meredith in the opening pages of the pilot—specifically her one-night stand with a man she meets in a bar who turns out to be Derek, her soon-to-be boss. Rhimes recalled, "I remember getting called into a room full of old men, and they brought us in to tell me that the show was a problem because nobody was going to watch a show about a woman who would sleep with a man the night before her first day of work. And they were dead serious."[30] Rhimes's producing partner Betsy Beers recalled her response to one executive asking, "What kind of woman would ever, ever do that?" She raised her hand and said, "That would be me."[31]

Of course, that would be countless women, not just Beers. But television's long and sordid history of minimizing or trivializing women's stories and positioning female characters as passive observers rather than active participants is often even more extreme in the case of storylines and imagery around women's sexual pursuits.³² In television's first half-century, discussion and depictions of women enjoying sex were taboo, if not off the table altogether. Rhimes addressed Hollywood's tendency to shame sex and promote violence in a 2015 conversation with *Women's Health*. " I find it fascinating that you can shoot someone in the face on network television, show the whole thing, watch their brains fly out of the back of their head, and no one blinks," she said. "But people are shocked when you show anybody having sex."³³ It was even shocking in the early days of *Grey's* to hear a character say *vagina*, which is why Rhimes and her team were asked by the network's Standards and Practices Department to come up with a euphemism for Bailey to say in a season 2 episode when she births her son.³⁴ (Ironic considering the title of the show that there would be such discomfort with characters naming this part of a woman's anatomy.) "Vajajay" has since entered the public lexicon, and the scene-stealing Bailey has remained a fan favorite of *Grey's*, with Wilson now entering her twentieth season on the show and more recently serving double duty as actor and director (directing twenty-four episodes to date).³⁵

Despite the network executives' initial concerns about Meredith's sex life, the dynamic and unruly female characters on *Grey's* immediately captured America's hearts. More than sixteen million viewers tuned in to watch the pilot on March 27, 2005,³⁶ and nearly eighteen million viewers returned the following week for episode 2.³⁷ As *New York Times* critic Kate Aurthur wrote in May 2005, "When you parse its ratings, 'Grey's Anatomy' underscores one of the real lessons of the current season . . . men will watch shows with a female lead. That goes against conventional wisdom, which dictates that it's easier to get women to watch shows aimed at men."³⁸

The Women Television Creators Who Preceded Shonda Rhimes

Rhimes's success in twenty-first-century network and streaming television stands on the shoulders of the ambitious women writers working in the twentieth century who pushed their way into television writers' rooms—often alongside their husbands or male writing partners, particularly in the early days of the industry—and most notably the women whose business savvy and persistence gained them access to the revered rank of "creator." But the vast majority of women television creators before Rhimes were white and mostly telling stories about white people. A select few women of color succeeded in getting their original series produced. Yvette Lee Bowser was the first Black woman to create and run a scripted television show, *Living Single* (1993–8), starring Queen Latifah. The series was a significant success for the Fox network, attracting viewers across demographics and ranking first place in Black[39] and Latina households,[40] making it all the more surprising when Fox canceled the series while it was still thriving in its fifth season. "If we were number one in Caucasian households, it would not have been canceled that way," Bowser remarked.[41] Perhaps not so surprising is that much like Rhimes's experience with Meredith, network executives were troubled by Bowser's character Maxine (Erika Alexander), who in the pilot script was aggressive and in touch with her sexuality. "I felt that a lot of the male executives were very threatened by her," Bowser said. "They wanted me to take that character completely out of the show."[42] Bowser compromised by moving Maxine from the brownstone where the other characters lived into a house across the street.[43] The series is noteworthy not only because of Bowser's glass-ceiling-breaking achievement as the first Black woman television creator but also because it centered on single Black women.

Despite the lack of ceremony when *Living Single* was canceled, Bowser's perseverance laid the foundation for women television writers of color coming up behind her. Winifred Hervey, who created *In the House* (1995–9) and *The Steve Harvey Show* (1996–2002), actually got her start in the industry before Bowser, writing for series like *Laverne & Shirley*, *Mork & Mindy*, *Benson*, and *The Cosby Show*, before executive producing seasons 2 and 3 of *The Fresh Prince of Bel-Air*. Hervey discussed with the Emmy's Television Academy Foundation her experience as the only woman writing for *The Cosby Show* in the earliest days of the series as well as oftentimes being the only minority writer on a show's staff.[44] Sara Finney-Johnson and Vida Spears (with Ralph Farquhar) created the hit sitcom *Moesha* (1996–2001) and followed that with the spin-off *The Parkers* (1999–2004). Mara Brock Akil,[45] who got her start writing for *Moesha*, created *Girlfriends* (2000–2008), which she developed under the guidance of seasoned television executive Kelly Edwards.[46] The late Eunetta T. Boone, who served as story editor on *The Fresh Prince of Bel-Air* and co-producer on *Living Single*, created *One on One* (2001–6) and its spin-off *Cuts* (2005–6). Felicia D. Henderson, who also got her start on *The Fresh Prince of Bel-Air* and *Moesha*, created the series *Soul Food* (2000–2004), based on the film by George Tillman Jr., though Henderson is not credited as creator of the show. Meg DeLoatch, who began her career writing for *Living Single*, created

Eve (2003–6) after racking up a slew of producing credits, including on Boone's *One on One*. And though *Grey's* star, producer, and director Debbie Allen (who plays Dr. Catherine Avery Fox) has not created a scripted television show, she has been one of the most powerful Black women in Hollywood since the mid-1980s, most notably producing *A Different World* (1988–93), for which she also directed dozens of episodes.[47] Whoopi Goldberg is another legendary multihyphenate working in the 1980s and 1990s, who entered the film and television industry after the success of her one-woman Broadway show, which she wrote. With Tammy Ader, she developed the female-centric series *Strong Medicine* (2000–2006), also serving as executive producer.

It is critical to note the role of mentorship in the careers of these trailblazing Black women television writers, directors, and producers from the 1990s and early 2000s. Much like *Grey's* has served as an incubator for Shondaland's most recent series creators—*HTGAWM* creator Peter Nowalk, *Station 19* creator Stacy McKee, and *Bridgerton* creator Chris Van Dusen have all been with Rhimes/Shondaland since the early days of *Grey's*—the television series in the 1990s produced by Black women created mentorship opportunities for emerging Black women television writers, several of whom went on to create their own shows, particularly after the success of *Grey's*.[48] Rhimes herself has noted that mentorship by prominent Black producer Debra Martin Chase, who produced *The Princess Diaries 2*, was instrumental in teaching her about the business.[49] But before *Grey's*, besides the female show creators detailed above, if television series written by women were picked up by the networks, these women were almost exclusively Caucasian.

Several of the earliest successful television shows were created by women, and because they were firsts in an emerging medium, these women developed standards and practices still followed by television writers today. Irna Phillips, who passed away in 1973, was likely the first woman to get a scripted series broadcast on television; her short-form and short-lived *These Are My Children* (1949) premiered on NBC in January 1949 and was canceled four months later.[50] Phillips was forty-seven when the series aired and was already firmly established as a creator of "radio stories," bringing in $250,000 annually (more than $3 million in today's dollars[51]) with a dedicated daily fan base of ten million female listeners from around the country.[52] Like Rhimes, Phillips was born and raised in Chicago. She is known for pioneering the soap opera genre, and after her first failed attempt, she created four shows that stayed on the air for decades: *Guiding Light* (1952–2009), co-created with Agnes Nixon; *As the World Turns* (1956–2010); *Another*

World (1964–99), co-created with William J. Bell; and her final show, *Days of Our Lives* (1965–), co-created with Ted Corday and Allan Chase, currently in its fifty-ninth season. Phillips's series leaned heavily on dialogue to carry the stories' action, a holdover from her days in radio and a practice still used in television today.[53] But even more significant is that Phillips was one of the first television creators to run multiple scripted serialized shows simultaneously, mapping the narrative and character arcs within and across episodes, seasons, and series. In the 1930s, while developing storylines for her daily radio program *Today's Children*, she had to find a way to plan and effectively stay ahead of the story threads. Phillips detailed her strategy for this in her unpublished memoir, *All My Worlds*,[54] which provides a fascinating glimpse into what has since become standard practice for television creators and showrunners working with staff writers to map stories for a season.

Two chapters in this volume discuss other historic female show creators: E. Deidre Pribram's chapter, "Ensemble Storytelling in *How to Get Away with Murder*," offers insights into pioneering television writer, producer, and actress Gertrude Berg, creator of *The Goldbergs* (1949–57), and the creative partnership between Lucille Ball and Jess Oppenheimer on *I Love Lucy* (1951–7);[55] and Chriss Williams's chapter, "Color-Aware Casting," traces the disruptive effects of *Lucy*'s depiction of an interracial couple on television. Madelyn (Pugh) Davis, though not a co-creator on *Lucy*, was a significant force behind the series and important to mention in detailing early women writers as she was one of television's first comedy writers, scripting all 181 episodes alongside her writing partner Bob Carroll Jr.[56] Marlo Thomas was also a key player in advancing women's roles both on- and offscreen with her groundbreaking television series *That Girl* (1966–71). Though she did not create or write for the series, she did develop (in fact, conceive) the show's concept and served as uncredited executive producer via her role as head of Daisy Productions.[57] Created by Sam Denoff and Bill Persky, *That Girl* was venerated as a feminist first, but for the most part, the episodes were written by men (of the fifty-six credited writers on the show, only eight were women).[58]

More women television writers began working in the 1970s after James L. Brooks and Allan Burns hired a staff of women writers for *The Mary Tyler Moore Show* (1970–7),[59] produced by MTM Enterprises, an independent production company that Moore established in 1969 with her then husband Grant Tinker. Also in 1969, Joan Ganz Cooney co-created *Sesame Street* (1969–) with Lloyd Morrisett, which is one of the longest-running series in the history of television outside the soap genre. Rarely mentioned in screenwriting scholarship is Blanche Hanalis, who was a prominent figure in 1960s and 1970s television, writing for multiple series before developing the hit show *Little House on the Prairie* (1974–83), based on the novels by Laura Ingalls Wilder.

Other notable television series created by women in the 1970s and 1980s include *Family* (1976–80, Jay Presson Allen), *The Facts of Life* (1979–88, Jenna McMahon and Dick Clair), *Cagney & Lacey* (1981–8, Barbara Avedon and Barbara Corday), *Dynasty* (1981–9, Esther Shapiro and Richard Alan Shapiro), *Scarecrow and Mrs. King* (1983–7, Eugenie Ross-Leming and Brad Buckner), *Kate & Allie* (1984–9, Sherry Coben), *The Golden Girls* (1985–92, Susan Harris), *Designing Women* (1986–93, Linda Bloodworth-Thomason), *L.A. Law* (1986–94, Terry Louise Fisher and Steven Bochco), *The Wonder Years* (1988–93, Carol Black and Neal Marlens), and *Murphy Brown* (1988–98, Diane English). Susan Harris and Jenna McMahon's work in these decades (and into the 1990s) is especially noteworthy as they both created multiple long-running shows. In addition to *The Golden Girls*, Harris created *Soap* (1977–81), *Benson* (1979–86), *Empty Nest* (1988–95), and *Nurses* (1991–4), among others; and McMahon (along with Clair) created *It's a Living* (1980–9) and *Mama's Family* (1983–90).

Many contemporary television viewers are familiar with Marta Kauffman's wide-reaching success in the 1990s with *Friends* (1994–2004, co-created with David Crane), but it's likely that few casual consumers of television are aware of women creators from the 1990s such as Susan Borowitz (*The Fresh Prince of Bel-Air*, 1990–6, co-created with Andy Borowitz), Deborah Joy LeVine (*Lois & Clark*, 1993–7), Beth Sullivan (*Dr. Quinn, Medicine Woman*, 1993–8), April Kelly (*Boy Meets World*, 1993–2000, co-created with Michael Jacobs), Winnie Holzman (*My So-Called Life*, 1994–5), Amy Lippman (*Party of Five*, 1994–2000, co-created with Christopher Keyser), and Dottie Dartland Zicklin (*Caroline in the City*, 1995–9, co-created with Fred Barron and Marco Pennette; and *Dharma & Greg*, 1997–2002, co-created with Chuck Lorre).

While this list is by no means exhaustive and may in fact read as impressive, it is important to recognize that these women television creators were the exception to the rule in the 1970s through 1990s as few women writers—even those with extensive writing credits—were able to get their original series produced.[60] By situating Shonda Rhimes's work in the past two decades in the context of women's work creating television series in the first five decades of the medium, we can better understand the magnitude of Rhimes's accomplishments.

Shonda Rhimes's Innovations in Television

To properly introduce Rhimes's contributions to the global television industries, it is necessary to detail the ways in which she broke barriers as a woman television creator and producer in the early 2000s, reimagining women's placement and portrayals in screen stories. Still, this engagement with *Grey's* and with Rhimes as a woman series creator-producer should be read as merely a launchpad for a wide variety of critical interrogations of Shondaland's television shows. As readers can see from the table of contents, the chapters in this volume span a range of topics, but they all have one thing in common: all are written by scholars interested in examining the ways in which Rhimes has disrupted the television industry, innovating the art form and/or business model of creating, producing, and marketing shows for global audiences. Each contributor to this collection has expertise in a unique area of scholarship, including screenwriting, television producing, legal studies, women in film/television, LGBTQ+ representation, speculative fiction/fantasy narratives, BIPOC representation, industry studies, and more. While not all Shondaland television series are covered in depth in this book, considerable attention is given to the most-watched shows, especially *Grey's*, *Private Practice*, *Scandal*, *HTGAWM*, and *Bridgerton*, offering new ways of thinking about how Rhimes's work has helped to transform the medium and the impact of these changes on viewers, as well as how Shondaland's series have evolved in the past two decades.

My goal with this collection is to offer emerging screenwriters and scholars of television—in addition to informed consumers of television—accessible essays that offer insights into both the craft and cultural significance of Rhimes's series. To that end, I commissioned short chapters on topics such as pilot pacing and structure, genre, various aspects of character and thematic representation, as well as the intricacies of Shondaland's business practices, which should appeal to and be useful to a cross-section of readers. Importantly, there is not one way or a correct way to read this book. Readers are encouraged to navigate directly to chapters covering facets of their favorite series or topics of interest to them. Or readers may read the collection from start to finish. Those who read the complete book are likely to discover fascinating correlations within and across the television series under examination.

Millions of viewers around the world binge (and re-binge) Shondaland's series each day. My hope is that this book will inspire casual viewers to become *critical* viewers, thinking deeply about the ways in which they are affected by the characters and storylines in these shows and how Rhimes and her team of collaborators go about crafting the stories for emotional impact and investment. The dark and twisty nature of Meredith as the central figure in Rhimes's first hit series is not only an early example of the types of complicated and emotionally layered characters audiences could expect to see from shows coming out of Shondaland; this depth of character also offers a window into what viewers look for in compelling character studies. The characters across all Shondaland's series run the gamut of human behaviors from polite to loving to selfish to cruel all the way up to (possibly) evil, but if there is an attribute that most of these characters share, it is their vulnerability—the characters' internal private battles are at some point (if not often) in each of the series made very public. Turns out, audiences delight in watching characters that read as honest and brave.

Five seasons into *Grey's*, after a lengthy courtship, Derek (aka "McDreamy") finally proposes to Meredith in the elevator of Seattle Grace Hospital (episode 19, written by Stacy McKee and aptly titled "Elevator Love Letter"). The walls are covered with brain CT scans, and Derek draws Meredith's attention to the "one in a million" patient's scan from the pilot episode. "This was the first surgery we ever scrubbed in together," he reminds her. "Our first save." He proceeds to walk Meredith through the history of their partnership in the operating room, detailing the reasons he fell in love with her (and her brain). "You say you're all dark and twisty," he muses, looking into her eyes. "It's not a flaw. It's a strength. It makes you who you are."[61]

Notes

1 *Grey's Anatomy*, season 1, episode 1, "A Hard Day's Night," created by Shonda Rhimes, aired March 27, 2005, on ABC.
2 See National Association of Broadcasters Hall of Fame, Shonda Rhimes, https://nab.org/hof/inductees/shondaRhimes.asp.
3 Shonda Rhimes, "My Year of Saying Yes to Everything," filmed February 2016, video, 3:42, https://www.ted.com/talks/shonda_rhimes_my_year_of_saying_yes_to_everything.
4 Ibid., 16:23.
5 Ibid., 17:50.
6 *HTGAWM* was created by Peter Nowalk, who began his career on *Grey's* and *Scandal*.
7 *Bridgerton* was created by Chris Van Dusen, who also began his career on *Grey's* and *Scandal*.

8. Lesley Goldberg, "Inside Shonda Rhimes' Second Netflix Pact: A 'Significant' Raise and New Revenue Streams," *The Hollywood Reporter*, July 12, 2021, https://www.hollywoodreporter.com/tv/tv-news/inside-shonda-rhimes-second-netflix-deal-1234980626/.
9. See IMDb Awards page, https://www.imdb.com/title/tt0172348/awards/?ref_=tt_awd.
10. Savannah Walsh, "'You're No Longer Britney Spears': How Crossroads Captured the Girl Beyond the Pop Star," *Vanity Fair*, October 18, 2023, https://www.vanityfair.com/hollywood/2023/10/youre-no-longer-britney-spears-how-crossroads-captured-the-girl-beyond-the-pop-star.
11. See IMDb Box office, https://www.imdb.com/title/tt0368933/.
12. Kate Aurthur, "A 'Grey's Anatomy' Lesson," *New York Times*, May 1, 2005, https://www.nytimes.com/2005/05/01/arts/television/a-greys-anatomy-lesson.html.
13. Meghan Casserly, "How 'Scandal's' Shonda Rhimes Became Disney's Primetime Savior," *Forbes*, May 8, 2013, https://www.forbes.com/sites/meghancasserly/2013/05/08/how-scandals-shonda-rhimes-became-disneys-primetime-savior/?sh=2f9b1e3f7d5a.
14. Rick Porter, "TV Ratings 2022–23: Final Seven-Day Averages for Every Network Series," *The Hollywood Reporter*, June 7, 2023, https://www.hollywoodreporter.com/tv/tv-news/tv-ratings-2022-23-every-primetime-network-show-ranked-1235508593/.
15. ABC Television Network, Press Release, "Season Program Rankings," May 31, 2006, https://web.archive.org/web/20141011060406/http://abcmedianet.com/web/dnr/dispDNR.aspx?id=053106_05.
16. Jenna Bans's *Off the Map* (2011) was another early medical drama produced by Shondaland, airing on ABC for one season. Bans was a writer and producer on *Private Practice*, *Grey's*, and *Scandal*. She also created *The Family* (2016) and the hit show *Good Girls* (2018–21). Paul William Davies's legal drama *For the People* (2018–19) aired on ABC for two seasons. He was a producer and executive story editor on *Scandal* and his Shondaland/Netflix miniseries, *The Residence*, is currently in production.
17. Writers Guild of America West, "Inclusion & Equity Report 2022," *WGAW*, https://www.wga.org/uploadedfiles/the-guild/inclusion-and-equity/Inclusion-Report-2022.pdf.
18. Martha Lauzen, "Boxed In: Women on Screen and Behind the Scenes on Broadcast and Streaming Television in 2022–23," Center for Study of Women in Television and Film, 2023, https://womenintvfilm.sdsu.edu/wp-content/uploads/2023/10/2022-23-Boxed-In-Report.pdf.
19. UCLA Entertainment & Media Research Initiative, "Hollywood Diversity Report 2023," 19, https://socialsciences.ucla.edu/wp-content/uploads/2023/11/UCLA-Hollywood-Diversity-Report-2023-Television-11-9-2023.pdf.
20. Carla Hay, "Black Women Showrunners Making Their Mark on Television," *Women's Media Center*, February 24, 2022, https://

womensmediacenter.com/news-features/black-women-showrunners-making-their-mark-on-television.

21 Samantha Bergeson, "Black Female Showrunners Chart 'the Shonda Effect' of 'Grey's Anatomy' Mega-Producer Shonda Rhimes," *IndieWire*, March 21, 2022, https://www.indiewire.com/features/general/shonda-rhimes-black-female-showrunners-sxsw-1234709859/.

22 See Beretta E. Smith-Shomade, *Shaded Lives: African-American Women and Television* (New Brunswick: Rutgers, 2002), for an important discussion of the representation of Black women on television pre-Shondaland.

23 Shonda Rhimes, "Oprah Talks to Shonda Rhimes," interview by Oprah Winfrey, *The Oprah Magazine*, December 2006, https://www.oprah.com/omagazine/oprah-interviews-greys-anatomy-creator-shonda-rhimes/all.

24 See Jeanine Basinger's seminal work on women's representation in film, such as *A Woman's View* (New York: Alfred. A Knopf, 1993), 43–4.

25 It's also worth noting that Meredith acknowledges early in the pilot (immediately after the teaser) that she is one of only six female interns out of twenty total. She states this to Cristina before even introducing herself, to which Cristina replies that one of the six is a model, which won't help with the "respect thing."

26 *Grey's Anatomy*, season 6, episode 11, "Blink," created by Shonda Rhimes, written by Debora Cahn, aired January 14, 2010, on ABC.

27 Shonda Rhimes, *Year of Yes* (New York: Simon & Schuster, 2015), 246.

28 Ibid.

29 Joy Press, *Stealing the Show* (New York: Simon & Schuster, 2018), 113.

30 Shonda Rhimes, "Shonda Rhimes and Betsy Beers on Finding Your Creative Partner," interview by Carly Zakin and Danielle Weisberg, *9 to 5ish*, the Skimm, October 26, 2022, https://www.theskimm.com/podcast/shonda-rhimes-betsy-beers-finding-your-creative-partner.

31 Press, *Stealing the Show*, 109.

32 For a fascinating early look at women's responses to representations of women characters on television, see Andrea Press's *Women Watching Television: Gender, Class, and Generation in the American Television Experience* (Philadelphia: University of Pennsylvania Press, 1991), 28.

33 *Women's Health*, "Shonda Rhimes Wants Her Daughters to Own Their Sexuality," September 21, 2015, https://www.womenshealthmag.com/life/a19910804/shonda-rhimes-game-changer/.

34 Press, *Stealing the Show*, 117.

35 See IMDB page, https://www.imdb.com/name/nm0933156/?ref_=tt_ov_st.

36 ABC Television Network, Press Release, "Weekly Program Rankings," March 29, 2005, https://web.archive.org/web/20081221202459/http://abcmedianet.com/web/dnr/dispDNR.aspx?id=032905_05.

37 ABC Television Network, Press Release, "Weekly Program Rankings," April 5, 2005, https://web.archive.org/web/20081227112430/http://abcmedianet.com/web/dnr/dispDNR.aspx?id=040505_07.

38 Aurthur, "A 'Grey's Anatomy' Lesson."
39 Alan Carter, "'Living Single' Is an Unexpected Hit," *Entertainment Weekly*, May 13, 1994, https://ew.com/article/1994/05/13/living-single-unexpected-hit/.
40 Steven Priggé, *Created By . . . Inside the Minds of TV's Top Show Creators* (Los Angeles: Silman-James Press, 2005), 160.
41 Ibid.
42 Ibid.,100.
43 Ibid.
44 See Hervey's interview with the Television Academy Foundation, https://interviews.televisionacademy.com/interviews/winifred-hervey.
45 Still a prolific force in the industry, Mara Brock Akil has created series such as *The Game* (2006–15), *Being Mary Jane* (2013–19), and *Love Is_* (2018).
46 Kelly Edwards, *The Executive Chair: A Writer's Guide to TV Series Development* (Studio City: Michael Wiese Productions, 2021), xv.
47 Imani M. Cheers, *The Evolution of Black Women in Television: Mammies, Matriarchs, and Mistresses* (New York: Routledge, 2018), 15. Additionally, it's important to note that Madeline Anderson, though not a television writer, is frequently credited as the first Black woman to produce and direct a syndicated television series.
48 As another example, Stacy A. Littlejohn began her producing career on *One on One* and went on to create *Single Ladies* (2011–15) for VH1. See interview in *Writing for the Screen* (Abingdon: Routledge, 2017), 42–52.
49 Shonda Rhimes (@shondarhimes), "Debra Martin Chase Set an Incredible Example for Me," X, November 1, 2019, https://twitter.com/shondarhimes/status/1190375214988722176?lang=en.
50 Elana Levine, *Her Stories: Daytime Soap Opera & US Television History* (Durham: Duke University Press, 2020), 22–3.
51 See inflation calculation for $250,000 in 1949 to 2024, https://www.officialdata.org/us/inflation/1949?amount=250000.
52 "Soap Comes to TV," *Pathfinder News Magazine*, February 9, 1949, https://archive.ph/20190307200950/http://www.oldmagazinearticles.com/article-summary/first_tv_soap-opera%23.XIF6f9LLfK5.
53 See also Jennifer Keishin Armstrong, *When Women Invented Television: The Untold Story of the Female Powerhouses Who Pioneered the Way We Watch Today* (New York: HarperCollins, 2021), and Annie Berke, *Their Own Best Creations: Women Writers in Postwar Television* (Oakland: University of California Press, 2022).
54 Irna Phillips's son donated her memoir to the Library of Congress in 2020. For more information, see Cary O'Dell, "The Queen of Soaps . . . Speaks for Herself," *Library of Congress Blogs*, March 16, 2022, https://blogs.loc.gov/now-see-hear/2022/03/the-queen-of-soaps-speaks-for-herself/.

55 According to data from IMDb, Goldberg's series premiered in August 1949, making Irna Phillips's series the first broadcast series on television.
56 See IMDb page, https://www.imdb.com/title/tt0043208/fullcredits?ref_=tt_ov_st_sm.
57 See interview with Marlo Thomas on the Television Academy Foundation, https://interviews.televisionacademy.com/shows/that-girl.
58 Ruth Brooks Flippen wrote twelve episodes of *That Girl* and received "story by" credit on one; Peggy Elliot wrote eight episodes; Helen Levitt and her husband/writing partner Alfred Levitt wrote six episodes; and the remaining female writers—Barbara Avedon, Irma Kalish, Treva Silverman, Lynne Farr, and Fai Harris—each wrote one episode. Apart from Harris, every woman writer on *That Girl* went on to have a significant career in television.
59 Anna Weinstein, *Writing Women for Film & Television: A Guide to Creating Complex Female Characters* (Abingdon: Routledge, 2023), 73.
60 Denise D. Bielby, "Gender Inequity in Culture Industries: Women and Men Writers in Film and Television," *Sociologie du Travail* 51, no. 2 (2009): 237–52.
61 *Grey's Anatomy*, season 5, episode 19, "Elevator Love Letter," created by Shonda Rhimes, written by Stacy McKee, aired March 26, 2009, on ABC.

Part I

HOW SHE WORKS
Creating Television Series

Chapter 1

SCANDAL AS A NEW SERIES MODEL

William Rabkin

If we were to watch the 1927 version of *The Jazz Singer* today, we might have any of a huge range of reactions. We might be impressed by the urgency of Al Jolson's singing, for instance, or appalled by the use of blackface, engaged by the family drama, or repelled by what now looks like dreadful overacting.

The one reaction we can't possibly have, though, is the one shared by audiences all over the country when it first premiered. They were astonished to see something completely new—a feature film in which the characters actually spoke and sang. A *talking* picture.

After almost a century of movies and television shows with synchronized dialogue, music, and sound effects, it's simply impossible to recreate the excitement that this first talkie inspired in its audience. That film changed the way movies were made forever, and the changes it wrought became so integral to every film that followed we simply accept that this is the way the art form has always been and don't think about all that had come before.

In much the same way, when we look back at the 2012 premiere of Shonda Rhimes's series *Scandal* (2012-18), it is essentially impossible to see how revolutionary that series was. At the time, it was heralded for being only the second drama in American television with a Black female lead—and the first since *Get Christie Love!* (1974-5) almost forty years earlier[1]—and one of a tiny number created and run by a Black woman.

But the show's greatest contribution to the art and craft of the television drama went unnoticed at the time and still is mostly so today. Because *Scandal* changed the way American television stories are told and, like *The Jazz Singer*, changed it so completely that we barely remember how they were told before.

More precisely, with *Scandal*, Rhimes demonstrated that both an episode and a season of television could move much faster than anyone had ever attempted and contain far more story than writers and broadcasters had thought audiences would accept. And once audiences (and creators) had gotten used to *Scandal*'s pace, everything that had come before began to feel impossibly slow. Within a handful of years, almost every series on network, cable, and streaming had adopted the new paradigm for storytelling.

What did that new paradigm look like, and how was it different from the one that dominated television for the previous sixty years? Let's examine several series belonging to the same genre as *Scandal*—the drama of politics.

The West Wing: *The Old Paradigm*

In season 1, episode 12 of Aaron Sorkin's *The West Wing*, "He Shall, from Time to Time . . . ," which aired January 12, 2000, President Bartlett (Martin Sheen) collapses on the eve of the State of the Union speech and is diagnosed with the flu. But when Chief of Staff Leo McGarry (John Spencer) suspects that there is something bigger going on, Bartlett admits that he has long suffered from relapsing/remitting MS, and that while his wife, daughters, and a few key national security personnel know this, he has hidden it from the American public through all his political campaigns. And of course, Leo must now also hide this truth, because revealing it would open Bartlett up to charges that might lead to impeachment.

In season 2, episode 1, "In the Shadow of Two Gunmen," which aired October 4, 2000, Bartlett is shot in an attempted assassination and rushed to the hospital, where an anesthesiologist has to be told the secret as a medical necessity.

Once he's recovered, Bartlett realizes that as his first term is coming to an end, he will need to tell the American people the truth about his condition. Over the course of the second season, he begins to tell his senior staff individually to get their assistance in planning the public revelation of his illness. In season 2, episode 22, "Two Cathedrals," the last episode of the season, Bartlett announces in a press conference that he is suffering from MS and does not give an answer when asked if he will run for a second term.

Bartlett's illness becomes a major plot point in many third season episodes as members of his staff are brought to testify before congress. Finally, in season 3, episode 11, "H. Con-172," which aired January 9, 2002, President Bartlett agrees to accept a bipartisan congressional censure for lying to the American public, while his wife Abbey (Stockard Channing) surrenders her medical license rather than face charges for violating medical ethics by treating her own husband for his MS.

Bartlett's failure to tell the truth about his MS was the primary scandal of the first three seasons of *The West Wing* and was the subject of multiple storylines. From its inception to its conclusion, it played out over forty-three episodes, two full seasons' worth.

And this was a show that one critic said "juggles fast-moving plots,"[2] while another worried that "it relies so heavily on relentless pacing that I fear it will soon wear thin with me."[3]

Now let's look at a more recent series in the same genre.

The Diplomat: *The New Paradigm*

The most successful political drama in the last few years is Debora Cahn's *The Diplomat* (2023–),[4] which stars Keri Russell as longtime state department employee Kate Wyler, who is unexpectedly named US ambassador to Great Britain after a terrorist attack in the Persian Gulf kills forty-one sailors on a British aircraft carrier.

Over the course of the eight episodes that make up the show's first season, all premiering April 20, 2023, Kate discovers that the real reason she's been chosen for this position is that the aging president is facing re-election and needs to replace his unpopular female vice president and is using this appointment to vet Kate for the job. And that there is a conspiracy within agencies of the Federal government led by her direct boss, Secretary of State Miguel Ganon (Miguel Sandoval), to undermine her in hopes of using her failure to damage the president and advance Ganon's own candidacy. And that her estranged husband Hal (Rufus Sewell), another diplomat with far greater experience, has been directly involved with the conspiracy to make Kate vice president but may be arranging it all in his own secret bid to become secretary of state.

Meanwhile, Britain's prime minister Nicol Trowbridge (Rory Kinnear) is planning a military strike against Iran in retaliation for the bombing until Iranian agents drug and kidnap Hal to put him on a phone call with the Iranian foreign minister who assures him that their country is innocent. Kate has to work all the levers of power to stop the United States and the United Kingdom from launching a military strike against Iran, and when she succeeds, she's rewarded by the Iranian ambassador with the name of the actual perpetrator, a Russian terrorist named Roman Lenkov. Kate manages to persuade the British that these

Russians are the real bad guys, but just as the prime minister is planning a series of retaliatory military strikes against Russia, the Russian ambassador gives Kate the terrorist's location in France—Lenkov is no friend of the Russian government, either.

Kate brokers a deal with the French government to allow the Brits to lead an international group to arrest the terrorist. But she learns from a French diplomat that the unit's actual orders have been to kill Lenkov and not arrest him. She realizes that the only person who can benefit from the terrorist's death is the one who hired him to blow up the British aircraft carrier—which means that the real villain all along has been the prime minister of the UK. Before she can reach out to Hal to tell him, he is blown up in a car bombing and we are left not knowing whether he will survive into a second season.

And that's just half the storyline. There is an intricate romantic subplot involving a triangle between Kate, Hal, and the UK foreign secretary. And maneuverings for and against Kate in the CIA's London station. And of course, the whole personal story of Kate learning how to transform herself from a direct, hands-on problem-solver to an ambassador skilled in the delicate art of diplomacy.

It's impossible to imagine how many seasons of *The West Wing* it would take to contain all the twists and turns in the first season of *The Diplomat*. And yet, at least one critic warned that "the slow pace might not appeal to everyone."[5] In terms of the pace of its storytelling, this show was hardly an outlier on its release. Just a few weeks earlier, Paramount Plus had started its weekly release of another eight-episode political thriller that moved even faster—*Rabbit Hole* (2023), created by Glenn Ficarra and John Requa.

Clearly something had changed in American television over the two decades between *The West Wing* and *The Diplomat*. I believe we can trace that change back to Shonda Rhimes and *Scandal*.

Tracking the Narrative Pace of Television Series

Before we talk about how Rhimes changed the pacing in television shows, it's worth taking a step back and describing exactly what the change was. It's easy to talk about stories moving faster or slower than each other, but often we're just speaking of our perception of momentum. What does it actually mean to say that a story is fast?

What I suggest is that we define narrative pace as the number of significant story turns divided by the amount of time in which they take place. This formula would apply to both individual episodes and entire series, although it's the latter that really concerns us here.

Narrative pace has always varied greatly not only between series but between episodes of a single show. On *Diagnosis Murder* (1993–2001), a show on which I served as showrunner in the late 1990s, we could go from a slow-moving cat-and-mouse story to a real-time thriller paced so fast its script ended up requiring more than twenty additional pages over our standard fifty-four just to fill our forty-three-minute running time.

But no matter how fast or slow our episodes moved, the narrative pace of our series was, like that of the vast majority of dramas that preceded us, close to zero. Our show existed in a narrative steady state, with a set of characters in a situation established in the pilot and rarely changing after that. A new character or location might be added along the way, and some number of episodes devoted to them to some extent, but ultimately they would be absorbed into the original narrative without making fundamental changes to it.

This was essentially the definition of a television series for most of the medium's first half-century. Serialized storytelling came to television drama in 1981 with Steven Bochco and Michael Kozoll's *Hill Street Blues* (1981–7). Although it seemed revolutionary at the time, with stories sprawling over multiple episodes instead of being resolved in a single hour, the series' overarching narrative actually moved very little. In fact, such movement would have violated the show's central theme, which centered on the futility of trying to make change in a dysfunctional system and the need to simply manage the chaos rather than attempt to reform it.

Television narrative took another step forward in the 2000s as shows like Joss Whedon's *Buffy, the Vampire Slayer* (1997–2003) established a new serialized/procedural format, under which the series would introduce an overarching storyline for the year in the opening episodes but then only touch on it lightly for most of the year before making it the principal focus in the last quarter or third of the season.[6]

What made *Buffy*'s new paradigm truly revolutionary was not the multiepisode story arcs but that Whedon used these extended storylines to change the status quo that originally defined the series. When the title character (Sarah Michelle Gellar) graduates from high school at the end of the third season—after the school principal turns into a monstrous serpent and eats many of the students—Buffy spends the next years struggling to make it first as a college student and then as a college dropout. When she sacrifices herself at the end of season 5 to save her little sister Dawn (Michelle Trachtenberg)—herself a major narrative turn since she hadn't existed in the previous four seasons and was indeed created by a mystical force—Buffy is actually dead for the sixth season premiere, and the major storyline of that year focuses on her struggle to fit in once she is resurrected.

But while these narrative shifts may be monumental in comparison to earlier drama series in which the characters, their relationships, and their positions in their shows stayed constant no matter how long the show ran, by today's standards, they were glacial. A major narrative shift came once a year and created a new status quo for the episodes to take place in.

The years after *Buffy*'s finale did little to change the drama's standard paradigm. If we look at the shows that premiered in the 2011–12 season, for instance, we can see that with the exception of *Scandal* there was very little to differentiate between the new dramas and almost anything that had come before. Michael Brandt and Derek Haas's *Chicago Fire* (2012–) follows a crew of firefighters as they race to emergency after emergency. There is some conflict between various characters, mostly sparked by the death of a colleague at the beginning of the pilot, but once that is established, it essentially never changes. *Chicago Fire* is almost entirely a pure procedural, with the only serialized elements being interpersonal relationships that can be examined from various angles without changing anything in the overarching story. But even a serialized drama like Mike Kelley's *Revenge* (2011–15), a modern-day adaptation of *The Count of Monte Cristo* in which an orphaned daughter returns incognito to the Hamptons home of the rich family responsible for her father's death and seeks revenge on them one by one, expended its narrative energy on a new victim in every episode and neglected any greater story development.

One could even say that Vince Gilligan's *Breaking Bad* (2008–13), which felt like such a radical departure from television's past when it first aired and was halfway through its run during the 2011–12 season, did little to change the drama's narrative style. Although the show's moral complexity and increasingly evil protagonist were indeed something new on television, the seasons' format was not significantly different from the *Buffy* paradigm, with a new "big bad" introduced at the beginning of a season and growing to dominate the storylines as episodes went by.

Scandal's Narrative Pacing

Scandal was truly something different. The show's first twenty episodes—seven in a brief midseason run starting in May 2012 and then the first thirteen of a full twenty-two-episode order beginning that fall—tell their story in a way that had never been seen on television before.

Not that a viewer would have expected this from the concept alone. A drama about Olivia Pope (Kerry Washington), a Washington DC "fixer" who helps a new client every week, it sounds like it could easily have been a standard procedural, a new way into a private detective series at a time when private detectives were decidedly out of fashion. Even if you read the synopses for those episodes, you can't detect anything particularly new: "Olivia Pope and Associates take on DC's finest madame when her list of clients threatens to send shockwaves through Washington's elite"; "The team tries to help a millionaire's son who has been accused of rape"; "When a plane crashes and all passengers, including a US senator, are killed, the team has to find the accident's cause."

It's not until you actually start watching *Scandal* that you begin to realize that this is—or was, anyway—a new storytelling paradigm for television drama.

The first thing you notice about *Scandal*—even before you meet its protagonist—is that it's built for speed. Story comes flying at the viewer, and the show isn't going to slow down for us to catch up. The first scene is a breathless blind date in an upscale bar. Except that we almost immediately are told that it's not what we think. Quinn Perkins (Katie Lowes), the woman we meet running in heels to the bar, is really here only to tell the exquisitely dressed Harrison (Columbus Short) that she isn't interested in blind dates but came because she didn't have his phone number to cancel, but before she can leave, Harrison informs her that it's not a date, it's a job interview. Only it can't be a job interview because Quinn hasn't applied for a job. She's leaving again when he insists she ask him who he works for. And when she does and he answers "Olivia Pope," she is desperately interested in the interview. Except that it isn't an interview, because Olivia has already instructed Harrison to hire her.

Then we meet Olivia Pope as she's riding up a warehouse elevator on her way to pay a ransom to a group of Ukrainian mobsters, only, as her associate Finch informs her, she's $3 million short, something that does not slow her down at all. Olivia manipulates the gangsters into taking the smaller payout and she then takes the package they were hired to retrieve. (Only much later do we discover that it contains the kidnapped—and, of course, adorable—baby of the Russian ambassador.)

This is followed by the quick title card that flashes by in lieu of an opening credits sequence. But it might as well have given us the clip of Al Jolson announcing "You ain't heard nothin' yet" before launching into his biggest hit. Because this is the moment that television storytelling started to change.

It's impossible to convey the pace of these scenes in a paragraph or two. But what is crucial to the storytelling style is that both of them pick up far closer to their stories' end than their beginning. We're thrown into Olivia's negotiation without any idea of why she's there or what she's buying or who has hired her, and we're in the middle of Quinn learning her date is not a date without ever believing that it was, or knowing what she thinks about it, or even who she is. It's not just that the story is moving, it's that the story has been moving for some time before we got there, and we can either run to catch up or let it get away from us completely.

Just take that first scene at the bar. In a more traditional television narrative, it's got enough turns for three or four scenes: Quinn is set up on a blind date by her friend; she doesn't want to go and wants to cancel but her friend can't or won't give her Harrison's phone number; she goes to the bar to apologize but he informs her it's not a date but a job interview; she has not applied for this job so it's clearly either a mistake or a lie from Harrison to cover that it actually is a date; the job is with Olivia Pope, whom Quinn idolizes; it's not actually an interview at all as it's really an offer.

If you took all these plot turns and intercut them with a couple of scenes leading up to Olivia's negotiation with the Ukrainians, you could easily fill an act of a standard 2012 television script.

But as I mentioned earlier, it's not the pace of the episodic stories that sets *Scandal* apart. There were earlier shows that attempted to move fast like this. The appeal of Robert Cochran and Joel Surnow's *24*, for example, which premiered on Fox in 2001 and ran for nine seasons, was almost entirely due to the speed of its narrative turns, with a major reversal coming at the end of every act—and just before every set of commercials. But often it seemed that *24*'s turns were there not to advance a storyline but simply for the sake of making the show feel like it was moving fast. Sometimes a twist at the end of one act would directly contradict the twist from the previous act, rendering everything that happened in between meaningless—except that the only real meaning here was the fact that the plot had twisted again.

What does set *Scandal* apart from everything that had come before was the pace of storytelling across the episodes. In the pilot, Quinn Perkins comes to work for Olivia Pope and Associates (OPA) as they are asked by Chief of Staff Cyrus Beene (Jeff Perry) to deal with former White House intern Amanda Tanner (Liza Weil), who claims that she was fired after sleeping with President Fitzgerald Grant (Tony Goldwyn). Olivia scares her off, but Quinn believes the girl. After talking to Amanda, Quinn brings back the information that Grant used to call her "sweet baby," which we learn is what Grant used to call Olivia during their lengthy affair. Yes, we just learned our protagonist was sleeping with the (very married) president of the United States. Olivia, now certain that Grant is guilty, takes Amanda on as a client and vows to help her.

Over the next few episodes, Olivia hides Amanda in a safe house, but the girl disappears, seeming to have run off. But Olivia's associate Huck (Guillermo Diaz), a former torturer and assassin for a top secret intelligence division, recognizes the hallmarks of the disappearance and declares that Amanda has been kidnapped. Indeed, hours later, her body is found in the river. And it is revealed that the assassin was hired by Cyrus Beene.

But just when Beene and the president think this crisis is over, Beene receives an audio sex tape of the president and Amanda along with a threat to release it if he doesn't step down. Olivia, now working for the president, manages to discover that the blackmail threat came from the chief of staff for the very conservative vice president, who hopes to see her installed in Grant's place.

That alone is a significantly faster pace than, say, *The West Wing*, but it's hardly revolutionary. But the next plotline down is. When OPA is working for Amanda Tanner, Cyrus Beene sets investigators on all of the associates, and once Quinn is fingerprinted, she's revealed to be a wanted fugitive, on the run for a terrorist bombing of software company Cytron in which her fiancée was killed.

Quinn becomes Olivia's new client just as President Grant is shot and critically wounded in an assassination attempt, for which Huck is almost immediately framed. Now Olivia has two associates to protect.

But it turns out that Olivia is directly involved with both cases. Through flashbacks, we learn that Olivia and the president fell hopelessly in love when she was working on his campaign. When it looked like he was going to lose a very close race, Olivia entered into a conspiracy with Beene, Grant's wife Mellie (Bellamy Young), billionaire donor Hollis Doyle (Gregg Henry), and campaign lawyer Verna Thornton (Debra Mooney) to steal the election by using Cytron voting machine software to flip a county in Ohio that would give them the state and thus the presidency.

But after the election, the software's designer realized what he'd unwittingly been a part of and blackmails Doyle—who hired an assassin to send a mailbomb to Cytron and frame the designer's fiancée for the crime. When Olivia Pope realized this, she had Huck drug and kidnap the fiancée and leave her in a Washington DC hotel along with documentation of a completely new identity . . . of Quinn Perkins.

And of course, that's just a fraction of what's going on. I don't have time to dive into the assassin's identity—except to say she was hired by Verna Thornton, who Grant has named to the Supreme Court but who is now dying of cancer and trying to atone for her part in the crime—or into the president murdering his Supreme Court appointee in the hospital.

Certainly, there are enough major story turns in these twenty episodes to keep *The West Wing* going for decades. But it's not just the twists that give *Scandal* its pace. It's that the show's present-day stories are not only moving at an incredible clip, the flashbacks move at the same pace. And most importantly that each new revelation about the past fundamentally changes the way we read what we're seeing in the present. We start out thinking that Quinn is just a new hire, more an audience-identification figure to bring us into this world than anything else; then she becomes a mystery client for Olivia and then she is Olivia's victim. With each new revelation, we are forced to reconsider everything we thought we knew about the stories and characters.

In a pre-*Scandal* series, the viewers sit in a fixed place and watch the story play out in front of them. *Scandal*'s narrative puts the audience on a platform that is moving, sometimes with the story, sometimes against it. Characters act in the present, but the meaning of their actions is determined by things in the past that we and they become aware of at various points in the narrative.

Unlocking the viewer from the fixed place outside the narrative flow is the essence of contemporary television storytelling. It's what makes shows like *The Diplomat* and *Rabbit Hole* so addictive.

And it turns out to be a style that is much better suited to streaming shows than it was for *Scandal*. It burns through story so fast that what might have fit into forty-four episodes now fills eight. This becomes a problem when a series is producing twenty-two episodes per year, as *Scandal* did. There are only so many ways a writer can believably twist a story, and in its later years, *Scandal* would begin to seem ludicrous—as when a storyline has Huck kidnapping and torturing Quinn, who has become his trusted friend (for reasons I can't remember), even pulling out her teeth with pliers, only to shortly afterwards feature a storyline in which Huck is upset because Quinn doesn't seem to want to be his friend anymore for reasons he can't understand.

Now, seeming ludicrous was always one of *Scandal*'s great pleasures. After all, the second season did feature a sitting Supreme Court justice putting out a hit on the president and him murdering her in return. But there's a point at which audiences are no longer willing to suspend their disbelief. And while *Scandal* did run for seven seasons, the 7.4 million viewers watching the final season[7] were down by almost half from the season 4 peak of 12.66.[8]

But that hardly diminishes the importance of Rhimes's achievement with *Scandal*. It's hard to imagine almost any of the streaming shows we are seeing today without its influence. The way she told stories is the way we all tell stories now. And when we see a series that defies the contemporary pace—something like Julian Fellowes's *The Gilded Age* (2022–), for instance—it feels like we're watching something that is as much a callback to a distant age as a contemporary silent movie like *The Artist* (2011). What was once the standard has become a quaint novelty, and what was revolutionary is now the norm.

Notes

1   Tanzina Vega, "A Show Makes Friends and History," *New York Times*, January 16, 2013, https://www.nytimes.com/2013/01/17/arts/television/scandal-on-abc-is-breaking-barriers.html.
2   Hal Boedeker, "Drama Is Missing in Tepid 'West Wing,'" *Orlando Sentinel*, September 22, 1999, https://www.newspapers.com/article/the-orlando-sentinel-west-wing-season-o/74729073/.
3   Tony Atherton, "Drama: Series' Pacing Is Relentless," *Ottawa Citizen*, September 21, 1999, https://www.newspapers.com/article/the-ottawa-citizen-west-wing-season-one/74730065/.
4   It's worth noting that Debora Cahn, creator of *The Diplomat*, got her start writing for *The West Wing*, *Grey's Anatomy*, and *Private Practice*. She is credited as writer on thirty-four episodes of *The West Wing*, seventeen episodes of *Grey's*, and three episodes of *Private Practice*.
5   Jeanine T. Abraham, "TV Review: Netflix's 'The Diplomat' Walks and Talks Its Way Through the World of Diplomacy," *Medium*, May 9, 2023, https://medium.com/@visableblackwoman/the-diplomat-walks-and-talks-its-way-through-the-world-of-diplomacy-e2ee003f4911.
6   Following the dictum of Andrew Hickey, author of the podcast *A History of Rock Music in 500 Songs*, there is no such thing as a "first" of any kind in art, and there are always earlier experiments before any great change. In the case of dramatic serialization, we can find examples in two *noir* police series from the 1980s: Michael Mann's *Crime Story* (1986–8) and Stephen J. Cannel and Frank Lupo's *Wiseguy* (1987–90). Chris Carter's

The X-Files (1993–2002, 2016–18) pushed the paradigm further by extending a set of continuing storylines about an alien invasion and a government conspiracy to cover it up across the show's entire initial run.

7   Lisa de Moraes, "2014–15 TV Season Series Rankings: Football and 'Empire' Ruled," *Deadline Hollywood*, May 21, 2015, https://deadline.com/2015/05/2014-15-full-tv-season-ratings-shows-rankings-1201431167/.

8   Lisa de Moraes and Patrick Hipes, "2017–18 TV Series Ratings Rankings: NFL Football, 'Big Bang' Top Charts," *Deadline Hollywood*, May 22, 2018, https://deadline.com/2018/05/2017-2018-tv-series-ratings-rankings-full-list-of-shows-1202395851/.

Chapter 2

THE ART OF DEVELOPING "HUMANISTIC" FEMALE CHARACTERS

Rosanne Welch

From Dorothy Dandridge to Princess Mia Thermopolis, Meredith Grey, Olivia Pope, and Queen Charlotte, Shonda Rhimes has injected feminism into all the characters she creates or caretakes in the projects created under the umbrella of her name. Before Rhimes's ascendance to the rank of television producer, female characters, women of color, and women over the age of forty often functioned as props to the male leads as opposed to fully realized characters in their own right. In the television series developed in Shondaland, women characters—whether leads or supporting—have become three-dimensional, often shown in authority, with families and lives outside their workplace, even when the shows are workplace oriented.[1]

Some critics have defined Rhimes's female characters solely as feminists, which can be viewed as a way to sideline her intentions as creative producer and television showrunner, deeming her only focused on and useful to female viewers.[2] I frame Rhimes's stories and characters (male and female) as "humanists," using the basic idea from the humanist chaplain of Harvard University, Greg M. Epstein, that humanism is a philosophy emphasizing the individual and their agency as human beings who can be good for the sake of being good. They share the responsibility to lead ethical lives of personal fulfillment.[3] Humanism celebrates the value of human thought (as opposed to divine reason), while feminism largely exists to advance ideas of gender equality in women's personal and professional worlds. Humanist beliefs stress the potential value and goodness of human beings, emphasize common human needs, and seek solely rational ways of aspiring to the greater good for humanity.[4]

"Women's rights are human rights" is a phrase first used in the 1980s, which found its most prominent usage as the title of then First

Lady Hillary Clinton's speech at the United Nation's Fourth World Conference on Women in Beijing in 1995.[5] Rodham Clinton said, "If there is one message that echoes forth from this conference, let it be that human rights are women's rights and women's rights are human rights," a concept that threads through most of the women of Rhimes's shows and seems a hallmark of Shondaland, as well. One example of this is when Rhimes allowed a writer under contract with Shondaland, Allan Heinberg, sabbatical time off to write the first *Wonder Woman* movie in 2016.[6] In that way, she served as creative midwife to Heinberg's version of the comic book heroine. Whether she's written or executive produced female characters into life through guiding other writers' scripts, Rhimes's messages have spoken to viewers around the globe.

Rhimes made her interest in showcasing humanism clear when she hired Dan Shapiro, Arnold P. Gold Professor of Medical Humanism and Chair of the College of Medicine's humanities department at Penn State Hershey, as a consultant for her first two medical dramas *Grey's Anatomy* (2005–) and *Private Practice* (2007–13).[7] Shapiro's program emphasizes producing compassionate, caring, humanistic physicians and was the first humanities department in a medical school in the United States. In hiring Shapiro as a consultant, Rhimes was able to bring the real-world philosophy of medicine to her fictional hospitals, presenting authentic depictions of humanism to her audiences. Of his work on both shows, Shapiro said,

> The writers are very respectful of the language; they understand that words are the therapist's scalpel. They may not always agree with me, but I feel I have very thoughtful colleagues at both shows.... To the extent that I can use it as a vehicle to educate the public about other issues that I care about, I want to do that.[8]

In 2016, Rhimes received the Personality of the Year Award at Mipcom, the television showcase at the Cannes Film Festival, a fitting honor since her slate of shows produced under the Shondaland banner at that time aired across 250 territories in sixty-seven languages.[9] Rhimes used her "Media Mastermind" keynote speech to explain (as if she needed to) her penchant for creating complicated female protagonists. "I'm writing heroines who talk like my mothers, like my friends ... I never felt that what they said was wild." She added: "I have always been amazed by the power and global reach of television.... It is an incredible feeling to know that audiences around the world have enjoyed the shows and characters that I have created."[10] She did not define her audience as solely a female one, and a deeper reading of her characters shows their larger, humanist influence.

This began in small ways in her early screenplays and ballooned when she began filling ABC with hit shows. For instance, though Rhimes was not the first writer to create Princess Mia—that honor goes to author Meg Cabot, whose novel was adapted for the screen as *The Princess Diaries* (2001) by screenwriter Gina Wendkos—Rhimes's focus on feminism and humanism in her characters came across in the sequel, *The Princess Diaries 2: Royal Engagement* (2004). A quick summary of the plot leans toward feminism with its discrimination against unmarried women: Newly twenty-one years old, Princess Mia Thermopolis is supposed to succeed her grandmother as the Queen of Genovia, but another noble who wants his nephew to be the new ruler advocates for an ancient law denying the crown to an unmarried woman. Already in this early work, Rhimes leaned into humanism by having Princess Mia go to Princeton. At first glance, Princeton is merely a fancy Ivy League university name to drop, but Rhimes went deeper. She sent the princess to the Woodrow Wilson School of Public and International Affairs at Princeton, a school whose motto is "In Service to the Nation & Humanity."[11] This choice belonged to the screenwriter as it is not a title in the Meg Cabot series.

Humanism (and Feminism) in Grey's Anatomy

Rhimes's pilot for *Grey's* indicates her focus on humanism on the very first page of the script with the name she chose for the hospital. While it is commonly known as "Seattle Grace," its full name is "Seattle Grace Mercy West Hospital."[12] Rhimes could have named the hospital for a famous woman, but she chose "grace," conjuring thoughts of bestowing honor, dignity, and "mercy," which means to compassionately treat those in distress using forgiveness, benevolence, and kindness. Rhimes then carefully constructed characters and stories imbued with those humanistic qualities. Every episode does not contain a comment on feminism, but nearly every episode involves a display of honor and dignity, often given to those least used to receiving such treatment, characters that find themselves in unexpectedly perilous situations. Likewise, the doctors and interns Rhimes imagined into Seattle Grace face daily affronts to their own humanity, often being asked to act like "gods" in the choices they must make to save lives—including their own.

For instance, while Cristina Yang's (Sandra Oh) intense interest in her career over marriage and family might read as a feminist statement, throughout her time on the series, Yang strongly advocates for her own individual potential and continually seeks rational solutions to the human problems she sees every day—in her patients and in her own life. It is only because she is a female that our first thought is that she is the embodiment of feminism. The very reason she works so hard to become a doctor comes from her humanist desire to help people avoid the sadness she experienced as a child when her father died in a car accident.[13] Even Yang's decision to have an abortion[14] (while that right was still guaranteed by the Constitution of the United States) can be read through the lens of humanism. Full bodily autonomy is considered a human right by Amnesty International[15] and the Human Rights Watch.[16] Their beliefs include the idea that it is essential that laws relating to abortion respect, protect, and fulfill the human rights of pregnant persons. People do not become less human when they become pregnant. Motherhood is not Yang's choice in life, and the abortion is her choice to make.

It can be argued that Miranda Bailey (Chandra Wilson) is a more central character in *Grey's* than Meredith Grey (Ellen Pompeo). For starters, Bailey begins her journey on the series as Meredith's immediate boss, a resident when Meredith arrives as an intern. Meanwhile, due to her stern and stone-faced demeanor, Bailey's subordinates refer to her as "The Nazi." Yet she is far from deserving such an epithet, showing her humanism to patients and eventually to the interns as well. She never backs down from a debate with her own boss if she feels a patient's health is at risk over a hurried decision, which eventually leads her to the position as the hospital's chief of surgery (see season 12, episode 1, "Sledgehammer," written by Stacy McKee).[17] Through Bailey's character, Rhimes can showcase a working wife and mother who, despite a few missteps, is able to manage it all—and remarkably well. Feminism is clearly displayed in Bailey's character, and in many episodes, she also demonstrates characteristics of deep humanism. For example, in season 5, episode 19, "Elevator Love Letter" (written by McKee), Bailey sits with Izzie Stevens (Katherine Heigl) in her hospital room while she awaits surgery for cancerous tumors that threaten her life. To make Izzie feel better, Bailey gives her colleagues work excuses to be away from the hospital while engaging Izzie in a conversation about the surgery she is preparing. Insisting that Izzie needs to keep her own knowledge fresh serves as a beacon of hope that she will indeed have a future.[18]

While Catherine Avery Fox (Debbie Allen) gives power and value to mature women of color (particularly over the age of sixty), an act of feminism, this character also depicts a female philanthropist dedicated to promoting the welfare of others with large donations of needed monies. A rarity on television, she offers a humanist perspective by being both a world-class surgeon and head of the Catherine Fox Foundation. In season 9, episode 16, "This Is Why We Fight" (written by Austin Guzman), when Seattle Grace faces bankruptcy and loses a possible investor, Fox steps forward to purchase the hospital so the staff of excellent surgeons can continue their own potential while being available to help the community.[19] In season 14, episode 21, "Bad Reputation" (written by Mark Driscoll), Catherine starts the Catherine Fox Foundation, under her maiden name, an organization dedicated to working toward equity in medical care for all.[20] In season 10, episode 24, "Fear (of the Unknown)" (written by William Harper), when a bomb goes off in a local mall and the large group of victims arriving at the hospital result in chaos, the wounds cause a pregnant April Kepner (Sarah Drew) to worry about bringing a child into this violent world. Catherine shares her humanistic perspective, telling April that parenthood is the path to making positive change since good people raising good children is a powerful contribution.[21]

Humanism (and Feminism) in Shondaland's Later Series

Private Practice, the spin-off of *Grey's*, includes a number of strong, talented, dedicated female characters, beginning with Naomi Bennett (Audra McDonald), the character credited with starting the story action by inviting *Grey's* character Addison Montgomery (Kate Walsh) to work in her patient-centric Los Angeles practice "Oceanside Wellness Group." With many of Rhimes's storylines revolving around the female characters' love lives more than their skillsets, feminist and humanist ideologies may not appear obvious. However, Rhimes's invention of a medical group that practices small-town medicine in a city as large as Los Angeles—with a focus on connecting patients and their families (see season 2, episode 1, "A Family Thing" written by Rhimes and Marti Noxon)[22]—echoes her humanistic choice of university for Princess Mia in *The Princess Diaries 2*. Also, the Oceanside Wellness Group recognizes that medicine involves ethics and requires group decisions whenever a case enters a morally or ethically gray area. Here, too, this stems back to the contributions Rhimes solicited from humanistic medical expert Dan Shapiro.

Each of Rhimes's first two hit shows center on a white woman, and the supporting casts of women of color carry the weight of the humanistic storylines from the backgrounds that Rhimes invented for them to their present-day life choices. When the network recognized Rhimes's hit-making abilities, she and her Shondaland team brought women of color into the leading roles of her next two successes, Olivia Pope (Kerry Washington) in *Scandal* (2012–18) and Annalise Keating (Viola Davis) in *How to Get Away with Murder* (2014–20), created by Peter Nowalk. Interestingly, as discovered through deep reads of each program, these women are more flawed and therefore often less able to stress the potential value and goodness of other human beings, less able to emphasize human needs, and more likely to seek solely rational ways of solving human problems. In other words, these lead characters are less humanistic, but their supporting characters carry that ideology.

With *Scandal*, Kerry Washington has made it clear in interview after interview that the character of Olivia Pope should not be considered a heroine of any kind.[23] Olivia arrives in the pilot episode as a Washington DC crisis manager. In the eight years the show aired on ABC, it earned (among other honors) the Peabody Award for Excellence in Television[24] and the NAACP Image Award for Outstanding Drama Series,[25] and the American Film Institute (AFI) named it "Television Program of the Year."[26] Through her position as the head of Olivia Pope and Associates, Olivia goes to extreme lengths to fix the scandals her clients find themselves enmeshed in, whether they are innocent or guilty. Either way, she powerfully orders them to behave in ways she advises, and they do. Olivia also threatens whomever she needs to—with whatever threat is required—to earn the outcome she desires. While there is much to admire about the control Olivia wields, she cannot be said to act in a humanistic ideology. Not even, often, in a feminist ideology. As mentioned, though, the supporting characters in *Scandal* often carry the work of embodying the humanistic ideology. For example, critics and fans described Attorney General David Rosen (Joshua Malina) as a "white hat" character "practically incorruptible in his quest for justice" from his first appearance through his untimely death. Even Scott Foley, who played Jake Ballard, defined Rosen as "the last vestige of truth and honor on this show."[27]

Annalise Keating in *HTGAWM* is another confident female protagonist. She has a formidable education in criminal law from Harvard and has a commanding presence as practitioner inside the courtroom. In an example of her humanism working hand in hand with feminism, in season 4, episode 5, "I Love Her" (written by Sarah L. Thompson), a flashback to 2002 explains how Keating and her associate Bonnie Winterbottom (Liza Weil) met. In that earlier era, Keating is told by her law firm partner to destroy Winterbottom, a rape witness on the stand. Keating does so, but in the aftermath, she quits her position at that firm and offers Winterbottom help with obtaining her law degree.[28] Also, with the supporting characters of *HTGAWM*, the Shondaland team makes some humanistic points, including female antagonists who learn their lesson and change for the better. For example, US attorney Tegan Price (Amirah Vann) starts out as a villain by constantly confronting Keating in court and supporting a questionable CEO. In season 4, episode 15, "Nobody Else Is Dying" (written by Nowalk), when Annalise proves to Tegan that her boss killed a district attorney, Tegan turns whistle-blower and begins working with Annalise and mentoring a new generation of young lawyers.[29]

By creating strong, complicated women characters for series such as *Grey's, Private Practice, Scandal*, and *HTGAWM*, Shondaland has brought Rhimes's ideology to millions of viewers around the world. Are her heroes feminists, humanists, or antiheroes? As with all good writing, Rhimes leaves that up to her audience to decide.

Notes

1 "Shonda Rhimes Doesn't Know Any Dumb and Weak Women," *Time*, October 18, 2016, https://time.com/4534973/shonda-rhimes-strong-female-leads/.
2 Lauren Wilks, "Is Grey's Anatomy on the Wave? A Feminist Textual Analysis of Meredith Grey and Cristina Yang" (BA thesis, Trinity University, 2012), http://digitalcommons.trinity.edu/infolit_usra/7.
3 Greg M. Epstein, *Good Without God: What a Billion Nonreligious People Do Believe* (New York: HarperCollins, 2009), xiii.
4 Ibid., xiv.
5 Hillary Rodham Clinton, "Women's Rights Are Human Rights," remarks to the U.N. 4th World Conference on Women Plenary Session, delivered September 5, 1995, Beijing, China, video, https://www.americanrhetoric.com/speeches/hillaryclintonbeijingspeech.htm.
6 Author interview with Allan Heinberg, January 14, 2023.
7 "Doctor Drama: Medical Humanities Professor Advises Two TV Shows," Penn State, May 8, 2009, https://www.psu.edu/news/medicine/story/doctor-drama-medical-humanities-professor-advises-two-tv-shows/.

8. Ibid.
9. Elsa Keslassy, "Shonda Rhimes Named Mipcom's Personality of the Year," May 31, 2016, https://variety.com/2016/tv/global/shonda-rhimes-named-mipcoms-personality-of-the-year-1201785508/.
10. Ibid.
11. *The Princess Diaries 2: Royal Engagement*, written by Shonda Rhimes, directed by Garry Marshall (2004), USA: Walt Disney.
12. *Grey's Anatomy*, season 1, episode 1, "A Hard Day's Night," created by Shonda Rhimes, aired March 27, 2005, on ABC.
13. *Grey's Anatomy*, season 5, episode 7, "Rise Up," created by Shonda Rhimes, written by William Harper, aired November 6, 2008, on ABC.
14. *Grey's Anatomy*, season 8, episode 2, "She's Gone," created by Shonda Rhimes, written by Debora Cahn, aired September 22, 2011, on ABC.
15. "Key Facts on Abortion," *Amnesty International*, https://www.amnesty.org/en/what-we-do/sexual-and-reproductive-rights/abortion-facts/#:~:text=Amnesty%20International%20believes%20that%20everyone,and%20if%20they%20have%20children.
16. "Q&A, Access to Abortion Is a Human Right," *Human Rights Watch*, June 24, 2022, https://www.hrw.org/news/2022/06/24/qa-access-abortion-human-right#:~:text=What%20is%20the%20Human%20Rights,right%20to%20access%20to%20abortion.
17. *Grey's Anatomy*, season 12, episode 1, "Sledgehammer," created by Shonda Rhimes, written by Stacy McKee, aired September 24, 2015, on ABC.
18. *Grey's Anatomy*, season 5, episode 19, "Elevator Love Letter," created by Shonda Rhimes, written by Stacy McKee, aired March 26, 2009, on ABC.
19. *Grey's Anatomy*, season 9, episode 16, "This Is Why We Fight," created by Shonda Rhimes, written by Austin Guzman, aired February 21, 2013, on ABC.
20. *Grey's Anatomy*, season 14, episode 21, "Bad Reputation," created by Shonda Rhimes, written by Mark Driscoll, aired April 26, 2018, on ABC.
21. *Grey's Anatomy*, season 10, episode 24, "Fear (of the Unknown)," created by Shonda Rhimes, written by William Harper, aired May 15, 2014, on ABC.
22. *Private Practice*, season 2, episode 1, "A Family Thing," created by Shonda Rhimes, written by Rhimes and Marti Noxon, aired October 1, 2008, on ABC.
23. "'Scandal's' Olivia Pope Is No Role Model, Kerry Washington Says (But OK to Dress Like Her)," *Los Angeles Times*, August 5, 2015, https://www.latimes.com/entertainment/tv/showtracker/la-et-st-kerry-washington-olivia-pope-scandal-role-model-20150805-story.html.
24. Lesley Goldberg, "'Scandal' Showrunner Shonda Rhimes on Peabody Win: 'A Complete Shock,'" *The Hollywood Reporter*, April 11, 2014, https://www.hollywoodreporter.com/news/general-news/scandal-showrunner-shonda-rhimes-peabody-694604/.

25 Aaron Couch and Arlene Washington, "NAACP Image Awards: The Winners," *The Hollywood Reporter*, February 22, 2014, https://www.hollywoodreporter.com/news/general-news/naacp-image-awards-winners-682585/.

26 Nellie Andreeva, "AFI Awards 2013: 'Orange Is the New Black', 'Masters of Sex', 'House of Cards' Among Top 10 TV Programs, 'Homeland' & 'Modern Family' Out," *Deadline*, December 9, 2013, https://deadline.com/2013/12/afi-fest-awards-2013-tv-full-list-649254/.

27 Natalie Abrams, "*Scandal* Cast Reacts to that Shocking Series Finale Death," *Entertainment Weekly*, April 20, 2018, https://ew.com/tv/2018/04/20/scandal-david-rosen-death/.

28 *How to Get Away with Murder*, season 4, episode 5, "I Love Her," created by Peter Nowak, written by Sarah L. Thompson, aired October 26, 2017, on ABC.

29 *How to Get Away with Murder*, season 4, episode 15, "Nobody Else Is Dying," created by Peter Nowak, written by Nowalk, aired March 15, 2018, on ABC.

Chapter 3

CRAFTING THE PILOT

Someone Arrives

Rani Deighe Crowe

There is a saying that every story is about somebody coming or going. In the pilots for Shonda Rhimes's *Grey's Anatomy* (2005–), *Private Practice* (2007–13), and *Scandal* (2012–18), each episode begins with someone arriving. In fact, "An ambitious woman starts a competitive new job" could be the opening of the logline for all three series pilots. Rhimes uses this entry point to set up her heroines' journeys in diverse professional worlds traditionally occupied by men where the protagonists must prove themselves (as not only capable but, in fact, exceptional), compete with colleagues, balance their career ambitions with love interests and relationships with other women, and also confront ethical dilemmas. Each pilot delivers a clear female point of view, introducing the stakes and forcing the newcomer to face self-doubt before demonstrating that she belongs. Each pilot introduces a love interest for the female lead, as well as a cohort of diverse supporting characters with their own goals, strengths, and weaknesses that will develop throughout the series. Rhimes adapts the traditional hero's journey[1] for a heroine's journey,[2] including tensions between the feminine and masculine and internal arcs that lead to self-realization.

In what follows, I will compare the pilot episodes for *Grey's*, *Private Practice*, and *Scandal* with a focus on the strategies Rhimes employed to set up her series for popular longevity, impactful female points of view, and space to explore relevant current events and social themes. I will also demonstrate how her pilots establish the themes for the series, plant seeds for plotlines, and introduce the characters with clear needs and wants that set up season- and series-long character arcs. The pilots for these television shows serve as solid models for developing popular series that can grow with the characters and audience.

Creating the World

The world of a series creates objectives and obstacles for the lead characters; provides reasons for stylistic art or cinematography choices; contributes to pacing, tone, and stakes; factors into the budget; and establishes rules and procedures within the show. A richly built world makes space for future story and relationship arcs and helps drive themes and plots. Rhimes's pilots define the specificities of each show's world.

Grey's borrows reliable medical series tropes and conventions established by its popular predecessors such as *St. Elsewhere* (1982–8, created by Joshua Brand and John Falsey), *ER* (1994–2009, created by Michael Crichton), and *Scrubs* (2001–10, created by Bill Lawrence) to create the frantic world of the hospital and tell stories about medical diagnoses and procedures, relationships between medical mentors and mentees, the balance of personal and professional life, and the complications of relationships in the workplace. *Grey's* differentiates itself by entering the world via the voiceover of Meredith Grey (Ellen Pompeo), a female surgeon protagonist at the beginning of her career in a more richly diverse world than much of television before it. We enter through Meredith's first day as an intern at Seattle Grace Hospital. *Private Practice*, a *Grey's* spin-off, takes us into the elite world of a Los Angeles private practice co-op through established *Grey's* character Addison Montgomery (Kate Walsh), a world-class neonatal surgeon. Addison leaves her job at Seattle Grace to make a life change by moving to Los Angeles. *Scandal* (2012), set in Washington DC, splits the protagonist in two and enters through Quinn Perkins (Katie Lowes), an idealistic young lawyer newly hired to work for Olivia Pope (Kerry Washington), the esteemed head of a team of lawyers who are "not a law firm" but rather fixers for the political elite.

Each pilot defines the specificities of the genre and setting for its show. *Grey's* is a medical drama set in a large hospital in Seattle. *Private Practice*, also a medical drama, takes place in Los Angeles in an elite private practice with a small group of doctors. *Scandal's* genre might be classified as a legal-political-detective drama hybrid. The series is set in Washington DC among politicians and lawyers and fixers. All three series offer images of the cities in which they are set. *Scandal* delivers sights of the Capitol as well as fast-paced dialogue reminiscent of Aaron Sorkin's *The West Wing* (1999–2006). It uses sound and visual editing transitions to simulate surveillance or press photography. All these worlds feature flawed protagonists and ensembles of supporting characters that envision themselves in their professions as heroic and above the law or playing God. The worlds with ensembles of complex characters set up the series for storylines with diverse representations, relationships, and social issues.

Introducing the Structure

All three series are one-hour network dramas, which means roughly forty-five minutes of screen time with commercial breaks. Rhimes uses a five-act structure, beginning with a new hire entering the world to orient them and the viewer to the other characters and rules of the world. All three shows have series and seasonal storylines and character arcs as well as episodic plots around specific cases (patients or clients). Both *Grey's* and *Private Practice* use a designated teaser to set up the episode, while *Scandal* folds the introduction into Act One.

Setup

The setup for a pilot script introduces viewers to the world, characters, theme, and any necessary exposition for the episode's plot to begin. The pilots become setups for the series.

The *Grey's* pilot teaser opens on a surgical montage with Meredith's voiceover: "The game. They say a person either has what it takes to play, or they don't. My mother was one of the greats. Me on the other hand—I'm kinda screwed."[3] It then cuts to reveal Meredith in her mother's house scrambling to dress and kick out the one-night stand lying next to her so she can make it to her first day of work as an intern at the hospital.

The device of the voiceover establishes Meredith as the protagonist and sets up the show dominantly through her point of view. It helps to establish her objective in her career as a doctor and sets up her mother as a driving force for her stakes. Introducing her image first, in a state of undress after a one-night stand as she scrambles to make it to her first day of work, sets up her conflict between her professional goals and personal desires and relationships. Seeing her first in her home, the house that was her mother's that she has just moved back into with the intention to sell, introduces her as a person with flaws and vulnerabilities. Previous medical pilots like *ER* and *St. Elsewhere* similarly take place over the course of one shift at the hospital, but they follow male doctors and are contained to the grounds of the hospital.

3. Crafting the Pilot

Next, we see Meredith driving to work, images of Seattle in the background, with the voiceover of Chief of Surgery Dr. Richard Webber (James Pickens Jr.) as Meredith rushes into a hospital room full of interns (mostly male). Dr. Webber's speech continues, describing "the game" they all want to play. The interns enter the operating room where they are awed by the space. Getting to "scrub in" is the goal for all of them. Now we see Dr. Webber. He tells them to look around at their competition. They do. They are worried, including Meredith. The teaser ends with her voiceover reiterating that she is "screwed."[4] The teaser sets up the exposition, Meredith's objective, obstacles (competition, self-doubt), stakes (living up to her mother), and the overarching thematic conflict (between personal and professional).

Private Practice starts with Addison leaving her position at Seattle Grace Hospital to start a new job at a private practice in Los Angeles. Dr. Richard Webber confronts "my Addison"[5] telling her not to leave, that she won't like a private Los Angeles co-op, that she is a world-class neonatal surgeon, that she lives to cut. This pushes Addison to defend her decision and explain her choice. As Addison proudly describes the brilliant doctors she will be working with, her words become voiceover as we glimpse images of the doctors' contrasting messy personal lives. This beginning shows what Addison is giving up and sets the stakes for this big decision to change her life. A brief montage of Los Angeles transitions us to Addison getting ready for work in her new house. Dancing and singing naked in her new free Los Angeles life, she looks up to see Sam (Taye Diggs) staring at her through the window. She throws on a robe and greets him outside to learn that he lives next door and didn't know she was moving to Los Angeles or was hired at the practice. She gets to work and realizes that Naomi (Audra McDonald) hasn't told any of the partners about Addison. The partners are upset that Naomi made a hiring decision without them. Now there is conflict, and Addison has something to prove. Addison gets oriented to the facilities and approach to medicine and realizes the immense change she is making. She begins to have doubts. While Meredith was a neophyte intern entering medicine with something to prove, Addison is already established as a respected surgeon, but the world of private practice will give her new things to learn, prove, and doubt. While *Grey's* starts in disembodied voiceover, *Private Practice* starts in action with Addison justifying her decision to leave. In her own voice, she states her objective, "to make a change,"[6] and introduces her new colleagues through her point of view.

Scandal deviates by introducing us through a different point of view than the series protagonist. Quinn is the young new hire looking up to

Olivia Pope, the series protagonist. Rhimes's protagonists are at different places in their career and power. While Meredith and Addison are both starting new jobs with other people in positions of authority, Olivia has established reputation and power through her firm, Olivia Pope and Associates (OPA). Both *Grey's* and *Private Practice* pilots begin and end with the protagonists outside their jobs in their personal space. We watch Meredith and Addison put on their professional masks and earn respect. We are introduced to them as women before we see them as professionals in their new jobs. Olivia, on the other hand, is introduced in professional action, already masked, and it is later in the episode that we see the vulnerable woman (when the mask drops). Quinn is the novice in *Scandal*. We first meet her in a personal moment and witness OPA through her naive eyes.

Practically, entering the series through a new hire allows Rhimes to provide exposition through legitimate character action orientation, introductions, explanations, and questions. It enables her to set up a point of view of the world, as well as establish stakes and objectives for the characters for the series. Meredith, Addison, and Quinn have something to prove in their new jobs. Meredith wants to make it as a surgeon in "the game" and live up to her mother's reputation. Addison wants to "make a change" in her life and her friend needs her to be there. Quinn wants to work with the Olivia Pope whom she admires, and she also wants to be a "gladiator in a suit."[7] Metaphorically, a new female hire acknowledges that women are still new in these fields—and seeing the story worlds from their perspectives (as well as watching them as protagonists) is still relatively new in media.

Plots

Each show has two to three cases for the episode, like most medical and crime procedurals. *Grey's* and *Private Practice* have patients who must be diagnosed and treated and ethical dilemmas the characters must face. *Scandal* has clients whose problems the team must investigate and fix. In all three shows, the season and series characters and relationship arcs are advanced through the episode plots. In each pilot, the protagonist comes to a decision or has an episode arc.

While the series enter through a new person's perspective and have a primary protagonist, they also establish the ensemble characters with their own objectives and obstacles so that characters and storylines can be alternated throughout the episodes. In *Grey's* pilot, we see the progression of the other interns, George (T. R. Knight), Izzie (Katherine

Heigl), and Cristina (Sandra Oh) through montage and cutting between storylines. *Private Practice* crosscuts between a fertility case with Sam and Naomi, a birthing patient with Addison and Pete (Tim Daly), and a mental health patient emergency with Violet (Amy Brenneman) and Cooper (Paul Adelstein). *Scandal* cuts between the different OPA team members' tasks on the case. This structure helps to build suspense and develops multiple characters and relationships in the series. This strategy also keeps things open for characters to come and go as the series progress.

Narrative Arcs

All three pilots juggle the episode cases, character arcs, and series- and season-long storylines. The three newcomers and Olivia Pope have episode arcs. Meredith moves from doubt and uncertainty ("I'm screwed") to confidence ("I'm a doctor"). She also manifests her arc through a decision. At the beginning of the episode, she tells Dr. Derek Shepherd (Patrick Dempsey) she is selling her mother's house. At the end of the episode, she tells her mother she has decided to keep the house.

Similarly, Addison moves from a defiant confidence and certainty (when talking to Webber) to awkward insecurity and uncertainty (when she learns her colleagues may not want her there) to a final confidence and certainty (when she asserts that she is a "world-class neonatal surgeon" and she is staying). Her arc further manifests through her action of dancing naked in her new house. When at the beginning of the pilot she gives up on dancing (when Sam sees her), at the end of the pilot, her final action is to pull down the blinds and dance naked as we see only her silhouette. It is an onscreen affirmation of her decision and action to change her life.

Quinn starts the episode with the job offer to work for Olivia Pope, whom she admires greatly. She has doubts and uncertainty as she witnesses and participates in work that feels less than heroic. She questions if they are really the good guys. Harrison (Columbus Short) assures her they are and that Olivia is "the best guy,"[8] but Quinn has to believe it. She smiles and says, "gladiator in a suit," demonstrating her acceptance and belief in Olivia and their mission. Olivia starts from a place of confidence and power in action in her job. An assignment from the White House and US president Fitzgerald Grant's (Tony Goldwyn) office exposes her vulnerability and personal relationship with the president. She chooses to believe him. Lying is a dealbreaker, she tells all her clients. After destroying the president's mistress and realizing he was lying, she decides to right the wrong she feels she has done. She tells the president's chief of staff (Jeff Perry) that his mistress is now her client. It is a threat, a reclamation of power, and a declaration of independence from Fitz's influence. It is an episode arc and the setup for the main storylines throughout the series.

The pilots introduce season and series storylines. *Grey's* introduces the love interest storyline with Derek, the other interns Meredith will compete with and develop relationships with, their mentors and antagonists in the supervising doctors, as well as Meredith's relationship with Cristina, who will eventually become "her person." Her final decision to keep the house means she will need roommates, which will further her relationship with the other interns. Lastly, the story thread about Meredith's mother establishes stakes for her professional career and relationships with more mature doctors, and it also creates an opening for later stories about her family. *Private Practice* sets up the personal issues of the doctors at Oceanside Wellness Group and their relationships with one another: Pete previously kissed Addison, Sam and Naomi recently went through a divorce, Cooper may be addicted to sex, Violet is struggling to get over an ex she has been stalking, Cooper has been a supportive and truthful friend to Violet, and Naomi is Addison's best friend who needs her. *Scandal*'s pilot sets up Stephen's (Henry Ian Cusick) impending engagement, Abby's (Darby Stanchfield) crush on Stephen, Quinn and Olivia's relationship, Olivia's relationship with Fitz and his White House staff members, and Olivia's guarded self, which will reveal itself periodically throughout the series.

In Rhimes's pilot scripts, the characters frequently alternate between professional and personal discussion within a scene, all the while setting up narrative arcs for the series. In *Grey's*, while Cristina and Meredith discuss a patient's symptoms to try to determine her condition, Cristina lists the conditions it can't be, and then says, "Are you seriously not going to tell me why you won't work with Shepherd?" Meredith says, "No. What about infection?" Cristina goes over the reasons it's not an infection, and then says, "Just tell me." Meredith tells her she can't comment or react, and then says, "We had sex." Cristina tries not to react. "What about an aneurysm?" she says. The diagnostic conversation continues until Cristina asks, "Was he good?"[9]

In *Private Practice*, Sam and Naomi are involved in a custody challenge of a dead patient's sperm, with both his wife and the girlfriend making claims for it. Through discussing their patients' rights and relationships, they pivot to issues remaining from their own marriage and divorce. While addressing their patients' problems, they come to realizations about their personal issues.

In *Scandal*, we first meet Olivia Pope as she rides in an elevator with Stephen on their way to retrieve a kidnapped baby from Ukrainian mobsters. Stephen tells her, "We're going to get killed." Olivia responds, "Did you propose? Weren't you going to ask her tonight?" He tells her that he was doing this (work) instead and redirects her to the fact that they are short on money. Olivia says, "So you flaked. Why are we short?" He explains the problem and threat and counters that he didn't flake, he is working for her. She tells him not to worry, the mobsters will take what they give them. She asks, "Did you at least buy the engagement ring?"[10]

Examining Rhimes's pilots, we can observe patterns in the strategies she uses to create her series and the ways in which she plants seeds for future storylines. While successful as genre television and procedural dramas, they are also platforms for character-driven stories exploring relationships, ethical dilemmas, and topical issues. The strategies detailed throughout this chapter can be considered by screenwriters developing their own series.

Notes

1 For further reading, see Joseph Campbell's *The Hero with a Thousand Faces* (2008) and Christopher Vogler's *The Writer's Journey: Mythic Structure for Writers* (2011).
2 See Maureen Murdock's *The Heroine's Journey: Woman's Quest for Wholeness* (1990) and Kim Hudson's *The Virgin's Promise: Writing Stories of Feminine Creative, Spiritual, and Sexual Awakening* (2009).
3 *Grey's Anatomy*, season 1, episode 1, "A Hard Day's Night," created and written by Shonda Rhimes, aired March 27, 2005, on ABC.
4 Ibid.
5 *Private Practice*, season 1, episode 1, "In Which We Meet Addison, a Nice Girl from Somewhere Else," created and written by Shonda Rhimes, aired September 27, 2007, on ABC.
6 Ibid.
7 *Scandal*, season 1, episode 1, "Sweet Baby," *Scandal*, created and written by Shonda Rhimes, aired April 5, 2012, on ABC.
8 Ibid.
9 *Grey's Anatomy*, season 1, episode, 1.
10 *Scandal*, season 1, episode 1.

Part II

SIGNIFICANT WORKS
Normalizing Diverse Representation

Chapter 4

COLOR-AWARE CASTING

Chriss Williams

The apology came swiftly. The *New York Times* (NYT) featured a story about Shonda Rhimes and how her characters break down stereotypes. Unfortunately, the writer suggested that if "Ms. Rhimes" were to write an autobiography, "it should be called 'How to Get Away with Being an Angry Black Woman.'"[1] Rhimes would have none of it. When a Twitter follower asked if she saw the article, Rhimes tweeted, "I've been too busy being angry and black. Also a woman. Takes up a lot of time."[2] Fortunately for television viewers, Rhimes occupies that time by creating television worlds where stereotypes like the "angry woman" are rarely seen. In Shondaland, we see diversity in her characters where folks play against such stereotypes. But I shouldn't use the term "diversity" because "Shonda really does not love the word *diversity*," Kerry Washington said. "She talks about abandoning the word *diversity* and replacing it with *normalizing*."[3]

In "normalizing" the world, Rhimes populates her shows with characters of all colors to force viewers to be "color aware" about the casting choices. But in being aware, Rhimes offers another truth of interracial friendships, relations, and workplaces: folks rarely talk about race. We see this in season 2 of *Grey's Anatomy* (2005–), the longest-running nighttime medical drama in television history, when Meredith Grey (Ellen Pompeo), who is white, discovers that her famous surgeon mother had an affair with the chief of surgery at Seattle Grace Mercy West Hospital, who is Black.[4] Meredith's reaction has everything to do with the shock of finding out about the affair and nothing to do with his race. In a 2005 interview with the *NYT*, Rhimes said that when she wrote the pilot, she "didn't specify the characters' ethnicities," so her casting process was wide open. "I'm in my early thirties, and my friends and I don't sit around and discuss race. . . . We're post-civil rights, post-feminist babies, and we take it for granted we live in a diverse world."[5]

By the time Shondaland's hit show *Bridgerton* (2020–) arrived on Netflix fifteen years later, Rhimes had successfully given viewers a world where race could be taken "for granted." But more, she was now aware of how race and diversity in her casting choices can force viewers to consider these issues in a new light. And by being casting aware, Rhimes is intentional with her choices. As *Bridgerton* creator Chris Van Dusen said, "I don't call the casting color blind, because I feel like the word color blind implies that color and race was never considered—and I don't think that's true for *Bridgerton* . . . I think color and race is very much a part of the show and very much a part of the conversation."[6]

"Color-blind" casting began in the theater in the 1950s and 1960s. Legendary theater producer-director Joseph Papp was an early proponent of casting actors without regard to race. "Papp was one of the first to cast Black and Hispanic actors in major classical roles . . . Joe wanted to fill the stage with the same kind of people he was going to fill the audience with, all the people of the city," said actor (and voice of Darth Vader) James Earl Jones. "He tried everything to open up the whole issue that you're casting human beings. He would cast Hamlet as a woman."[7]

By 2015, color-blind casting in theater took a turn toward "color aware" with Lin-Manuel Miranda's Tony- and Pulitzer Prize-winning Broadway smash *Hamilton*. Miranda's decision to cast nonwhite actors as America's Founding Fathers was the whole point of the show. President Obama knew this when, in 2016, he invited the cast to perform at the White House. In his introduction, he said, "with a cast as diverse as America itself, including the outstandingly talented women [. . .] the show reminds us that this nation was built by more than just a few great men—and that it is an inheritance that belongs to all of us."[8]

Miranda recounted the origin of *Hamilton* in an interview with Terry Gross:

> I think it's incredibly meaningful to then populate our live show with Black and brown artists, one, because hip-hop is a Black art form. It was created by Blacks and Latinos in the South Bronx in the '70s . . . And also, it's our country, too. You know, the line we've always said is this is a story of America then told by America now.[9]

Some, however, believed this directive to specifically cast Black and brown actors ran afoul of New York City's Human Rights Law that forbids discrimination in hiring based on race in a casting notice. The Actors' Equity Association also questioned the casting notice, but the producers were undeterred and defiant in their response: "[i]t is essential to the storytelling of 'Hamilton' that the principal roles, which were written for nonwhite characters (excepting King George), be performed by nonwhite actors . . . [w]e will continue to cast the show with the same multicultural diversity that we have employed thus far."[10]

For Miranda and Rhimes, being color aware in casting *is* the point. They want us to see color—and ethnicity and gender as well. They are not color "blind." They see race and they want everyone else to see it, too.

We're in This Together

In Rhimes's normalized world, she seeks to challenge modern perceptions of the role that race and gender should play. A dramatic example of this was when she explored the power dynamic of interracial love and the fraught history of white men sexually involved with Black women on *Scandal* (2012–18) in season 2, episode 8 ("Happy Birthday Mr. President," written by Rhimes). As secret lovers President Fitzgerald "Fitz" Grant (Tony Goldwyn), who is white, and his communication director, Olivia Pope (Kerry Washington), who is Black, walk through the crowded White House corridors, they share a terse conversation about the state of their relationship. Olivia drops a bomb, telling the President, "I'm feeling a little, I don't know, Sally Hemings/Thomas Jefferson about all this."

Later, alone, Olivia and Fitz have one of the most memorable moments in the show's history. Fitz confronts Olivia about her comment and tells her the truth about his feelings for her:

```
        FITZ
You're playing the race card
because I'm in love with you?
Come on! Don't belittle us. It's
insulting and beneath you and
designed to drive me away. I'm not
going away.

        OLIVIA
I don't have to drive you away.
You're married and you have
children. You're the leader of the
Free World. You are away by
```

definition. You are away. You're
unavailable.

          FITZ

So this is about Mellie?

          OLIVIA

No, no, no! This is . . . I smile at
her and take off my clothes for
you. I wait for you. I watch for
you. My whole life is you. I can't
breathe because I'm waiting for
you. You own me, you control me, I
belong to you.

          FITZ

You own me! You control me. I
belong to you. You think I don't
want to be a better man? You think
that I don't want to dedicate
myself to my marriage? You don't
think I want to be honorable? To
be the man you voted for? I love
you. I'm in love with you. You're
the love of my life. My every
feeling is controlled by the look
on your face. I can't breathe
without you. I can't sleep without
you. I wait for you. I watch for
you. I exist for you. If I could
escape all of this and run away
with you? There's no Sally or
Thomas here. You're nobody's
victim, Liv. I belong to you. We're
in this together.[11]

He walks away leaving her shattered. Television has never depicted a scenario like this before: A white man—and not just any white man, the president of the United States of America—declaring that a Black woman "owns" him. This scene burns with the passion and intense love they share.

But more, by evoking the relationship between President Thomas Jefferson and Sally Hemings, the enslaved woman Jefferson owned and had children with, Rhimes offers no history lesson—you either know who Sally Hemings is or you don't. So, depending on your knowledge of Jefferson and Hemings, you take the scene as a direct reference to America's racial history, or you just enjoy the passion.

Color-aware casting allows moments like this where racial or ethnic issues do not require long discussions or any discussion—a knowing nod or reference lets those in the know see that the television characters, despite not directly addressing racial issues, are still very much aware of them.

The Wig Comes Off

If *Scandal* saw an interracial couple trying to be together (the state of their relationship was left open-ended in the finale), Shondaland's next series, *How to Get Away with Murder* (2014–20), created by Peter Nowalk, features a successful and glamorous Black female lead married to a white man. With this, we get to go into the bedroom in a very intimate way, revealing issues Black women face that previously were never seen on screen.

In 2019, California became the first state to pass the CROWN Act.[12] CROWN stands for "Create a Respectful and Open Workplace for Natural Hair," and it bans discrimination against people with natural hairstyles in the workplace. Holly Mitchell, who served as a State Senator for California from 2013 to 2020, introduced the bill, describing the law as being about "inclusion, pride and choice." "[t]his law protects the right of Black Californians to choose to wear their hair in its natural form, without pressure to conform to Eurocentric norms." For Black women and many women of color, wearing their hair the way they want, without fear of repercussions, is a step closer to bringing their "authentic selves" to work. By 2023, nineteen states followed California's lead in passing their own versions of the CROWN Act.[13]

But five years before the passage of California's CROWN Act, Shondaland brought this issue to an international audience in *HTGAWM*'s season 1, episode 4 ("Let's Get to Scooping," written by Erika Green Swafford), an episode that ends with what journalist Shania Russell calls "one of the most memorable revelations in the series."[14] Annalise Keating (Viola Davis), a gifted law professor and glamorous defense attorney "who's been radiating power since she first stepped into the frame—sits down in her bedroom and strips away her makeup and wig." Russell adds that Annalise is "a force of nature, terrifying her students and colleagues alike, with a pristine reputation and picture-perfect success, trophy husband and all."

But this evaporates when she stares at her reflection in the mirror at the conclusion of the episode. Lost between who she wants the world to believe she is and who she really is, Annalise begins to reveal herself to the viewer—but more, she empowers herself by baring her authentic self. She starts with her jewelry, dropping it onto her vanity like spare change. Then, she reaches behind her head and slowly at first, and then in one swift motion, she takes off her wig revealing her close-cropped natural hair. She peels off her long eyelashes and wipes off her makeup as the music throbs. This is not some sad-sack, woe-is-me moment. This is a defiant and visual "hear me roar." It's made even more potent because her white husband is watching—and by his look, we wonder if this might be the first time he has seen his wife in her natural beauty.

In an interview with the *Wall Street Journal*, Davis admitted that the scene was her idea:

> I just wanted to deal with her hair. It's a big thing with African-American women. . . . You start when you're just a young girl. Do you twist it? Do you leave it natural when it's so hard to take care of? Then you start wearing wigs but every night before bed you've got to take the wig off and deal with your hair underneath. And it's a part of Annalise that I needed the writers to deal with because I've never seen it, ever, on TV and I thought it would be very powerful. It's part of her mask.[15]

Annalise's mask would get a new crown in season 3, episode 5 ("It's About Frank," written by J. C. Lee) when Oscar-nominated actress Mary J. Blige appears as a hairdresser, delicately giving Annalise a weave. The *Huffington Post* called the episode "Un-be-weave-able," proclaiming, "Mary J. Blige Gave Viola Davis a Sew-In on TV and It Was Historic."[16]

By showing intimate moments such as these—moments that women of color have but rarely have opportunities to see on television—*HTGAWM* normalizes them. Shondaland and *HTGAWM* were five years ahead of the CROWN Act, helping women of color bring their "authentic" selves to work and into our homes.

4. Color-Aware Casting

History of Visibility/America Accepts

Before we could have a white president on television declare that a Black woman "owns" him or a Black woman take off her wig or get a weave, we had to simply *see* Black folks on television. Donald Bogle details the early history of Blacks on television in his book, *Primetime Blues: African Americans on Network Television*:

> [a]t the tail end of the Depression, a former blues singer, then appearing in a Broadway drama, was asked by the NBC radio network to perform on an experimental broadcast for a new medium. She agreed—and made broadcast history. The year was 1939. The woman was Ethel Waters. The program was *The Ethel Waters Show*. The new medium then in development was called television . . . as the evening's headliner, the mighty Ethel Waters, midway in what would be a long, turbulent, and illustrious career, had become—at this very early time—the first African American to star in her own program on the tube. Television hasn't been the same since.[17]

Ethel Waters was followed by Anna May Wong, who in 1951 was the first Asian American to have a leading role in a television series, *The Gallery of Madame Liu-Tsong* (1951).[18] That same year, television's first interracial couple appeared on the groundbreaking show *I Love Lucy* (1951–7), which starred Lucille Ball and her real-life husband Desi Arnaz, of Cuban descent. In 1956, Nat King Cole was the first African American to host a national show, *The Nat "King" Cole Show* (1956–7). Bill Cosby followed in 1965, the first Black actor to have a leading role in a television series, *I Spy* (1965–8). In 1968, Diahann Carroll was the first Black actress to star in her own series, *Julia* (1968–71), also notable in that Julia was one of the first nondomestic roles for a Black actress.[19]

In 1977, ABC pushed the boundaries of race and diversity, testing America's appetite for seeing it on television. This watershed event was the twelve-hour miniseries based on Alex Haley's epic best-selling novel *Roots*. As writer Darin Strauss explains, the series was important because "a Black family were the heroes, and the dads from some of America's favorite shows—'The Brady Bunch,' 'The Waltons,' 'Bonanza'—played racists . . . the finale on ABC remains the third highest-rated television episode ever."[20]

I Love Lucy was the first series to demonstrate just how accepting America would be of interracial marriage on the small screen, however, and it was critical for nonwhite viewing audiences. Journalist Raj Tawney explains, "[a]lthough my father was an immigrant from India and my mother was of Puerto Rican and Italian descent; the idea of belonging to a flavorful, multiethnic household, just like the Ricardos, gave me a reason to feel proud of my own mixed identity."[21]

But Ball had to get creative to convince the network to cast her husband in the show. Strauss explains that CBS initially hired a white actor to play Ball's husband, and so, "Lucille Ball produced, paid for and starred in a number of live performances with [her real-life Cuban husband] Desi in vaudeville theaters across the country."[22] These live shows were successful, proving to CBS's network executives that America was ready for its first interracial marriage on television.

Diversity as a Business Model

Shondaland owes a lot to Lucille Ball and Desi Arnaz and their production company, Desilu Productions. Desilu was Hollywood's first independent production company and introduced a new business model to television, producing classic shows like *The Andy Griffith Show* (1960–8), *My Three Sons* (1960–72), and *The Dick Van Dyke Show* (1961–6).[26] Desilu's *Mission Impossible* (1966–73) and *Star Trek* (1966–9) were especially lauded for their interracial casting. Desilu didn't announce their desire to produce shows with interracial casts—they just did it, knowing from their experience with *I Love Lucy* that America would be accepting.

There's a direct line from Desilu's interracial casting to Shondaland's network shows such as *Grey's Anatomy*, *Scandal*, and *HTGAWM*. In 2017, Shondaland expanded its reach when Rhimes signed a multiyear contract with Netflix, a deal potentially worth between $300 and $400 million. *Bridgerton* was the first series from this deal, and in 2021, Rhimes and Netflix extended her deal to include feature films, podcasting, audio, live events "as well as potential gaming and VR content." But more, Rhimes's partnership with Netflix furthers her work to see diversity behind the lens by "investing in and providing the financial and technical infrastructure to bolster diversity programs to increase industry workplace representation for underrepresented groups both domestically and in the UK."[23]

Bridgerton: *Alternative History*

For *Bridgerton*, Rhimes and Van Dusen only needed a jumping-off point to bring color to their version of 1810s British royal court. For it, they "returned to a historical debate that Sophie Charlotte zu Mecklenburg-Strelitz, born in 1744, is said to have had African ancestors—which means she could indeed have been the first Black British queen."[24] As Ellen Harrington, director of the German Film Institute, noted, Rhimes and Van Dusen's casting of "people of Color as members of the royal court was a conscious decision to reinterpret and retell history."[25] Vernā Myers, Netflix's vice president of inclusion strategy, said that Rhimes's color-aware casting was a result of Netflix supporting diverse showrunners and encouraging an "inclusion lens" to be applied to decisions. "[i]t's exciting," Myers said. "It's interesting, it brings up a lot of conversation, and some controversy."[26]

One point of controversy was summarized in a *NYT* headline that declared: "'Bridgerton' Takes On Race. But Its Core Is Escapism." In the story, critic Salamishah Tillet explains that the characters of *Bridgerton* never seem to forget their Blackness and understand it as one of the many facets of their identity: "[t]he show's success proves that people of color do not have to be erased or exist solely as victims of racism." However, this, she concludes, "risks reinforcing the very White privilege it seeks to undercut by enabling its White characters to be free of racial identity."[27]

Similarly, critic Eric Deggans stated that the "show seems ambivalent about race. You know, while a lot of the characters don't talk about race that much and seem to act as if race doesn't matter,"[28] Carolyn Hinds was more direct in her critique, writing, "the problem in 'Bridgerton' comes when the characters' race is practically ignored for almost the entire show, except for a few vague references in their dialogue—using words like 'us' and 'them.'"[29]

But this criticism proves the point of how far we've come—or better, how Shondaland's color-aware casting choices have pulled us along. For *Bridgerton*, the overriding issue of race and how it's infused into its world is summed up about halfway through season 1 when the Black Duke of Hastings's aunt, Lady Danbury, tells him (and the viewer), "[l]ook at our queen. Look at our king. Look at their marriage. Look at everything it is doing for us, allowing us to become. We were two separate societies divided by color, until a king fell in love with one of us. Love, Your Grace, conquers all."[30]

And in Shondaland's universe, love is all you need.

Notes

1 Alessandra Stanley, "Wrought in Rhimes's Image," *New York Times*, September 18, 2014, https://www.nytimes.com/2014/09/21/arts/television/viola-davis-plays-shonda-rhimess-latest-tough-heroine.html.

2 Lorena O'Neil, "Shonda Rhimes Criticizes *New York Times* over 'Angry Black Woman' Line," *Hollywood Reporter*, September 19, 2014, https://www.hollywoodreporter.com/news/general-news/shonda-rhimes-criticizes-new-york-734314/.
3 Taylor Ferber, "Why Shonda Rhimes Doesn't Like the Word *Diversity*," *Vulture*, November 18, 2017, https://www.vulture.com/2017/11/scandal-shonda-rhimes-doesnt-like-the-word-diversity.html.
4 Christina Dugan Ramirez, "'Grey's Anatomy' Set to Become the Longest-Running Primetime Medical Drama on TV—Surpassing 'ER'!," *People*, February 28, 2019, https://people.com/tv/greys-anatomy-longest-primetime-medical-drama/.
5 Matthew Fogel, "'Grey's Anatomy' Goes Colorblind," *New York Times*, May 8, 2005, https://www.nytimes.com/2005/05/08/arts/television/greys-anatomy-goes-colorblind.html.
6 Jennifer Mass, "'Bridgerton' Switched Book Characters' Races for Series—Just Don't Call the Casting 'Color Blind,'" *TheWrap*, December 21, 2020, https://www.thewrap.com/bridgerton-colorblind-cast-queen-charlotte-black-mixed-race/.
7 Laura Wolff Scanlan, "Joe Papp and the Transformation of American Theater," *Humanities* [online] 43(2), June 3, 2022, https://www.neh.gov/article/joe-papp-and-transformation-american-theater.
8 Former president Barack Obama, "Remarks by the President at 'Hamilton at the White House,'" *White House*, March 14, 2016, https://obamawhitehouse.archives.gov/the-press-office/2016/03/14/remarks-president-hamilton-white-house.
9 "'The Past Isn't Done with Us' Says 'Hamilton' Creator, Lin-Manuel Miranda," *NPR*, Fresh Air, June 29, 2020, https://www.npr.org/transcripts/884592985.
10 Robert Viagas, "Civil Rights Attorney Slams *Hamilton* for Casting Notice—AEA Responds," *Playbill*, March 30, 2016, https://playbill.com/article/civil-rights-attorney-slams-hamilton-for-casting-notice-aea-responds.
11 *Scandal*, season 2, episode 8, "Happy Birthday, Mr. President," created by Shonda Rhimes, written by Rhimes, aired December 6, 2012, on ABC.
12 Nicole Chavez and Faith Karimi, "California Becomes the First State to Ban Discrimination Based on Natural Hairstyles," *CNN*, July 3, 2019, https://www.cnn.com/2019/07/03/us/california-hair-discrimination-trnd/.
13 Shannon Dawson, "Here Are All of the States that Have Successfully Passed the CROWN Act," *Newsone*, March 21, 2023, https://newsone.com/4383979/the-crown-act-states/.
14 Shania Russell, "Viola Davis and the Power of Removing Annalise Keating's Wig on How to Get Away with Murder," *Slashfilm.com*, April 13, 2022, https://www.slashfilm.com/830842/viola-davis-and-the-power-of-removing-annalise-keatings-wig-on-how-to-get-away-with-murder/.

15 John Jurgensen, "Viola Davis on the Shocking 'How to Get Away with Murder' Ending," *Wall Street Journal*, October 17, 2014, https://www.wsj.com/articles/BL-SEB-84222.
16 Taryn Finley, "Mary J. Blige Gave Viola Davis a Sew-In on TV and It Was Historic," *HuffPost*, October 21, 2016, https://www.huffpost.com/entry/mary-j-blige-viola-davis-weave_n_580a1d5ae4b02444efa2ca2d.
17 Donald Bogle, *Primetime Blues: African Americans on Network Television* (New York: Farrar, Straus and Giroux, 2001), 1.
18 It's believed that all copies of this show were destroyed as there are no known copies available. See Nicole Chung, "The Search for Madame Liu-Tsong," *Vulture*, September 5, 2017, https://www.vulture.com/2017/09/the-search-for-the-gallery-of-madame-liu-tsong.html.
19 Essence Gant, "15 Black Actresses Who Made History," *Black Enterprise*, February 1, 2020, https://www.blackenterprise.com/black-actresses-who-made-black-history/.
20 Darin Strauss, "An 'I Love Lucy' Lesson: The Elites Always Misjudge Americans' Tolerance," *The Hill*, August 15, 2020, https://thehill.com/opinion/civil-rights/512033-an-i-love-lucy-lesson-the-elites-always-misjudge-americans-tolerance/.
21 Raj Tawney, "Was I Love Lucy Ahead of Its Time?" *Television Academy*, March 22, 2019, https://www.emmys.com/news/online-originals/was-i-love-lucy-ahead-its-time.
22 Strauss, "An 'I Love Lucy' Lesson."
23 Peter White, "Shonda Rhimes Extends Deal with Netflix, Adds Feature Films & Gaming To Pact," *Deadline*, July 8, 2021, https://deadline.com/2021/07/shonda-rhimes-extends-deal-with-netflix-adds-feature-films-gaming-1234788724/.
24 Christine Lehnen, "'Bridgerton' and the Art of non-traditional Casting," *dw.com*, March 25, 2022, https://www.dw.com/en/netflix-hit-series-bridgerton-and-the-art-of-non-traditional-casting/a-61246176.
25 Ibid.
26 Lanre Bakare, "'Something You've Never Seen Before': Netflix Diversity Chief on Bridgerton's Casting," *Guardian*, January 22, 2021, https://www.theguardian.com/tv-and-radio/2021/jan/22/something-youve-never-seen-before-netflix-diversity-chief-on-bridgertons-casting.
27 Salamishah Tillet, "'Bridgerton' Takes on Race. But Its Core Is Escapism," *New York Times*, April 2, 2021, https://www.nytimes.com/2021/01/05/arts/television/bridgerton-race-netflix.html.
28 "Netflix's 'Bridgerton' Is 1st Project from Shonda Rhimes' Production Company," *NPR*, January 11, 2021, https://www.npr.org/2021/01/11/955557294/netflixs-bridgerton-is-1st-project-from-shonda-rhimes-production-company.

29 Carolyn Hinds, "'Bridgerton' Sees Race Through a Colorist Lens," *Observer*, January 1, 2021, https://observer.com/2021/01/bridgerton-sees-race-through-a-colorist-lens/.

30 Liv Facey, "'Queen Charlotte' Achieves Black Regency Escapism Without Ignorance," *Teen Vogue*, May 9, 2023, https://www.teenvogue.com/story/queen-charlotte-a-bridgerton-story-balances-race-history-regency-romance-op-ed.

Chapter 5

BLACK MATERNAL BODIES ON THE SCREEN

Shondaland and the New Representational
Paradigm of Black Motherhood

Zsuzsanna Lénárt-Muszka

The representations of Black women and mothers on the small screen—especially women who are pregnant, breastfeeding, or contemplating an abortion—have changed dramatically in the past few decades. As recently as 1993, singer Vanessa Williams was expected to hide her pregnant belly during the televised Grammy Awards Ceremony;[1] in the same year, Aunt Viv had to wear maternity tent dresses on *The Fresh Prince of Bel-Air* (1990–6), and there were virtually no mainstream portrayals of Black women caring for their newborns or practicing any other embodied act of care related to new motherhood. Yet, two years prior, heavily pregnant Demi Moore—a white actress—graced the covers of *Vanity Fair*, posing nude with her belly exposed. While the photo was certainly controversial (with some even deeming it immoral),[2] the fact remains that a white woman's pregnant body was considered worthy of display, while Black women's pregnancies were erased from view. Additionally, where white mothers are often portrayed as "nurturers," Black women's depictions tend to be filtered through centuries of history and tainted by stereotypes that cast them as lazy, greedy, inattentive mothers, unfit to care for their children.[3] When Black women and mothers were not erased, they were animalized, exoticized, and either oversexualized or degendered and deemed not feminine enough.[4]

Many of these underlying assumptions are linked to how the Black mother was conceptualized and treated throughout American history. Starting from the Middle Passage, the notion of motherhood meant something vastly different for Black American women than it did to white ones. While individual enslaved women's circumstances might have differed, what unified their experiences was the pervasive occurrence of reproductive rights violations.[5] In a distressing cycle of systematic rape and enforced reproductive labor, enslaved women were routinely required to generate more capital throughout the Southern regions, not only through their work on plantations but through giving birth to as many children as possible, who would become enslaved themselves.[6] Even after Emancipation, Black women's reproductive rights were curtailed in various forms, apparent in, among others, a high number of women being pressured into sterilization and contraception.[7] Maternal rights disparities continue to endure even as we move into the twenty-first century and so do racist stereotypes and the scarcity of media representation.[8]

In the past few years, however, the cultural tendency to idealize white mothers while vilifying Black ones has started to dissipate, and with it, the images of Black maternal bodies have also certainly begun to diversify. A striking number of these visual representations celebrate positive images of Black motherhood and/or show young Black women and mothers as complex individuals whose bodies—whether pregnant, giving birth, nursing, or even undergoing an abortion—are nothing to be ashamed of. Undoubtedly, Black television mogul Shonda Rhimes is single-handedly responsible for the post-millennial ubiquity of these varied images. Shows created and/or produced by Rhimes, including medical dramas *Grey's Anatomy* (2005–) and *Private Practice* (2007–13) as well as the political thriller *Scandal* (2012–18), depict a significant number of situations arising from women characters getting pregnant, experiencing and making decisions regarding pregnancy, childbirth, and breastfeeding, and featuring mothers from all walks of life, races, and ethnicities, prominently among them Black women and girls.

This chapter explores the aesthetics and politics of a variety of scenes from *Grey's Anatomy*, *Private Practice*, and *Scandal* that feature Black women navigating the embodied aspects of new motherhood. Apart from exploring why these representations might be considered groundbreaking, I will also comment on their historical and contemporary social contexts and the changing landscape of media representations that have arisen in no small part thanks to the work of Rhimes.

Pregnancy, Abortion, and Miscarriage

Pregnancy is quite often dramatized on *Grey's*. Season 18, episode 6 ("Every Day Is a Holiday (with You)," written by Meg Marinis) offers viewers a fascinating and complicated depiction of Black motherhood in modern America. Ashley, a pregnant mother of four, is so overworked that she doesn't see a doctor despite long-term abdominal pain.[9] The fact that her doctors believe her and don't try to trivialize her suffering counters the long-lasting beliefs that Black people are less susceptible to pain,[10] while the fact that she doesn't get medical care in time comments on how members of disadvantaged communities are prevented from seeking care because of a lack of time, financial hardship, or inadequate access to health care, evident in long waiting times and overcrowded hospitals.[11] Even though Ashley only needs an appendectomy, she requests a hysterectomy or tubal ligation (procedures that would prevent another pregnancy). Crucially, the medical staff respects her wishes and grants her complete bodily autonomy, thereby normalizing Black women's right to making their own reproductive choices. This storyline shows a striking similarity with an early episode involving a subplot featuring a white mother.[12] On the one hand, Ashley's inclusion speaks to the increase in racial diversity on the small screen; on the other hand, it has an inescapable historical dimension as it sets up a satisfying contrast with the repeated curtailment of Black women's rights. The fact that Ashley needs an appendectomy and requests a hysterectomy is also a matter of some irony; medically unjustified postpartum hysterectomies performed on Southern Black women in the first half of the twentieth century were so common that they earned the colloquial term "Mississippi appendectomies."[13]

Other instances of Shondaland depicting pregnancy and maternal autonomy attempt to normalize both the physical symptoms and the individual woman's right to choose. Even though Miranda Bailey (Chandra Wilson) fears a heart attack and menopause when she experiences severe hot flashes and mood swings early in her pregnancy, she later treats these symptoms as healthy, run-of-the-mill manifestations of hormone level fluctuations.[14] The pregnancies of a teenage girl (Cheyenne in season 2[15]) and of a sixty-something woman (Adele Webber in season 3[16]) are depicted without judgment and moralizing overtones, as is surrogacy (Rina in season 3[17]). These portrayals work to remove the stigma associated with Black teenage pregnancy and pregnancy out of wedlock without explicitly discussing these issues. In the few instances when abortion is discussed or portrayed in Shondaland, race is there only in the background. In *Scandal*'s season 5, episode 9 ("Baby, It's Cold Outside," written by Mark Wilding), Olivia Pope (Kerry Washington) has an abortion, which is shown with an overhead close-up that focuses on her face but mostly obscures the emotional reality of the procedure.[18] While Olivia's status as the Black "mistress" of a white president is often discussed on the show, the abortion itself is not framed in terms of race. The scene's strength lies exactly in its treatment of abortion as an everyday procedure, a strategy that was hailed and lambasted by the press.[19] In *Private Practice*'s season 3, episode 11 ("Another Second Chance," written by Kathy McCormick and Krista Vernoff), Maya's abortion is debated in terms of morality and choice, with race not factoring into the discussion.[20] The same is true of Adele's[21] and Bailey's[22] miscarriages and Gina's emergency hysterectomy[23] in *Grey's*, with no discussion of these characters' Blackness. Notwithstanding, even when no overt references are made to the mothers' race, Shondaland intentionally populates the screen with Black characters, which serves to validate Black women getting quality reproductive health care in all walks of life.

Childbirth

When it comes to scenes of childbirth, Shondaland series have also been groundbreaking in diverse portrayals of Black women. Although the brief childbirth scene in *Grey's* season 17, episode 5 ("Fight the Power," written by Zoanne Clack)[24] emphasizes Jo's—a white doctor's— perspective, it shows the new mother's joy and love for her newborn, contributing to the fight against stereotypes that cast Black women as uncaring mothers. *Grey's* scenes involving Avi,[25] Sheryll,[26] or Bailey[27] in labor and giving birth emphasize the intense physicality of the process and shed light on its emotional impact. When Bailey's water breaks suddenly, she is unfazed and refuses to treat childbirth like an illness.[28] She goes through the process on her own terms, refusing to take pain medication or to start pushing until her husband gets there. As a result, her obstetrician implies that Bailey is not rational because she's a woman in labor, which, instead of demeaning Bailey's intellectual ability, is rather a comment on the emotional toll labor can have. Her obstetrician, Addison (Kate Walsh, who returns to the series from *Private Practice*), acknowledges that Bailey is a competent person who is doing her best in an impossible situation, and she deserves assistance, not judgment.

All in all, in the aforementioned three scenes, neither the dialogue nor the cinematography sugarcoat childbirth. The camerawork does not shy away from showing sweat or disheveled hair, and the audience is not spared the vocality of labor either; the women grunt and scream while experiencing intense pain. This representational strategy highlights that the realities of labor are powerful yet quotidian and that Black women going through labor belong on the screen without judgment.

Scenes of childbirth on *Grey's*, including C-sections (see Rina,[29] Sarah,[30] or Blair[31]), in which a Black mother is shown to be in the care of a compassionate doctor, are also important in the representation of Black women's pregnancy. Enslaved women have endured prolonged experimentation within the realm of gynecology and obstetrics for centuries. Most notoriously, procedures spearheaded by white male surgeon J. Marion Sims during the nineteenth century were conducted without anesthesia, aiming to find a cure for the vesicovaginal fistula, a postnatal condition.[32] The unwarranted procedures routinely carried out on Black women as recently as the twentieth century frequently served the educational needs of young, predominantly white, male physicians.[33] So while Shondaland's series do not try to pretend that Black women no longer face medical racism, the impact of showing positive examples of Black women treated competently, often by doctors who are themselves women of color, is noteworthy. Even when doctors (including a Black man) discuss on *Grey's* what a great learning opportunity a particular procedure to be carried out on a pregnant Black woman is, they treat this patient with respect; her well-being and wishes are priorities.[34]

Breastfeeding

There haven't been many fictional representations of breastfeeding on television, let alone involving Black women. *Grey's* was among the first shows that tackled portraying this inescapably embodied practice. In season 2, episode 9 ("What Have I Done to Deserve This?" written by Stacy McKee), Bailey returns to work as a new mother with her breastmilk leaking and leaving visible marks on her shirt.[35] The way Bailey treats this incident contrasts heavily with how the men around her view it. The chief of surgery (Richard Webber) is exasperated to the point of being speechless when he sees the stains, but Bailey maintains eye contact with him and does not attempt to cover up the stains, making the viewer feel there is nothing unnatural about the situation. Similarly, in two other scenes involving Webber and another male colleague, Derek Shepherd (Patrick Dempsey), Bailey takes breastfeeding and milk leakage as merely a fact of life, thereby removing the stigma from it. Breastfeeding has often been looked at as something private, shameful, and even repulsive, which, coupled with the deep-seated racist assumptions about Black (female) bodies being excessive, grotesque, and hyper-embodied,[36] adds to these scenes' potency: Bailey's defiant posture and unapologetic eye contact show that milk—even if it is leaking—is nothing to be ashamed of. Additionally, the practice of wet nursing—which started during slavery but continued into the twentieth century—meant that the breastmilk of Black women was used for the nourishment of white infants, often to the detriment of their own babies.[37] Therefore, portraying Bailey with her milk belonging only to herself and her baby was not only revolutionary in the history of television but also significant from the perspective of the historical mistreatment of nursing Black mothers. These representations also move away from the twentieth-century images of the Black mother as someone perpetually in crisis, suffering in silence from poverty and abuse;[38] instead, they characterize motherhood as a site from which triumph and joy can also emerge while simultaneously normalizing various aspects of (not) becoming a mother. When crises inevitably occur in medical dramas, the characters are still mostly multidimensional and come from all walks of life, thus offering viewers a wide range of images and representation.

Postpartum Conditions

Grey's also attempts to normalize a host of postpartum conditions. In season 2, episode 22 ("The Name of the Game," written by Blythe Robe), when Bailey experiences a surge of hormones after giving birth, she treats her emotional outbursts as completely ordinary; she implies that just because her physical state compels her to feel certain emotions, she is more than able to continue working.[39] To discourage a male colleague from meddling with her patient, she sarcastically says that she does not know what she might be capable of if she were to experience another sudden rush of hormones.[40] Whereas the show treats these strong sensations with humor, it approaches more serious postpartum conditions with sensitivity and empathy. In season 17, episode 11 ("Sorry Doesn't Always Make It Right," written by Julie Wong), Hollie has severe depression related to her recent childbirth experience and the Covid pandemic, and her husband stays with their sick newborn at the hospital, with Hollie recovering at home.[41] Crucially, neither her family members nor the doctors shame her for not being beside her baby; instead, she receives support and understanding whether her depression stems from the emotional aftermath of the pandemic or has physical—hormonal—causes.

These representations do a lot to combat negative stereotypes against mothers in general, but in particular, Black mothers. The Western discourse on motherhood, rooted in a patriarchal framework, has been constructed and informed by an amalgamation of theories, convictions, and vested interests, chiefly among them beliefs that have historically relegated women to the "nature" pole within the nature/culture spectrum and deemed them irrational and overly emotional, contrasting with the traditionally male domains of rationality and logic. Additionally, Western racism has thought of Black individuals as intellectually inferior, engendering a perception that extends to Black women, attributing to them an even greater degree of irrationality and an excess of emotions.[42] This is highlighted by stereotypes like the angry Black woman, an image in which biases come together to suggest that Black women are naturally prone to emotional outbursts and irrational behavior. Through Black characters such as Bailey and Hollie, viewers get a sense that even when new Black mothers experience emotional intensities, they can still be capable and loving mothers.

Conclusion

Not only has Shondaland ushered in a new era that broadens the representational paradigm of early Black motherhood, Rhimes's work has also resulted in a renewed focus on the Black maternal body in television shows across the spectrum, including major networks' primetime series created by and starring people of color. In scenes that were unimaginable prior to *Grey's*, in contemporary television Black women are shown getting abortions (*Empire*, 2015–20[43]), coping with postpartum depression (*Black-ish*, 2014–22[44]), or being in intense labor and tussling with the decision to give up their babies for adoption (*Empire*[45]). In 2019, a major plotline on *The Resident* (2018–23) focused on a Black woman who dies from complications of a C-section after her care is delayed and her and her husband's concerns are dismissed while white patients are given priority.[46] Two years later, *New Amsterdam* (2018–23) dedicated an entire episode to the issue of medical racism affecting Black women; it dramatizes cases in which they face difficulties with breastfeeding, VBAC (vaginal birth after C-section), and sexual trauma leading to pregnancy.[47] Both episodes comment on racial bias—both conscious and unconscious, both individual and systemic—

explicitly through character dialogue while also not shying away from using intimate shots that bring into relief the embodied aspects of the women's pain and joy.

Simultaneously, there has been an ongoing shift in the self-representation of Black superstars who are increasingly embracing their maternal bodies. A striking number of their visual representations celebrate positive images of joyful Black mothers. The pregnant and postpartum bodies of Black superstars such as Beyoncé, Kelly Rowland, Kerry Washington, Keke Palmer, Cardi B, and Rihanna have been proudly shown and celebrated both in public and on social media. More and more Black celebrities are making their public appearances and social media posts an integral part of their own narrative. A prominent example of how culture has shifted is Serena Williams's 2017 *Vanity Fair* cover that evokes Demi Moore's iconic portrait, featuring a Black, aestheticized, idealized pregnant body in a triumphant pose.[48] Beyoncé's performance at the 2017 Grammy's and her postpartum social media posts are also groundbreaking since they honor the Black maternal body as something glamorous and worthy of celebration. After seeing the aforementioned Grammy's performance—one that emphasizes Beyoncé's pregnant belly—Vanessa Williams remarked in a nostalgic tweet, "They never showed my pregnant belly when I sang my nominated 'Save the Best for Last'—Oh how times have changed!"[49] Indeed, these photographs and public appearances, whether eroticized or drawing on religious or classical iconography, are subversive since they put the Black body on a pedestal instead of the scaffold, and in doing so, they resist centuries of erasure and violence.

The clear line from *The Cosby Show*'s (1984–92) well-known and "perfect" television mom, Clair Huxtable, to the contemporary, much more varied images of Black women and mothers on a variety of screens also testifies to the evolving media landscape, all no doubt owing a lot to Rhimes's work. Characters such as Bailey, whether heavily pregnant, in labor, or coping with their changing postpartum bodies, are portrayed in all their dignity, humanity, and beauty. Whether they need life-saving C-sections or opt not to have any (more) children, these women are shown making decisions that prioritize their own well-being and autonomy, with their doctors respecting their wishes. The portrayal of their experiences challenges societal expectations, highlights the importance of reproductive health, and ultimately empowers Black individuals and communities. These powerful images on the screen serve as a form of resistance, acknowledging the dignity of Black mothers while challenging the status quo.

Notes

1 Vanessa Williams (@VWOfficial), "They Never Showed My Pregnant Belly when I Sang My Nominated 'Save the Best for Last'—Oh How Times Have Changed! Kudos Beyoncé!-- #Grammys," *Tweet*, February 13, 2017, https://twitter.com/VWOfficial/status/830977023577300992.
2 George Lois, "Flashback: Demi Moore," *Vanity Fair*, last modified June 22, 2011, https://www.vanityfair.com/news/2011/08/demi-moore-201108.
3 Julia S. Jordan-Zachery, "Mythical Illusions: Cultural Images and Black Womanhood," in *Black Women, Cultural Images, and Social Policy* (New York: Routledge, 2009), 26–48.
4 Venetria K. Patton, *Women in Chains: The Legacy of Slavery in Black Women's Fiction* (New York: State University of New York, 2000), xii.
5 Jennifer L. Morgan, *Laboring Women: Reproduction and Gender in New World Slavery* (Philadelphia: University of Pennsylvania Press, 2004), 3.
6 Jennifer L. Morgan, "Partus Sequitur Ventrem: Law, Race, and Reproduction in Colonial Slavery," *Small Axe* 22, no. 1 (2018): 1, muse.jhu.edu/article/689365.
7 Angela Y. Davis, *Women, Race and Class* (New York: Vintage, 1983), 177–9; Harriet A. Washington, *Medical Apartheid: The Dark History of Medical Experimentation on Black Americans from Colonial Times to the Present* (New York: Doubleday, 2006), 197.
8 Latoya Hill, Samantha Artiga, and Usha Ranji, "Racial Disparities in Maternal and Infant Health: Current Status and Efforts to Address Them," *Kaiser Family Foundation*, last modified November 1, 2022, https://www.kff.org/racial-equity-and-health-policy/issue-brief/racial-disparities-in-maternal-and-infant-health-current-status-and-efforts-to-address-them/.
9 *Grey's Anatomy*, season 18, episode 6, "Every Day Is a Holiday (with You)," created by Shonda Rhimes, written by Meg Marinis, aired November 18, 2021, on ABC.
10 Sophie Trawalter, Kelly M. Hoffman, and Adam Waytz, "Racial Bias in Perceptions of Others' Pain," *PLOS ONE* 7, no. 11 (2012): 1–7, https://doi.org/10.1371/journal.pone.0048546.
11 Wayne J. Riley, "Health Disparities: Gaps in Access, Quality and Affordability of Medical Care," *Transactions of the American Clinical and Climatological Association* 123 (2012): 167, https://www.ncbi.nlm.nih.gov/pmc/articles/PMC3540621/.
12 *Grey's Anatomy*, season 2, episode 23, "Blues for Sister Someone," created by Shonda Rhimes, written by Elizabeth Klaviter, aired April 30, 2006, on ABC.
13 Dorothy E. Roberts, *Killing the Black Body: Race, Reproduction, and the Meaning of Liberty* (New York: Pantheon Books, 1997): 90.

14 *Grey's Anatomy*, season 16, episode 4, "It's Raining Men," created by Shonda Rhimes, written by Mark Driscoll, aired October 17, 2019, on ABC.

15 *Grey's Anatomy*, season 2, episode 15, "Break on Through," created by Shonda Rhimes, written by Zoanne Clack, aired January 29, 2006, on ABC.

16 *Grey's Anatomy*, season 3, episode 24, "Testing 1-2-3," created by Shonda Rhimes, written by Allan Heinberg, aired May 10, 2007, on ABC.

17 *Grey's Anatomy*, season 3, episode 24, "Testing 1-2-3," and season 3, episode 25, "Didn't We Almost Have It All?," created by Shonda Rhimes, written by Tony Phelan and Joan Rater, aired May 17, 2007, on ABC.

18 *Scandal*, season 5, episode 9, "Baby, It's Cold Outside," created by Shonda Rhimes, written by Mark Wilding, aired November 19, 2015, on ABC.

19 Sarah Kliff, "*Scandal* Showed a Realistic Abortion on Television," *Vox*, last modified November 20, 2015, https://www.vox.com/2015/11/20/9769634/scandal-abortion-shonda-rhimes.

20 *Private Practice*, season 3, episode 11, "Another Second Chance," created by Shonda Rhimes, written by Kathy McCormick and Krista Vernoff, aired January 14, 2010, on ABC; *Private Practice*, season 3, episode 12, "Best Laid Plans," created by Shonda Rhimes, written by Lara Olsen and Patricia Carr, aired January 21, 2010, on ABC.

21 *Grey's Anatomy*, season 3, episode 25, "Didn't We Almost Have It All?"

22 *Grey's Anatomy*, season 16, episode 9, "Let's All Go to the Bar," created by Shonda Rhimes, written by Kiley Donovan, aired November 21, 2019, on ABC.

23 *Grey's Anatomy*, season 6, episode 19, "Sympathy for the Parents," created by Shonda Rhimes, written by Allan Heinberg, aired April 1, 2010, on ABC.

24 *Grey's Anatomy*, season 17, episode 5, "Fight the Power," created by Shonda Rhimes, written by Zoanne Clack, aired December 10, 2020, on ABC.

25 *Grey's Anatomy*, season 15, episode 22, "Head Over High Heels," created by Shonda Rhimes, written by Bridgette Burgess, aired April 18, 2019, on ABC.

26 *Grey's Anatomy*, season 10, episode 16, "We Gotta Get Out of This Place," created by Shonda Rhimes, written by Jeannine Renshaw, aired March 20, 2014, on ABC.

27 *Grey's Anatomy*, season 2, episode 16, "It's the End of the World," created and written by Shonda Rhimes, aired February 5, 2006, on ABC; *Grey's Anatomy*, season 2, episode 17, "As We Know It," created and written by Shonda Rhimes, aired February 12, 2006, on ABC.

28 *Grey's Anatomy*, season 2, episode 16, "It's the End of the World."

29 *Grey's Anatomy*, season 3, episode 24, "Testing 1-2-3"; *Grey's Anatomy*, season 3, episode 25, "Didn't We Almost Have It All?"

30 *Grey's Anatomy*, season 7, episode 14, "P.Y.T. (Pretty Young Thing)," created by Shonda Rhimes, written by Austin Guzman, aired February 10, 2011, on ABC.
31 *Grey's Anatomy*, season 11, episode 16, "Don't Dream It's Over," created by Shonda Rhimes, written by Andy Reaser, aired March 19, 2015, on ABC.
32 Washington, *Medical Apartheid*, 70; Durrenda Ojanuga, "The Medical Ethics of the 'Father of Gynaecology', Dr. J. Marion Sims," *Journal of Medical Ethics* 19, no. 1 (1993): 28–30. http://www.jstor.org/stable/27717250.
33 Roberts, *Killing*, 92.
34 *Grey's Anatomy*, season 9, episode 21, "Sleeping Monster," created by Shonda Rhimes, written by Bronwyn Garrity, aired April 25, 2013, on ABC.
35 *Grey's Anatomy*, season 2, episode 19, "What Have I Done to Deserve This?" created by Shonda Rhimes, written by Stacy McKee, aired February 26, 2006, on ABC.
36 Janell Hobson, "The 'Batty' Politic: Toward an Aesthetic of the Black Female Body," *Hypatia* 18, no. 4 (2003): 88. http://www.jstor.org/stable/3810976.
37 Emily West and R. J. Knight, "Mothers' Milk: Slavery, Wetnursing, and Black and White Women in the Antebellum South," *Journal of Southern History* 83, no. 1 (2017): 37, https://doi:10.1353/soh.2017.0001.
38 Jennifer C. Nash, *Birthing Black Mothers* (Durham: Duke University Press, 2021), 4.
39 *Grey's Anatomy*, season 2, episode 22, "The Name of the Game," created by Shonda Rhimes, written by Blythe Robe, aired April 2, 2006, on ABC.
40 *Grey's Anatomy*, season 3, episode 5, "Oh, the Guilt," created by Shonda Rhimes, written by Zoanne Clack, Tony Phelan, and Joan Rater, aired October 19, 2006, on ABC.
41 *Grey's Anatomy*, season 17, episode 11, "Sorry Doesn't Always Make It Right," created by Shonda Rhimes, written by Julie Wong, aired April 8, 2021, on ABC.
42 Jonathan Crane, "Exploding the Myth of Scientific Support for the Theory of Black Intellectual Inferiority," *Journal of Black Psychology* 20, no. 2 (1994): 189, https://doi.org/10.1177/00957984940202007.
43 *Empire*, season 4, episode 12, "Sweet Sorrow," created by Lee Daniels and Danny Strong, written by Eric Haywood and Jamie Rosengard, aired April 11, 2018, on Fox.
44 *Black-ish*, season 4, episode 2, "Mother Nature," created by Kenya Barris, written by Corey Nickerson, aired October 10, 2017, on ABC.
45 *Empire*, season 4, episode 13, "Of Hardiness Is Mother," created by Lee Daniels and Danny Strong, written by Dianne Houston and Carlito Rodriguez, aired April 18, 2018, on Fox.

46 *The Resident*, season 2, episode 20, "If Not Now, When?" created by Amy Holden Jones, Hayley Schore, and Roshan Sethi, written by Jones, Tianna Majumdar-Langham, and Chris Bessounian, aired April 15, 2019, on Fox.
47 *New Amsterdam*, season 3, episode 8, "Catch," created by David Schulner, written by Erika Green Swafford, aired April 20, 2021, on NBC.
48 Buzz Bissinger, "Serena Williams's Love Match," *Vanity Fair*, last modified June 27, 2017, https://www.vanityfair.com/style/2017/06/serena-williams-cover-story.
49 Williams, "They Never Showed My Pregnant Belly."

Chapter 6

REWORKING THE "MONSTROUS MOTHER" FOR THE MODERN ERA

Louise Coopey

When asked about "strong female characters" in interviews, Shonda Rhimes has consistently and vehemently pushed back against the label by articulating a long-held belief that her "female characters get to be everything [. . .] [M]aybe in the past, they've been very one-dimensional, but like women, like girls, like all of us, they are fully dimensional in all ways."[1] Rhimes's commitment to diversity and her belief in the need to develop and nurture her characters manifest in woman-centric narratives like *Grey's Anatomy* (2005–), a long-running medical drama that positions the complex and multidimensional titular character Meredith Grey (Ellen Pompeo) at its heart. A skilled surgeon, Meredith's career forms the basis of the show. However, it is the nature and quality of Meredith's relationships that provide audiences insight into who she is, including her mother's influence on her life and career. Her mother, renowned surgeon Ellis Grey (Kate Burton), is introduced in Rhimes's pilot episode, "A Hard Day's Night," and the prominence of the relationship between Meredith and Ellis in *Grey's* is evident from the outset.

The first line of the voiceover that opens the pilot is spoken by Meredith about her mother: "My mother was one of the greats."[2] The immediacy of the introduction informs viewers just how significant Ellis is in Meredith's life, in terms of both her character arc and the wider narrative strands that form the fabric of the show. However, it also establishes a framework through which women tell their stories about balancing their careers with having a family "beyond simple notions of positive or negative images."[3] Through Dr. Ellis Grey's character, Rhimes champions the complexities of motherhood, womanhood, and a woman's power to choose.

Initially, Ellis Grey is positioned from Meredith's perspective and is presented as a "monstrous mother," a figure that is constructed within and threatens the hierarchical power wielded by the patriarchy through her reluctance to conform and resistance to social control.[4] Ellis ostensibly values her surgical career above her family, although her presence on screen slowly begins to challenge reductive representations of motherhood associated with working mothers. Rhimes uses a range of televisual tools and devices to slowly add layers to Ellis's identity, including flashback, third-party memories, and dialogue. Each of these tools contributes to the exploration of the dynamic between the characters and the generational shift between the experiences of mother and daughter, pushing back against representational boundaries.

This chapter explores the way *Grey's* maps what Latham Hunter refers to as the "contentious, complicated terrain of motherhood" through Ellis.[5] Her nuanced and multidimensional characterization illustrates the representational possibilities for women who are also mothers. In other words, women who are mothers are not *only* mothers, and Rhimes challenges depictions of one-dimensional tropes of motherhood and their generational specificity. Rhimes reworks the monstrous mother trope for the modern era by exploring Ellis's choices while simultaneously holding her to account for the detrimental impact of her decisions on her daughter.

The Grey Method (of Parenting)

The mother has historically been a consistent representational paradigm on television, mirroring the figure's importance to traditional gendered roles in society and serving to reinforce patriarchal desires to control and contain women through visual culture. Representational categories into which mothers have been shoehorned have typically subordinated them and guided how they are presented on screen. Not so with Rhimes's characters, though. Ellis Grey is an example of how Rhimes's mother characters tend to exceed boundaries that gendered social and cultural hierarchies have set to contain them.

Ellis's experiences of motherhood began in the late 1970s, meaning that she would have been subjected to and influenced by contemporaneous attitudes toward the mother, particularly through second-wave feminist thought that emerged out of the 1960s and 1970s. Second-wave feminism, E. Ann Kaplan argues, broadly focuses on the mother from the perspective of the daughter, therefore following familiar patterns of social and cultural relations that reinforced the binary and patriarchal categorization of mothers into "good" and "bad": "[F]eminism was in part a reaction against our mothers, who had tried to inculcate the patriarchal 'feminine' in us, much to our anger. This made it difficult for us to identify with Mothering and to look from the position of the Mother. Unwittingly, then, we repeated the patriarchal omission of the Mother."[6] The inability of the daughter to identify with the mother forms the basis of Ellis's relationship with Meredith, and the distance created through that emotional barrier has the unintended effect of casting the mother as monstrous. Not that blame should be attributed to Meredith. Rather, both women approach their relationship with entirely different, and competing, perspectives. Meredith does not see her mother as a complex individual with desires and needs of her own initially, but Rhimes's unraveling of the relationship as the show progresses leads to a recognition of that individuality on the part of both daughter and audience. Ellis appears monstrous from a distance initially but challenges that reductive label when examined more closely.

Depriving the mother of her own nuanced identity as a woman first narrows the representational possibilities, meaning that the mother is either idealized as a "good," nurturing, and selfless individual or derided as a "bad," neglectful, and selfish mother who is concerned only for herself.[7] However, Rhimes's commitment to character development renders it quickly apparent that Ellis Grey's approach to motherhood does not fit neatly into existing representational frameworks of mothers on screen. So much so, the duality of Ellis's identity—the career-focused woman and distant "bad" mother—is introduced in the first episode. Eight minutes into "A Hard Day's Night," Ellis's achievements are foregrounded through Meredith's peers discussing her being "royally inbred," owing to her status as a "Grey." Izzie Stevens (Katherine Heigl) identifies Ellis as "one of the first big chick surgeons," while Cristina Yang (Sandra Oh) points out that she won the Harper Avery Award, a fictional award for surgical excellence, twice.[8] They can all identify with Ellis as surgeons, are awestruck by her achievements, and aspire to be like her. The audience is therefore encouraged to see Ellis through her achievements at work, her ambition and refusal to conform to traditional gender roles, which aligns her with the bad mother and monstrous mother types and marks her as a disruptor of gendered norms.[9]

Meredith's perspective ostensibly reinforces this categorization eight minutes before the end of the episode. In a conversation with fellow surgical intern George O'Malley (T. R. Knight), Meredith dispassionately recalls that Ellis tried to dissuade her from going to medical school because she did not have what it takes to be a surgeon. Where good mothers are expected to nurture their child's emotional development and provide unconditional love and support,[10] the rhetorical distance Meredith puts between herself and the memory places emphasis on Ellis's inability to fulfill her daughter's needs. The distance is compounded at the end of the episode by the revelation that Ellis has Alzheimer's disease and is in a care home. However, the emotional disconnect between the past and present is a common theme that resonates in the moments that *Grey's* explores Meredith's childhood. We see her navigating hospital corridors alone as a small child and Ellis leaving her on a carousel after an argument with her lover, a young Richard Webber (J. August Richards). Meredith refers to Ellis driving her father away and moving her across the country at a moment's notice. All of the corresponding flashbacks and memories give the impression that Meredith was lonely and neglected, creating the sense that Ellis is a mother who damaged her daughter emotionally, the distance between them creating fear and contempt. Ellis's development is therefore filtered through the impact her parenting has on Meredith, balancing the formative experiences that shape the latter's childhood and the enduring legacy of Ellis's choices as Meredith navigates adulthood.

Unusually for a minor character, Ellis's influence is pervasive in the early seasons of the show, but her characterization is also developed as the show progresses through Rhimes's creative decision to give Ellis herself a voice. Empowering her to speak lends Ellis agency over her own experiences and allows her to communicate in the present and past alike instead of maintaining Meredith's power over her mother's narrative. Those experiences are recounted through reconstructions of her own memories, thus interrogating the space between "motherhood and professionhood."[11] Putting Ellis's version of events across diminishes her monstrosity as a neglectful and dangerous mother, while paradoxically confirming her absolute refusal to conform to the demands established by patriarchal discourse.[12] She is humanized as a woman who makes mistakes as a mother, though trying her best, while also attempting to be the best version of herself in her medical career—a duality that is indicative of complexity and an example that Meredith ultimately follows.

Affording the Monstrous Mother a Voice

Feminist media scholar Kathleen Rowe Karlyn claims that "[t]he feminist struggle for social transformation and justice can only benefit from our continued willingness to think about the institutions of motherhood, and to reflect on and strengthen our generational connections."[13] The potential for social transformation and strengthening of generational connections is dependent on the ability of the mother to challenge existing tropes. *Grey's* provides space for that because it does not demand women fit into narrowly defined categories that regulate their behavior. Instead, the world of *Grey's* provides scope for the characters to explore who they are and make choices without the "risk of being positioned as mad or bad" should they fail to live up to the impossible standards expected of them.[14] Even where Ellis's behavior is far from exemplary, the audience is privileged with the knowledge that her maternal concerns come from a place of love, even if she is unwilling or unable to reveal that side of herself to Meredith. Her monstrosity is diminished by her complexity.

Ellis's interactions with Meredith in season 3, episode 14 ("Wishin' and Hopin," written by Tony Phelan and Joan Rater) offer insight into the relationship between mother and daughter. They also provide insight into Ellis's character on her own terms instead of through Meredith's eyes. At the start of the episode, Meredith arrives at the nursing home Ellis resides in to find that she is temporarily lucid, a state that lasts for the duration of the episode and gives viewers a real-time view of what Ellis is like and how she interacts with her daughter (rather than simply taking Meredith's word for it). In truth, Ellis is overbearing, forthright, and unnecessarily harsh when speaking to her daughter, and this is markedly different from her interactions with other doctors and interns. For instance, with Meredith avoiding her after her admission, Ellis asks Cristina whether her daughter has chosen a specialty, a question she considers to be the "most personal" a surgeon can be asked in contrast to the frivolousness of whether she has a boyfriend.[15] While Cristina avoids revealing any information about Meredith to Ellis, the question irrevocably labels her an unconventional mother, and the snippet of dialogue offers significant insight into the mother–daughter relationship. It complicates Meredith's observation that Ellis prioritizes her career ahead of her. The question is indicative of maternal interest, but asking Cristina and not Meredith is a symbol of the distance between them. It is not the result of neglect or disinterest, but rather the outcome of an inability to relate to and empathize with each other. Ellis is not monstrous, but she is misunderstood.

In reworking the monstrous mother trope to include the complexity and nuance present in her characterization, Ellis's identity is grounded in the struggles and barriers she faced in her career, and most prominently in her need to continually fight for what she wants. In season 6, episode 15 ("The Time Warp," written by Zoanne Clack), Ellis articulates her frustration with those struggles in a flashback: "I gave birth to a child, Richard. That makes me a mother. It doesn't make me inept. It doesn't make me less of a woman. It doesn't make me less of a surgeon. No matter how much everyone wants it to."[16] This response to the rampant sexism in Seattle Grace Hospital in 1982, where Ellis (the younger iteration of whom is played by Sarah Paulson) is the only woman surgeon, explains not only how she gains a reputation for being monstrous but also why she is how she is. She is forthright and harsh because she must appear strong to resist those who would marginalize her, which impacts her focus and ability to balance motherhood and professionhood without losing part of herself. The use of a flashback in this episode allows Ellis the opportunity to speak for herself, presenting her truth. The complicated terrain of motherhood necessitates a series of choices on Ellis's part, but it also highlights her flaws and her problematic approach to her role as "mother."

The scene that defines the relationship between Ellis and Meredith and highlights the tension that arises from the former's choices occurs in "Wishin' and Hopin'" and begins with Ellis expressing a desire to know what her daughter's life is like. Meredith offers up the information that she has a boyfriend first, displaying the frivolousness that Ellis previously expressed disdain for, before her mother interrupts her curtly and asks her whether she has chosen a specialty. Instead of being satisfied that Meredith is expressing her own happiness, Ellis quickly becomes frustrated and belittles her:

> What happened to you? You've gone soft. Stammering about a boyfriend and saying that you're waiting to be inspired. You're waiting for inspiration? Are you kidding me? I have a disease for which there is no cure. I think that would be inspiration enough! [...] Anyone can fall in love and be blindly happy, but not everyone can pick up a scalpel and save a life. I raised you to be an extraordinary human being, so imagine my disappointment when I wake up after five years and discover that you're no more than ordinary. What happened to you?[17]

This speech is uncomfortable to watch, with Meredith's composure slipping gradually as the camera switches from Ellis's face to her own. The shift in her body language is subtle, unlike that of Ellis, who stands over her daughter and becomes more animated as her monologue progresses. Although Ellis appears to have the power over Meredith in this interaction, largely through her attempts to control her and her demands that Meredith disrupt gendered roles as she did herself, her monstrosity slips when it becomes apparent that Ellis is, in fact, power*less*. Speaking to Richard Webber (the older iteration of whom is played by James Pickens) immediately before losing lucidity to Alzheimer's once again, Ellis expresses her powerlessness through maternal concern for Meredith in an unconventional and yet distinctly Ellis way: "[S]he's got so much more to learn and I won't be able to teach her."[18] There is no singular, definitive way to show maternal support, but this is indicative of her concern for Meredith and how she will cope without her. Ellis is not a typical mother, but she *is* a mother and much more besides. It is the complexity of her characterization that reveals such layers and expands the representational possibilities for women who are also mothers on screen. Indeed, Meredith excels where Ellis struggled. She finds a balance between her career and parenthood later in *Grey's*, learning from her mother's experiences and mistakes. Here, the generational connection is apparent and celebrated by Rhimes.

More Extraordinary Than Ordinary

Ellis Grey is ultimately one of Rhimes's most extraordinary characters. Despite being a minor presence on screen, her influence is pervasive because she heavily influences the way Meredith sees herself and understands her own identity. In this respect, she has the impact expected of a mother. However, it is Ellis's complexity—her nuanced and multilayered characterization—that challenges the representational paradigm of the monstrous mother, allowing Meredith to ultimately follow in her footsteps without facing the same labels and prejudices. The importance of affording the monstrous mother a voice and humanizing her is achieved through a variety of devices to ensure a shifting of perspectives. There is no absolute and singular representation of the figure, which makes a compelling case for empowering women to decide who they are by exceeding boundaries imposed by the dominant patriarchal order that has historically sought to contain them. The generational shift between Ellis and Meredith is ultimately what allows the latter to break free from the constraints that Ellis had no choice but to deal with, while *Grey's* itself demonstrates why television is a compelling medium for exploring the archetype of the monstrous mother and pushing back against representational boundaries. It has the narrative time and space, along with a series creator and showrunner willing to embrace such complex representation.

Ellis is flawed as a human and as a mother, but she does the best she can. The complicated nature of her character is a credit to Rhimes and her determination to explore woman-centric narratives in the context of historical and present-day struggles. Ellis is domineering and pushy as a mother, but her identity is formed through her own experiences and a desire for Meredith to overcome similar challenges should she face them. Ultimately, through *Grey's*, Rhimes provides space to explore the complexities of motherhood, how mother–daughter relationships can shape girls as they mature into womanhood, and the universal struggle to balance motherhood and professionhood.

Notes

1. Samantha Sutton, "Shonda Rhimes Says She Isn't Creating 'Strong Female Characters,'" *Coveteur*, September 19, 2017, https://coveteur.com/2017/09/19/shonda-rhimes-strong-female-characters-ryan-murphy-beauty/.
2. *Grey's Anatomy*, season 1, episode 1, "A Hard Day's Night," created and written by Shonda Rhimes, aired March 27, 2005, on ABC.
3. Elana Levine, "*Grey's Anatomy*: Feminism," *How to Watch Television*, edited by Ethan Thompson and Jason Mittell (New York: New York University Press, 2013), 139.
4. Marilyn Francus, *Monstrous Motherhood: Eighteenth Century Culture and the Ideology of Domesticity* (Baltimore: Johns Hopkins University Press, 2013), 10; Jane Ussher, *Managing the Monstrous Feminine: Regulating the Reproductive Body* (London: Routledge, 2006), 4.
5. Latham Hunter, "Motherhood, Prime-time TV, and *Grey's Anatomy*," in *Mediating Moms: Mothers in Popular Culture*, edited by Elizabeth Podnieks (Montreal: McGill-Queens University Press, 2012), 323.
6. E. Ann Kaplan, "The Case of the Missing Mother," *Heresies* 16 (1983): 81.
7. Adrienne Rich, *Of Woman Born* (New York: W.W. Norton & Co, 1976), 110–27; Kaplan, "The Case of the Missing Mother," 81.
8. *Grey's Anatomy*, season 1, episode 1, "A Hard Day's Night."
9. Katherine Kinnick, "Media Morality Tales and the Politics of Motherhood," *Mommy Angst: Motherhood in American Popular Culture*, edited by Ann C. Hall and Mardia J. Bishop (Santa Barbara: ABC-CLIO, 2009), 3.
10. Rebecca Feasey, *From Happy Homemaker to Desperate Housewives: Motherhood and Popular Television* (London: Anthem Press, 2012), 2.
11. Hunter, "Motherhood, Prime-time TV, and *Grey's Anatomy*," 321.

12 Barbara Creed, "Horror and the Monstrous-Feminine: An Imaginary Abjection," *Screen* 27, no. 1 (1986): 49.
13 Kathleen Rowe Karlyn, *Unruly Girls, Unrepentant Mothers: Redefining Feminism on Screen* (Austin: University of Texas Press, 2011), 5.
14 Ussher, *Managing the Monstrous Feminine*, 1–2.
15 *Grey's Anatomy*, season 3, episode 14, "Wishin' and Hopin'," created by Shonda Rhimes, written by Tony Phelan and Joan Rater, aired February 1, 2007, on ABC.
16 *Grey's Anatomy*, season 6, episode 15, "The Time Warp," created by Shonda Rhimes, written by Zoanne Clark, aired February 18, 2010, on ABC.
17 *Grey's Anatomy*, season 3, episode 14, "Wishin' and Hopin'."
18 Ibid.

Chapter 7

RESPECTABILITY IN SHONDALAND

Villainous Queerings

Sébastien Mignot

In addition to all the reasons that make Shonda Rhimes exceptional in today's televisual landscape that have already been mentioned and which warrant the writing of this book, she has been called a "fierce and longtime advocate of LGBT equality" and has received awards from LGBTQ+ organizations such as the Gay and Lesbian Association Against Defamation (GLAAD)[1] and the Human Rights Campaign (HRC).[2] In her acceptance speech for the GLAAD Golden Gate Award, Rhimes used the adjectives *complex* and *layered* to describe the character of Cyrus Beene from her hit show *Scandal* (2012–18).[3] Indeed, part of what makes her work distinctive from the bulk of LGBTQ+ images produced in recent decades is arguably her emphasis on creating well-rounded, multifaceted characters. In that sense, she was one of the first showrunners to depart from a long representational tradition that has tended—albeit for legitimate reasons—to confine most LGBTQ+ characters to simplistic narratives of respectability, especially on network television.[4]

Respectability politics can be defined as follows: "a politics informed by a conviction that marginalized groups must demonstrate that they adhere to normative values before they will be accepted or granted rights by dominant groups."[5] To the notable exception of radical activist groups (like Against Equality), most mainstream organizations have favored this approach, at least from the 1960s onward.[6] As many scholars have demonstrated, respectability politics is ambivalent at best; while asserting the compatibility of given social groups with existing norms, it often ends up effecting secondary marginalization for those deemed less deserving within that same group and/or who find themselves at the intersection of multiple forms of oppression.[7]

7. Respectability in Shondaland 87

It is therefore easily conceivable that Rhimes's intersectional identity and personal experiences as a Black woman may have made her more keenly attuned to such ideas and more likely to take them into account when approaching matters of representation.

A great variety of LGBTQ+ characters populate the vastness of Shondaland—Rhimes's televisual queendom. In fact, as GLAAD argued in its 2020-1 report on the state of LGBTQ+ representation on television, four creatives including Rhimes were responsible for 17 percent of all LGBTQ+ characters.[8] This chapter will focus on three gay male[9] characters in two Shondaland network series: Cyrus Beene (Jeff Perry) from *Scandal* and Connor Walsh (Jack Falahee) and Oliver Hampton (Conrad Ricamora) from *How to Get Away with Murder* (2014-20).[10] The thematic affinities between these two shows and the similarities between the characters motivated this choice of corpus.[11] Both *Scandal* and *HTGAWM* blur the lines of morality and righteousness. The upcoming analysis aims to examine the various ways in which these three characters revisit notions of respectability and subvert existing tropes about gay men, in particular, that of the "gay villain."

Respectability

As the titles of these two shows indicate, antinormativity is a pervasive feature of these diegetic universes. Indeed, in portraying most of their characters involved in morally dubious, unethical, or downright wrong political or legal skullduggery, both shows question notions of right or wrong, of legitimacy and lawfulness.

As mentioned, the politics of respectability has been the overall strategy of mainstream LGBTQ+ organizations since the beginning of the LGBTQ+ movement. As early as the 1970s, organizations like the Gay Media Task Force realized the critical importance of cultural representation in achieving that goal.[12] However, in spite of the prevalence of this strategy over the years, and perhaps because of the somewhat recent hard-won victories of the LGBTQ+ movement and the growing acceptance of gays and lesbians, it has come under mounting criticism in recent years.[13] The successive seasons of *Scandal* and *HTGAWM* unfold axiologically complex narratives in which respectability politics get both mobilized and challenged.

At the beginning of *Scandal*, Cyrus Beene is the White House chief of staff[14] serving under Republican president Fitzgerald Grant. His function should, in all likelihood, prescribe that he abide by strict standards of respectability. Yet, in the first few episodes of the first season, he hires a hit man to get rid of a White House aide who had sexual relations with the president and is turning out to be somewhat of an inconvenience to the administration. This is the first in a long list of hits placed by Cyrus over the course of the series. Cyrus's rhetoric for justifying these actions is always couched in a language of necessity and duty, done in the name of protecting what the characters refer to as "the republic." Cyrus is portrayed as a henchman who must get his hands dirty so that the president does not. His actions are purportedly in service of this high purpose and contribute to fostering a climate of moral ambiguity that precludes simple definitions of respectability and is reminiscent of what Jason Mittell terms "relative morality" in his analysis of antihero characters.[15] This characterization is interesting as openly gay characters are not so common in political dramas, especially in such high-ranking positions.[16] This show makes the days of the Lavender Scare seem long gone when the presence of gays and lesbians in government was considered a threat to national security.[17]

This aspect of Cyrus's character conjures the trope of the "gay helper."[18] Using the actantial model[19] to examine Cyrus's actions in the series, we notice that he is often situated as a helper, whether it be in the help he provides the president, the "republic," or when he is hired as campaign manager and then as vice president for future late president-elect Francisco Vargas. Be that as it may, instead of sticking to the commonplace "gay helper" narrative, the show problematizes and subverts the trope and uses it to complexify Cyrus's character. The "gay helper" trope partakes of a logic of respectability inasmuch as such characters must prove themselves useful and help the narrative move forward. Nevertheless, Cyrus is no subservient minion. On the contrary, in acting of his own volition, oftentimes incurring the president's disapproval, he claims agency in this seemingly auxiliary function.

Cyrus appears to be sincere in his willingness to help make other people presidents. His enthusiasm seems particularly genuine regarding Vargas's run for office in season 5. However, as early as season 2, in a vociferous confession to his husband about rigging the election that put President Grant in the Oval Office, he forcefully declares that being gay has prevented him from fulfilling his destiny of becoming POTUS.[20] This scene is significant in Cyrus's character elaboration as it lays the ground for an ulterior development linked to the narrative arc of Vargas's assassination. (This point will be further explored later in the analysis.)

Sex

As Suzanna Danuta Walters argues, when gay characters are represented as helpers, they often end up being desexualized and compelled to serve as "moral centers" for their straight counterparts.[21] One of the most common ways gay men have been shown as respectable on screen is by thoroughly desexualizing them, especially on network television (cable channels are overall more adventurous, broadcasting more risqué content).[22] This is especially true of older gay men (older bodies indeed tend to be shown—if ever—in nonerotic ways), who remain few and far between on television. For instance, the representation of Cyrus's sexuality is not as graphic and explicit as Connor and Oliver's in *HTGAWM*, but it is still somewhat of a rarity in today's televisual landscape.[23] Aside from complaints about the show's bottom-shaming blunders,[24] *HTGAWM*, created by Peter Nowalk under the Shondaland umbrella, has been praised for being particularly daring in its depiction of gay sex for a network show.[25] As opposed to a myriad of other series featuring gay men, it did not simply suggest sexual intercourse by showing pre- or postcoital kisses and caresses. A rimming scene from the pilot has even entered the annals of television history, as it were.[26] The show is also one of the only ones to portray a serodiscordant couple on television. Oliver finds out that he is HIV-positive in season 1, and the topic of living with HIV receives nonsensationalistic treatment over the course of the series. In this regard and in others, the show can at times be said to showcase elements of queer pedagogy[27] and has the merit of trying to educate viewers about sex with people living with HIV (PLWH) and addressing the stigma associated with HIV, including within the gay community.

Connor, who might initially be perceived as a "promiscuous gay man,"[28] has an interesting trajectory regarding sex. At first, he uses sex to obtain privy information to help solve the cases Annalise Keating (Viola Davis) has the "Keating Four"[29] work on. In fact, that is how he meets Oliver, who eventually becomes his husband. The exclusive dimension of the "Coliver"[30] relationship is never absolutely clear, but neither of them is shown engaging in consensual nonmonogamy (CNM), except in season 6, episode 4 ("I Hate the World," written by Matthew Cruz), when they have a threesome as a recently married couple. This scene goes to show that their marital relationship does not espouse traditional respectability politics, which tend to recreate heteronormative romantic and sexual configurations.

Marriage

Respectability politics was particularly prevalent when same-sex marriage was still the main political aspiration of most mainstream LGBTQ+ organizations.[31] Access to marriage as a family institution seemed to demand from gays and lesbians that they conform to strict moral standards to assuage the fears of "middle" Americans.[32] The "sanctity" of the institution of marriage was not spared by *HTGAWM*'s general antinormativity. For example, instead of casting doubts about the viability of their relationship, Connor and Oliver's respective misdeeds reinforce their mutual fidelity, making them literal "partners in crime."

Cyrus, too, is a married man. In fact, he ties the knot three times over. These conjugal iterations flesh out Cyrus's character and provide an interesting take on the institution. At the beginning of *Scandal*, Cyrus is happily married to journalist James Novak. In the context of one of his investigations, James comes to be seen as a potential threat and meets an untimely demise as a result. Season 4, episode 17 ("Put a Ring on It," written by Chris Van Dusen) goes into greater detail about Cyrus's successive experience with wedlock.[33] In a predictable turn of events, Cyrus's first marriage was to a woman named Janet. Flashbacks into the past of older gay men commonly show them in closet narratives, and this one is no different. The episode connects all three marriages together and, in so doing, illustrates just how imperfect they have all been—even Cyrus's love marriage to James. His third and last marriage offers an interesting take on respectability politics—and particularly, respectability *in* politics. Indeed, Cyrus is explicitly coerced into marrying Michael Ambruso—a sex worker hired to take him down—to avert a political scandal. In this instance, the prescriptiveness of respectability ends up being precisely what dents the "sanctity" of marriage.

Children

In the discourse that opposed same-sex marriage,[34] one of the common arguments used by opponents to the notion centered on the welfare and protection of children. As a result, allusions to "the figure of the child," as queer theorist Lee Edelman termed it,[35] came to be a convenient maneuver to assign gays and lesbians to strict standards of respectability. Cyrus evinces a relative disinterest in his parenting duties and in children in general. This fact is made clear on various occasions throughout *Scandal*. James and Cyrus's adoption of their daughter Ella is not a mutual desire to be parents. It is James who wants a child, and only when he is about to find out the truth about Cyrus rigging the presidential election does Cyrus relent to James's wishes. In fact, later in the series, in season 2, episode 13 ("Nobody Likes Babies," written by Mark Wilding),[36] Cyrus expressly states his dislike for babies. In the antepenultimate episode of the last season ("People Like Me," written by Van Dusen and Nicholas Nardini),[37] Cyrus turns into somewhat of an archvillain and is being held prisoner in the bowels of the White House in the company of his longtime friend and godmother to his daughter, Olivia Pope (Kerry Washington). In a desperate attempt to get information from Cyrus, Olivia enquires about Ella's well-being. The evocation of the figure of the child in this interrogation can be interpreted as an unsuccessful strategy on Olivia's part to get Cyrus to capitulate before the particularly strict respectability prescriptions aimed at gay and lesbian parents. Indeed, Cyrus sees through Olivia's tactic, declaring: "You think you can guilt me into becoming a better person by bringing up my daughter, Liv? It won't work." Cyrus, a gay man, embraces being a villain and a bad father in the same utterance, and in so doing rejects being assigned to exemplariness.

Villains?

The axiologically troubled diegetic environment of these two shows complicates the labeling of characters as heroes, villains, or antiheroes. The symbolism of the "white hat" in *Scandal* epitomizes the complexity of ascribing rigid categories of good and evil to the characters. Frequent mention of the "white hat" is made throughout the series, including in episode titles,[38] pointing to the moral fluctuations of the characters.

Be that as it may, these complex and morally ambivalent characters must be put in historical perspective. Indeed, for decades, a long representational tradition in television showed queer-coded villains[39] or represented gay characters as either victims or villains.[40] As early as the 1970s, activists started lambasting such depictions for being homophobic. These characters' homosexuality was usually used as a pathologizing factor that explained and contributed to their villainy. Gradually, with the increasing momentum of respectability politics, gay villains virtually disappeared from audiovisual representations. In recent years, though, a new kind of gay villain has started creeping back on screen in mainstream cultural artifacts such as *The Wire* (2002–8), *Dexter* (2006–13), *Breaking Bad* (2008–13), and its spin-off *Better Call Saul* (2015–22), among others.[41] This new kind of gay antagonist differs from older iterations of gay villains insomuch as their homosexuality is often one of the features that make them relatable—and sometimes even likeable.[42]

Thanks to Rhimes's ambition to break away from strict standards of respectability and to portray "complex" and "layered" characters, Shondaland has produced characters that question these seemingly straightforward moral categories. Now, to what extent can our three characters be said to be actual villains?

The case of Oliver in *HTGAWM* is interesting as he is characterized as a good Samaritan from the beginning of the show, always trying to help others, sometimes putting himself at risk in so doing. Connor initially believes Oliver to be compliant, somewhat of a people-pleaser, and as such, he is presented as deprived of agency. However, as the narrative unfolds season after season, the purported people-pleaser with apparent low self-esteem chooses to join the team in their transgressions. Connor tries to stop Oliver from becoming a criminal as the rest of the group, but on various occasions, Oliver asserts his willingness to commit these morally reprehensible actions. In breaking free from the script of goodness that Connor assigns to him, Oliver claims agency. His trajectory, when examined through the lens of his ethnicity, is particularly illuminating. Indeed, Asian Americans are often associated with the myth of the "model minority": "a racial group distinct from the white majority, but lauded as well assimilated, upwardly mobile, politically nonthreatening, and definitively not-black."[43] Thus, in embracing a life of crime, Oliver defies a double injunction to abide by strict standards of respectability, both for being Asian and gay.

Despite their various misdeeds and breaches of morality, both Connor and Oliver remain largely likeable characters due to their endearing love relationship and the relative rectitude they display when the rest of the ensemble does not. For example, Connor is often the moral compass of the group, pointing to the immoral nature of the actions the "Keating Four" are contemplating. Unlike Connor and Oliver, Cyrus ends up being the ultimate antagonist in *Scandal*. His character's moral bankruptcy seems absolute in the last season of the series. However, the serial format of the narrative allows for a complex buildup of different layers of character elaboration, and by the end of the show, viewers are well-acquainted with the intricacies of Cyrus's temperament and personal history. This long process of sedimentation allows for a complex apprehension of the character's evolution. Mittell's elaboration on Murray Smith's model of viewer engagement with fictional characters in television narratives provides an interesting analytical lens to apprehend Cyrus's trajectory. One of the three main prongs of this approach centers on viewer allegiance: "the moral evaluation of an aligned character where we find ourselves sympathetic to their beliefs and ethics, and thus emotionally invested in their stories."[44] The question of moral allegiance in antinormative shows like *Scandal* or *HTGAWM* is complex and particularly prone to fluctuation. Viewer allegiance toward Cyrus is likely to shift over the various serial installments. When Cyrus works as Vargas's campaign manager, for instance, and is then chosen to be on the ticket, he tries to wear the proverbial "white hat" for a while because he genuinely believes that Vargas is a righteous candidate deserving of the Oval Office. After a somewhat hubristic private dialogue with his hit man-lover, Tom, in which Cyrus states that he wants to be president, Vargas gets killed. Tom falsely confesses to the murder to get revenge on Cyrus, who has since ended things with him. Due to his apparent motive and well-known hunger for power, Cyrus is initially believed to be responsible for Vargas's death and winds up imprisoned pending trial. In this sequence, Rhimes plays with the commonly held notion that characters in television serial narratives are allowed less room for "character transformation" than in more "stand-alone narrative forms."[45] Cyrus is believed by the rest of the ensemble to be incapable of such transformation, and this negation of change in Cyrus's character can be interpreted as causing "character overhaul." This along with the traumatic experience Cyrus has in prison are two decisive factors in Cyrus's moral dereliction that eventually turn him into the show's ultimate archvillain. In the aforementioned conversation between Cyrus and Olivia in season 7, episode 16, Cyrus asserts that the course of events has had no effect whatsoever on his character, that he has always been the power-hungry political fiend he is at that moment. During this quasi-monologue, the camera shoots Cyrus through various glass bell jars, creating the optical illusion of a blurred, fragmented self. The camera literally reminds viewers of the various layers that make Cyrus the complex character that he is, contradicting the simple narrative Cyrus unfolds in this moment.

Conclusion

Over her entire oeuvre, Rhimes challenges and subverts long-standing representational tropes. She shows a fierce determination to avoid simplistic narratives of identity, and in writing or shepherding to the screen full-fledged, complex gay villains in leading roles, Rhimes emancipates these characters from the understandable yet dehumanizing and mechanical adoption of respectability politics as the unsurpassable strategy to fight damaging homophobic stereotypes. Rhimes is, without a doubt, the most active and prolific LGBTQ+ ally on television today. She has expressed her discontent with being the exception rather than the rule in this respect and urges her fellow straight makers of culture to be more committed in the way they approach and represent diversity.[46] May they listen and follow her lead.

Notes

1. GLAAD has been a national media watchdog focusing on LGBTQ+ representation since 1985. Every year, they issue a report titled *Where We Are on TV* which examines and reviews the state of LGBTQ+ representation across the vastness of the televisual landscape.
2. The HRC is a national LGBTQ advocacy group and lobbying organization.
3. You may find the speech here, https://www.youtube.com/watch?v=iHp2WvspFfs.
4. Deborah A. Fisher et al., "Gay, Lesbian, and Bisexual Content on Television: A Quantitative Analysis Across Two Seasons," *Journal of Homosexuality* 52, no. 3–4 (2007): 167–88.
5. Dara Z. Strolovitch and Chaya Y. Crowder, "Respectability, Anti-Respectability, and Intersectionally Responsible Representation," *PS: Political Science & Politics* 51, no. 2 (April 2018): 340.
6. Ibid., 341.
7. Ibid., 340.
8. GLAAD, "Where We Are on TV 2020–2021," 2021.
9. Due to differences in the history of representational dynamics between gays and lesbians, this chapter will only focus on the portrayal of gay men.
10. It must be said that Rhimes is credited in these two shows in different capacities: she is "creator" of *Scandal* and "executive producer" on *HTGAWM*. As such, she might not have been as involved in the creative process of the second show. However, the show is, by all accounts, considered part of Shondaland.
11. To further illustrate the closeness between these two shows, mention can be made of two crossover episodes, one in each show. Olivia Pope from *Scandal* is featured in *HTGAWM*'s season 4, episode 13, "Lahey v. Commonwealth of Pennsylvania," and Annalise Keating from *HTGAWM* appears in *Sandal*'s season 7, episode 12, "Allow Me to Reintroduce Myself."

12 Stephen Tropiano, *The Prime Time Closet: A History of Gays and Lesbians on TV* (New York: Applause Theatre Book Publishers, 2002), 73.
13 This statement about the unprecedented acceptance of gays and lesbians must be nuanced. The reinvigoration of anti-LGBTQ+ sentiment and resurgence of anti-LGBTQ+ legislation in the United States in recent years put things into perspective. A Gallup poll from 2023 indicates that the number of respondents who declared same-sex relations were "morally acceptable" has declined from 71 percent in 2022 to 64 percent in 2023. Gallup, Inc., "Fewer in U.S. Say Same-Sex Relations Morally Acceptable," *Gallup.Com*, June 16, 2023, https://news.gallup.com/poll/507230/fewer-say-sex-relations-morally-acceptable.aspx.
14 Cyrus later becomes Mellie Grant's vice president.
15 Jason Mittell, *Complex TV: The Poetics of Contemporary Television Storytelling* (New York: New York University Press, 2015), 143.
16 In some of the most successful television serial political dramas, gay characters are not so common in such high ranking positions. A gay congressman is featured in *The West Wing* (1999–2006), but he is a Republican who is opposed to gay marriage and claims that his gay identity has no bearing on his political leanings. *House of Cards* (2013–18) might have provided an interesting counterexample with Frank Underwood's character. Underwood's sexuality is never explicitly labeled, but he is shown having sex with both men and women. His sexual fluidity remains, however, closeted throughout the entire show.
17 The Lavender Scare was a moral panic in the United States that happened in the 1950s at the same time as the Red Scare. It consisted of a government-led campaign to identify and purge homosexual individuals from federal employment and the military, resulting in thousands of LGBTQ+ individuals being dismissed from their jobs. Back then, homosexuals were believed to be communist sympathizers and more prone to becoming potential spies.
18 For more information on this trope, you may consult GLAAD, "Where We Are on TV 2017–2018," or TV Tropes, "Gay Best Friend," *TV Tropes*, accessed September 1, 2023, https://tvtropes.org/pmwiki/pmwiki.php/Main/GayBestFriend.
19 For more information, see Algirdas Julien Greimas, "On Meaning: Selected Writings in Semiotic Theory," *Theory and History of Literature*, vol. 38 (Minneapolis: University of Minnesota Press, 1987).
20 *Scandal*, season 2, episode 13, "Nobody Likes Babies," created by Shonda Rhimes, written by Mark Wilding, aired February 7, 2013, on ABC.
21 Suzanna Danuta Walters, *All the Rage: The Story of Gay Visibility in America* (Chicago: University of Chicago Press, 2001), 296.
22 *Queer as Folk* (Showtime, 2000–2005) is a good example of this. Contemporary shows broadcast on the Big Three (ABC, NBC, and CBS)

were infinitely tamer when they ventured to show gay characters in sexual activity at all.
23 More recently, series like *The White Lotus* (HBO, 2021–) have attempted to remedy this shortage.
24 J. Bryan Lowder, "Why Are How to Get Away with Murder's Gay Sex Scenes Full of Bottom Shame?" *Slate*, October 28, 2014, https://slate.com/human-interest/2014/10/why-are-how-to-get-away-with-murders-gay-sex-scenes-full-of-bottom-shame.html.
25 Alex Abad-Santos, "How to Get Away with Murder Has the Hottest Gay Sex on Television. That's Progress," *Vox*, November 13, 2014, https://www.vox.com/2014/11/13/7213021/how-to-get-away-with-murder-gay-sex.
26 Rimming scenes had appeared on cable television in *Queer as Folk* more than ten years before *HTGAWM* aired its first season.
27 For further information, see Ava Laure Parsemain, *The Pedagogy of Queer TV*, Palgrave Entertainment Industries (Cham: Springer International Publishing, 2019), doi:10.1007/978-3-030-14872-0.
28 "All Gays Are Promiscuous," *TV Tropes*, accessed September 1, 2023, https://tvtropes.org/pmwiki/pmwiki.php/Main/AllGaysArePromiscuous.
29 This is the name given by the fan community to the ensemble of Annalise Keating's students working with her.
30 Portmanteau contraction of both the names Connor and Oliver. This term is used quite extensively in fan communities of *HTGAWM*.
31 Strolovitch and Crowder, "Respectability, Anti-Respectability, and Intersectionally Responsible Representation," 340.
32 "Commitment: The Answer to the Middle's Questions on Marriage for Gay Couples—Third Way," *Thirdway.Com*, accessed September 1, 2023, https://www.thirdway.org/pocket-card/commitment-the-answer-to-the-middles-questions-on-marriage-for-gay-couples.
33 *Scandal*, season 4, episode 17, "Put a Ring on It," created by Shonda Rhimes, written by Chris Van Dusen, aired March 26, 2015, on ABC.
34 For example, former president George W. Bush and former Pennsylvania representative Rick Santorum have used such arguments.
35 Lee Edelman, *No Future: Queer Theory and the Death Drive* (Duke University Press, 2004), doi:10.1215/9780822385981.
36 *Scandal*, season 2, episode 13, "Nobody Likes Babies," created by Shonda Rhimes, written by Mark Wilding, aired February 7, 2013, on ABC.
37 *Scandal*, season 7, episode 16, "People Like Me," created by Shonda Rhimes, written by Chris Van Dusen and Nicholas Nardini, aired April 5, 2018, on ABC.
38 *Scandal*, season 2, episode 1, "White Hat's Off," created by Shonda Rhimes, written by Jenna Bans, aired September 27, 2012, on ABC; season 2, episode 22, "White Hat's Back On," written by Rhimes, aired May 16, 2013, on ABC.

39 Vito Russo, *The Celluloid Closet: Homosexuality in the Movies* (New York: Harper & Row, 1981).
40 Larry Gross, *Up from Invisibility: Lesbians, Gay Men, and the Media in America* (New York: Columbia University Press, 2002), 254.
41 Tim Molloy, "The Rise of the New Gay Villains," *TheWrap*, November 27, 2012, https://www.thewrap.com/rise-new-gay-villains-66701/.
42 Ibid.
43 Ellen D. Wu, *The Color of Success: Asian Americans and the Origins of the Model Minority* (Princeton: Princeton University Press, 2014), 2.
44 Mittell, *Complex TV*, 134.
45 Ibid., 141.
46 Shonda (@shondarhimes) Rhimes, "You Know What Bugs Me? I'm the Only Straight Person on This List. That s Not Okay. It's Like the Same Problem with ANY Kind of Diversity. White People Don't Do Their Job..." *Twitter*, January 14, 2021, 10:58PM, https://twitter.com/shondarhimes/status/1349838213779636224.

Chapter 8

FROM FAMILY SHAME TO DOCTOR'S PRIDE

Shifting Trans Narratives on *Grey's Anatomy*

Kara Raphaeli

Jackson Avery (Jesse Williams) walks into a Grey Sloan Memorial boardroom and greets his mother, world-class urologist Catherine Avery (Debbie Allen). Catherine is sitting with another woman, laughing over a breakfast spread of pastries, fruit, and coffee. She introduces the woman to Jackson as "a dear old friend of mine."[1] The friend is Michelle Velez (Candis Cayne), one of the top plastic surgeons in the nation. Jackson has read her publications and is excited to sit down and talk to her about cell grafting. In a scene that lasts less than two minutes, Velez explains to the Averys that she wants to enlist them both for an experimental form of vaginoplasty. It is only at the end of the scene, when Jackson expresses confusion as to why a surgeon of her caliber couldn't do the surgery herself, that Velez reveals she intends to be the patient.

This scene is revolutionary for *Grey's Anatomy* (2005–). Though Velez is a trans woman and vaginoplasty patient, she is first introduced as a successful surgeon and afforded the same respect and class that all female surgeons are given at Grey Sloan—and by developing the surgery herself, she is in control of her own body rather than at the mercy of others. The storyline is remarkable because for the first eleven seasons of *Grey's*, trans characters were depicted through harmful caricatures. In this chapter, I will look at the different trans characters on the show, connecting the shifts in storylines to both the changing cultural attitudes toward trans people and the personal experiences of *Grey's* showrunners.

Grey's takes a complicated perspective toward patients. On the one hand, as part of Shonda Rhimes's goal of presenting greater diversity,[2] the show has repeatedly pushed back against an array of negative stereotypes toward minoritarian groups, including disabled people. On the other

8. From Family Shame to Doctor's Pride   99

hand, to do so, *Grey's* replicates negative attitudes in order to challenge them.[3] Furthermore, it is useful to keep in mind that within disability studies, illness is regarded under the larger umbrella of disability. Thus, we can understand the patients on *Grey's* to all be either disabled or suspected of disability (e.g., symptom-free but waiting for test results after a car accident). The exceptions are women in labor, as they are engaged in a natural part of life, albeit one that requires medical assistance.

As disability theorist Rosemary Garland Thomas writes, in our culture the physically disabled body is seen as an "embodiment of corporeal insufficiency and deviance."[4] Therefore, *Grey's* has a pathologizing perspective toward patients' bodies by definition. By this, I mean that any disease, injury, illness, visual difference, or disability is assumed to be an obstacle toward normativity, and the patient's body is a site for the surgeons to reinscribe normative standards through gory surgeries and even violent actions.[5] As such, the patients are stripped of a certain level of humanity through the surgeon's eyes. This is what I call the pathologizing gaze.[6] The pathologizing gaze in *Grey's* is often established through interns' expressions of shock, repulsion, or other discomfort in response to particularly "freakish" patients, while the more seasoned residents and attendings can control themselves and show a greater degree of humanity while still perceiving the patients as needing to be fixed.

Unlike other minoritarian groups, trans people must rely on medical intervention in the form of hormone replacement therapy (HRT) and surgeries to attain their transition goals. In the early seasons of *Grey's*, this reliance places trans characters under the care of surgeons who pathologize transness (i.e., view the trans patient as someone needing to be fixed) rather than treating transness as an aspect of identity and experience independent from pathology, much as the show has always treated homosexuality as normative.[7] In 2014, a swell of media attention collectively referred to as "the transgender tipping point" discouraged treating trans characters as oddities. The media shift combined with increased knowledge on the part of *Grey's* producers led to the introduction of positive, nonpathologized depictions of trans people.

Trans Characters in the Early Seasons

November 6, 2006, *Grey's* aired its first episode featuring a transgender patient in season 3, episode 7, "Where the Boys Are" (written by Mark Wilding). In it, Donna Gibson (played by trans actress Alexandra

Billings) is a patient of Mark Sloan (Eric Dane) awaiting a vaginoplasty. In the first two scenes, we learn that Donna, thirty-seven, began her transition two years earlier, and that her wife, Vicky, is still struggling to share her life with a trans woman rather than a man. In fact, it is Vicky, not Donna, who is the focus of this storyline in the episode. The story is told from her point of view, and through dialogue and camera shots, viewers are encouraged to see Donna as a puzzle rather than a person.

We first meet Donna and Vicky as Sloan and Meredith Grey (Ellen Pompeo) enter a patient room with an empty bed. Instead of a gowned patient, we see two women who look similar: thirties, long brunette hair, slightly lowcut V-neck tops (sexy but no cleavage showing). The women are unpacking identical overnight bags. They could be sisters. Sloan greets them before Meredith has stepped into the room, and Donna announces, "She's still having some penis issues."[8] This line of dialogue is an enigma as there is no context to understand it. Seeing Meredith's confusion, Vicky explains, "Dr. Sloan is planning to remove my husband's penis this afternoon."[9] As Sloan is the only man in the room, Meredith asks, "And your husband is . . . ?" Donna pipes up, "Right here."[10] With this line, Donna smiles wryly; she is entertained by Meredith's confusion and unbothered being referred to as Vicky's husband rather than her wife. It's at this moment that the show takes its first commercial break, leaving the audience to process Donna's transness.

Returning from commercials, the camera focuses on Donna's high-heeled feet, crossed at the ankle, and then sweeps up her body as Meredith reads her medical file, which deadnames her (refers to Donna by her birth name rather than her chosen name). The contradiction between the shapely feminine body and the male name serves to further "other" Donna.

Like many episodes in the first few seasons, Sloan, as an attending, models a professional, respectful bedside manner toward a nonnormative patient. As he speaks to Donna, he holds her hand and assures her that surgery will go smoothly. Meanwhile, Meredith, the inexperienced intern, is the viewer's stand-in. And so, through their interaction, the audience is silently told that transgender people should be treated with respect but that shock and discomfort are reasonable reactions toward them as they are abnormal—and hence, pathologized. This message is reinforced by the fact that as Meredith continues to stumble on pronouns when discussing Donna's surgery, Vicky reassures her, "You're doing very well. Better than I did when I first found out."[11]

8. From Family Shame to Doctor's Pride   101

Halfway through the episode, Sloan and Meredith deliver bad news: Donna's presurgery labs show breast cancer, and she will have to stop hormone replacement therapy and start cancer treatments. Trying to process the situation, Donna asks, "So the hormones I've been taking are essentially giving me cancer?"[12] While it is true that trans women have an increased risk of breast cancer compared to men, their risk is still lower than for cis women.[13] Yet through this storyline, *Grey's* pathologizes transness further by turning it into the cause of disease and using the trans character to articulate that connection. Trans women ironically being diagnosed with cancers in sex organs is, in fact, a trope within medical shows. Billings, the actress who portrays Donna, was on an episode of *ER* (1994–2009) the previous year, playing a trans woman with testicular cancer.[14] This commonly deployed trope dehumanizes trans women by focusing on them only in relation to sex organs.

The cancer leads Sloan to cancel Donna's vaginoplasty since, as he says, "There'd really be no point. Once we stop the hormones, your breasts will shrink, your facial hair will grow back."[15] As he delivers this news, the camera focuses on Donna's disappointed face. Sloan's dismissal is both factually incorrect and a reinforcing of a physiological model of transness rather than a psychological one. Donna insists on having the vaginoplasty, against Sloan's advice. He pleads with her that he is trying to save her life, and Donna replies, "As a man. I'm not a man. I'll fight the cancer. I'll just fight it as a woman."[16] This is a powerful moment, a chance for a trans woman to stake a claim on her womanhood. But it is undercut by Vicky, who deadnames Donna in anger and storms out. Donna's response is to turn to Sloan and say, "I need Vicky to love me. But I need her to love *me*."[17]

Why does Donna need Vicky to love her? Meredith and Vicky have two one-on-one scenes in which Vicky articulates her difficulty with Donna's transition and why she won't leave her. From a cis perspective, there is a big question as to why Vicky would want to stay with Donna. She explains to Meredith that "She's my best friend. She knows me. She loves me. She's . . . my husband. At the end of the day, its Donna. Even when she hurts me. Even when I hate her."[18]

At no point does this episode encourage the viewer to question how Donna has hurt Vicky. Why does Vicky hate Donna? It seems likely that Vicky views Donna's intent to live authentically as selfish because it has upended Vicky's expectations for her life. Similarly, at no point does the show encourage the viewer to question what is loveable about Vicky. Throughout the episode, we see Vicky misgendering and deadnaming Donna. She is unsupportive and, at best, resigned to Donna's transition.

Vicky is not shown to be kind and loving toward Donna—we are simply meant to assume that as a trans woman, Donna is lucky to have a beautiful and normative partner.

Many patients' stories on *Grey's* function as a reflection of situations that the surgeons of Seattle Grace (and later Grey Sloan Memorial) are experiencing. However, the show's only male trans patient reflects the state of the hospital at large. In season 9, episode 14, "The Face of Change" (written by Stacy McKee), Seattle Grace experiences a significant financial setback and is seeking investors to stay open. In order to lure investors, the hospital is rebranding, and Alex Karev (Justin Chambers) and Jackson Avery are being considered for the position of "brand ambassador" for the hospital; this is the literal "face of change" that the episode title is referencing. Throughout the episode, Karev and Avery have photographers following them, taking photos and asking them questions about their surgeries. It is through the photographer's questions that the trans patient, played by cis woman Rachel Brosnahan, is introduced. Viewers are not asked to sympathize with any one character in the way we are asked to sympathize with Vicky; each character in this trans subplot remains foreign to the viewer, distanced by the intermediate photographers' cameras.

We first see Brian Weston (Brosnahan), the patient, and his girlfriend Jess (Matt Pascua), who is trans herself, being photographed with Avery. When the photographer misgenders them, Brian helpfully clarifies, "I'm the him, she's the her. Um, no, I was born a her and Jess was a him—I get it, it's confusing."[19] He says this with a friendly smile on his face. As with Donna, the message is that even the trans patient agrees they are an oddity and a source of mental disruption for the cis normates. The photographer then asks, "What exactly is today's surgery? A full gender reassignment?"[20] If this episode were developed today, with *Grey's* writers addressing the topic of transness with knowledge and a sense of educational responsibility, the phrase "full gender reassignment [surgery]" would either be omitted or included only so that a surgeon would have the opportunity to explain that there is no such thing as a "full gender reassignment"; there are many types of gender-affirming surgeries, and choosing how one modifies one's body is an individual patient's choice. However, this episode aired on February 7, 2013, a year before the "transgender tipping point" of 2014, and as such, neither surgeon corrects the photographer. Instead, Brian responds, "Oh no, nothing so drastic yet. Today we're just chopping off my boobs."[21] He says this while cupping his chest. It is understandable that as a cis actress, Brosnahan would find this action acceptable; however, most trans men who seek top surgery suffer from dysphoria about their chests. As such, a trans masculine patient would be unlikely to refer to their chest as "boobs" or cup their chest, which brings attention to their silhouette.[22]

Fortunately for Brian, there are no last-minute medical complications for the surgery he's been saving up for over the past four years. The complication is an emotional one; Brian's father shows up unexpectedly to try to stop the surgery. First, Mr. Weston accuses Jess of brainwashing Brian, and then physically attacks Karev, shoving him into a wall and yelling, "Are you the one who wants to hack my little girl into pieces?!"[23] The photographer is taking shot after shot of this moment, this regressive response to "the face of change." Once Mr. Weston calms down, he attempts to talk Brian into postponing the surgery, first gently and then losing his temper, deadnaming Brian and yelling, "I don't want you *mutilating* yourself!"[24] It is at this point that Brian kicks his father out of his hospital room. This is the last we see of Brian. We don't see him recover; we don't see his euphoria. Once again, this is not the trans patient's story but rather the story of how transness affects cis people.

Mr. Weston is loud and angry, not likeable in the way that Vicky is. The framing of the episode makes it clear that he is in the wrong but also that it is understandable he is struggling with Brian's transition. Karev's voiceover at the end of the episode sums it up:

> Change is a funny thing. Not everyone can handle it. It can sneak up on you. Your whole world is transformed. You realize the ground beneath you has shifted. Things are uncertain. And there's no turning back. The world around you is different now. Unrecognizable. And there's nothing you can do about it.[25]

A Transition in Transitions

On May 29, 2014, *Time* published a cover story about actress Laverne Cox, the breakout star of the Netflix drama *Orange Is the New Black* (2013–19), created by Jenji Kohan. Titled "The Transgender Tipping Point," Katy Steinmetz's article suggested that Cox's success represented a larger moment of increased social acceptance of trans people.[26] Steinmetz pointed to a greater acceptance of trans people in the younger generation, including Facebook expanding its gender options for users (rolled out in February 2014). While much has been written about the failure of this imagined tipping point to occur, trans visibility in media did blossom. In 2014, Joey Soloway's *Transparent* (2014–19) was released by Amazon Studios, and in 2015, the Wachowski sisters' *Sense8* (2015–18) aired on Netflix, both series featuring trans characters in leading roles and receiving critical acclaim and commercial success. Media attention toward trans people coincided with *Grey's* executive producers Joan Rater and Tony Phelan's teenage son coming out as trans.[27]

We can see the effect of the tipping point on *Grey's* writers by looking at the portrayal of Rosalind Warren (Benjamin Patterson) in season 11, episode 12, "The Great Pretender" (written by Mark Driscoll), which aired just seven months after Steinmetz's article was published. Rosalind is Ben Warren's (Jason George) closeted sibling—meaning Ben is unaware that his sibling is not a cis man nor that her chosen name is Rosalind.[28] Like Donna, Rosalind's transition is the cause of her illness. However, Rosalind's organ damage is due to using DIY hormones rather than having prescription HRT. Rosalind's storyline is transitional between the earlier transphobic plots and later plots such as the one with Dr. Michelle Velez. The episode is still problematic; Rosalind is played by a cis male actor, her hormones are the source of her illness, and her loved one is of greater focus than she is.

The focus of Rosalind's story is Ben Warren's struggle to accept his sister. Warren feels deceived by the fact that Rosalind knew she was a girl since age five but would not confide in him despite how close they were. He tells Miranda Bailey (Chandra Wilson), "If this was anyone else, it wouldn't even be an issue. But I told him everything. [. . .] But now he's got the biggest thing in his life and he waited twenty-five years to tell me. How's that supposed to make me feel?"[29] The idea that trans people are deceivers is a dangerous stereotype, as it gives people permission to react to trans people with violence. Indeed, trans panic is a defense strategy that lawyers take on behalf of defendants who have murdered trans people.[30] Through Rosalind, the episode challenges such imagery because Warren's hurt is understood as a poor reaction. Bailey models best practices by correctly gendering Rosalind, reminding Warren that Rosalind's transition isn't about him but her personal growth. "This is her song, so get off the stage and let her sing it," Bailey chides. During a tense talk between the siblings, Rosalind explains that "[e]very day of my life [I was] pretending. Benji, I'm tired of pretending. I just wanna be happy with who I am."[31] This framing of pretransition as a life of pretending suggests that the act of transition is living one's truth rather than being deceitful.

The episode ends unsatisfactorily, a rift remains between the siblings, who had been very close until that morning. Although Rosalind does not appear again on *Grey's*, her relationship with Warren comes up in conversation several times over the course of the season, and they eventually do reconnect (albeit offstage) in season 11, episode 15. Rosalind is the final character whose transness is pathologized on *Grey's*. Moving forward, transness is portrayed much like any other minoritarian identity on the show: a single aspect of a three-dimensional character.

Transitioning into the Future

The most impactful way that *Grey's* has depathologized trans people is to introduce trans doctors. Michelle Velez is the second trans doctor on the show, and Casey Parker (played by trans actor Alex Blue Davis) is the first. Parker is one of six new interns introduced in season 14. Parker's transness is only revealed in the fourth episode in which he appears. Instead, what we first learn about Parker is that he is a vet who served two tours in Iraq specializing in cybersecurity prior to medical school. In his intern interview, he explains to Richard Webber (James Pickens Jr.) and Bailey, "one day I caught some shrapnel, and I woke up on a cot in a CSH tent. I watched three combat surgeons save thirty-seven soldiers in six hours. I counted. I kept score. I thought, 'that's not a bad way to spend your time.'"[32] In this telling, Parker is shown as polite, composed, aspiring, while all the other intern interviewees are by turns pompous, accidentally rude, out of touch, and unprepared.

In episodes 8 and 9, "Out of Nowhere" (written by William Harper) and "1-800-799-7233" (written by Andy Reaser), the hospital computers have been hijacked by a virus and Bailey awaits very slow FBI intervention. Parker refuses to help hack the virus, revealing that he was convicted of hacking a federal server in his past, and part of his sentence is that he cannot engage in such behavior again. But as patients' lives are threatened by malfunctioning ventilators, Parker relents and single-handedly regains control of the hospital. Once the crisis is averted, Bailey asks him about his conviction, and he explains that he hacked into the DMV to change his gender marker. The camera focuses on Bailey's surprised but undisturbed face. Parker smiles and continues, "I'm a proud trans man, Dr. Bailey. But I like for people to get to know me before they find out my private medical history." Bailey murmurs her understanding, leans in and touches his chest in a way she would never touch a female surgeon, signaling that she sees Parker as a man, then adds, "Thank you for your service, Dr. Parker."[33]

In a 2018 interview with *The Hollywood Reporter*, showrunner Krista Vernoff explained that she worked with Alex Blue Davis to write this scene to make sure it was properly authentic to the trans experience. She learned a good deal about trans people a few years prior, after Phelan and Rater's son, Tom, came out as trans in high school. Tom Phelan's transition left Vernoff wanting to "illuminate [the trans] experience" for *Grey's* viewers.[34]

Vernoff continued her allyship in 2019 when she introduced nonbinary gender identities late in season 15. In episode 18, "Add It Up" (written by Alex Manugian), 22-year-old Toby Donnelly and their mother Kari arrive at the hospital after sustaining injuries in a snowmobile crash. Kari is paralyzed by the accident, for which Toby feels guilty. However, Toby's presence also serves as a source of education for Richard Webber. Because Jackson Avery and Taryn Helm (Jaicy Elliot) are adept at using they/them pronouns, Toby is spared the work of educating Webber. When Webber complains about Toby's pronouns to Avery and Helm, they push back against him. While Toby is in the CT machine, Webber asks, "Do we really have to use this . . . plural thing? Even when she can't hear us?" Avery corrects him, "While *they*—they can't hear us. Okay? Yeah, it's not that complicated."[35] In the end, Webber concedes that although it is difficult for him to keep up with a changing world, he understands that it is important for people to be referred to as they wish. Thus, Toby's three-episode arc uses Webber's well-established respectful-yet-cranky attitude toward younger generations to offer viewers a perspective of tolerance and acceptance toward nonbinary people.

Most recently, nonbinary actor E. R. Fightmaster has had a recurring role as Kai Bartley, a medical researcher and Amelia Shepherd's (Caterina Scorsone) love interest. When Bartley is first introduced to Shepherd and Meredith early in season 18, they are both familiar with Bartley's research and know their pronouns, sidestepping any clunky explanations of their gender identity. In fact, Bartley never discusses their gender identity. In season 18, episode 7, "Today Was a Fairytale" (written by Julie Wong), Shepherd and Bartley get to know each other before kissing for the first time; they discuss topics such as methods of dealing with stress, the specter of failure, and how they came to their respective careers.[36] Gender is never mentioned, suggesting that it is the very least important fact about Bartley. Later in the season, when Teddy Altman (Kim Raver) discusses her young son's fluid gender exploration, Shepherd shares that being with Bartley has opened up her imagination so that she sees that "people don't need to be constantly defined in order to be loved unconditionally. And since I've started viewing the world that way, I've never felt more like myself."[37]

Just as Meredith Grey has matured over the course of nineteen seasons from a hapless intern to a world-renowned surgeon, *Grey's* has also grown up; the writers have replaced harmful trans stereotypes with groundbreaking and sensitive recurring trans characters. Such representation directly leads to improvement in the lives of trans people, as the majority of Americans do not personally know any transgender person and, as such, form their opinions of trans people from media representations.[38] *Grey's* rejection of harmful caricatures extends beyond trans characters to depictions of a variety of disabilities—particularly visual differences and intersex patients, both of which were plentiful in the first ten seasons but thankfully lacking since.[39] The legacy of *Grey's* is helping its fans envision a far more inclusive and empathetic world than most other shows on television.

Notes

1 *Grey's Anatomy*, season 14, episode 12, "Harder, Better, Faster, Stronger," created by Shonda Rhimes, written by Kiley Donovan, aired February 8, 2018, on ABC.
2 Brooke Marine, "Shonda Rhimes Speaks to the Moment," *W*, February 7, 2022, https://www.wmagazine.com/culture/shonda-rhimes-interview-2022.
3 Gesine Wegner, "Relocating the Freakshow: Disability in the Medical Drama," *Zeitschrift für Anglistik und Amerikanistik* 67, no. 1 (2019): 19–36.
4 Rosemarie Garland-Thomson, *Extraordinary Bodies: Figuring Physical Disability in American Culture and Literature* (New York: Columbia University Press, 2017), 21.
5 A few examples: Dr. Izzie Stevens removes a clot from a patient's chest at his bedside (S01.E06); EMT Matthew Taylor performs an emergency tracheostomy (S10.E11); Dr. Meredith Grey performs brain surgery on a plane experiencing turbulence (S13.E20).
6 This stripping of humanity is examined in some episodes and is found to be necessary so that doctors don't get emotionally invested in a way which is destructive to their work, but also dangerous if it prevents them from caring about a patient enough to fight for them. In S13.E08, Dr. Webber creates a backstory for a Jane Doe so that the other doctors will fight harder for her.
7 In the third episode of the series, we meet Mr. Mackie, a gay older Black man who is an old friend of Chief Webber and who unabashedly and repeatedly hits on George. Not only is he a character who is treated with

respect, but he is in fact the first patient in the series who is afforded time to develop a three-dimensionality.
8 *Grey's Anatomy*, season 3, episode 7, "Where the Boys Are," created by Shonda Rhimes, written by Mark Wilding, aired November 9, 2006, on ABC.
9 Ibid.
10 Ibid.
11 Ibid.
12 Ibid.
13 Andrea Fehl et al., "Breast Cancer in the Transgender Population," *Journal of the Advanced Practitioner in Oncology* 10, no. 4 (2019): 387–94. doi:10.6004/jadpro.2019.10.4.6.
14 *ER* S11.E10. Other examples include a trans man who is forced to detransition on *Saving Hope*, S02.E09; a trans woman with prostate cancer on *Chicago Med* S02.E03; and a trans woman with a prostate infection on *Code Black* S02.E02.
15 *Grey's Anatomy*, season 3, episode 7, "Where the Boys Are."
16 Ibid.
17 Ibid.
18 Ibid.
19 *Grey's Anatomy*, season 9, episode 14, "The Face of Change," created by Shonda Rhimes, written by Stacy McKee, aired February 7, 2013, on ABC.
20 Ibid.
21 Ibid.
22 A much more realistic portrayal of a trans boy discussing his chest is seen a year later on ABC's *The Fosters*, when Cole, a trans boy, is housed in a shelter with girls and not allowed medical transition. Ironically, Cole is played by Tom Phelan, the son of Tony Phelan and Joan Rater, two executive producers on *Grey's*.
23 *Grey's Anatomy*, season 9, episode 14, "The Face of Change."
24 Ibid.
25 Ibid.
26 Katy Steinmetz, "The Transgender Tipping Point," *Time*, May 29, 2014, https://time.com/135480/transgender-tipping-point/.
27 Lisa Palmer, "'The Fosters' Star on the Rise of Transgender Television: 'It's Not Going to Do a Lot,'" *The Hollywood Reporter*, July 13, 2015, https://www.hollywoodreporter.com/tv/tv-news/fosters-transgender-tom-phelan-interview-808424/.
28 Although Ben's sibling does not share that she's chosen the name Rosalind until her last scene, in this chapter she is referred to as such because deadnaming a trans person is an act of violence which should not be modeled even with fictional characters.
29 *Grey's Anatomy*, season 11, episode 12, "The Great Pretender," created by Shonda Rhimes, written by Mark Driscoll, aired February 19, 2015, on ABC.

30 "The Gay/Trans Panic Defense: What It Is, and How to End It," American Bar Association, accessed October 27, 2023, https://www.americanbar.org/groups/crsj/publications/member-features/gay-trans-panic-defense/.
31 *Grey's Anatomy*, season 11, episode 12, "The Great Pretender."
32 *Grey's Anatomy*, season 14, episode 4, "Ain't That a Kick in the Head," created by Shonda Rhimes, written by Mariana Hope, aired October 12, 2017, on ABC.
33 *Grey's Anatomy*, season 14, episode 9, "1-800-799-7233," created by Shonda Rhimes, written by Andy Reaser, aired January 18, 2018, on ABC.
34 Leslie Goldberg, "How 'Grey's Anatomy' Wants to Change the Portrayal of Trans Characters on TV," *The Hollywood Reporter*, January 18, 2018, https://www.hollywoodreporter.com/tv/tv-news/greys-anatomy-transgender-storyline-explained-alex-blue-davis-interview-1075535/.
35 *Grey's Anatomy*, season 15, episode 18, "Add It Up," created by Shonda Rhimes, written by Alex Manugian, aired March 21, 2019, on ABC.
36 *Grey's Anatomy*, season 18, episode 7, "Today Was a Fairytale," created by Shonda Rhimes, written by Julie Wong, aired December 9, 2021, on ABC.
37 *Grey's Anatomy*, season 18, episode 17, "I'll Cover You," created by Shonda Rhimes, written by Kiley Donovan and Emily Culver, aired May 12, 2022, on ABC.
38 Brooke Migdan, "Fewer Than 1 in 3 Adults Personally Know Someone Who Is Transgender: Poll," *The Hill*, April 8, 2022, https://thehill.com/changing-america/respect/equality/3262,939-fewer-than-1-in-3-adults-personally-know-someone-who-is-transgender-poll/.
39 For a look at depictions of people with visual differences, see Gesine Wegner's article "Relocating the Freak Show: Disability in the Medical Drama."

Chapter 9

RESTORATIVE VERSUS RETRIBUTIVE JUSTICE

Themes from *How to Get Away with Murder*

Sara Correia-Hopkins and Cate Correia-Hopkins

Despite the prominence of crime drama, representations of restorative justice (RJ) are few and far between in popular culture. Instead of asking the typical guiding questions of retributive approaches (what laws have been broken, by whom, and what punishment they deserve), restorative justice asks what harms have been suffered, by whom, and who has the ability and responsibility to address them.[1] One exception to this lack of television representation, however, is in Shondaland's *How to Get Away with Murder* (2014–20), created by Peter Nowalk. In season 6, episode 7, "I'm the Murderer" (written by Laurence Andries),[2] lead character and lawyer Annalise Keating (Viola Davis) is assisted by several of her students, including Gabriel Maddox and Asher Millstone, in the case of the murder of an orphaned Black sixteen-year-old young man. Ryan Fitzgerald is shot dead in class at his Catholic high school by his closeted gay teacher, David Golan. At first, it is suggested that David shot Ryan in self-defense, under the mistaken belief that Ryan was about to wield a gun. It transpires that Ryan knew about David's sexuality, providing a motive for the shooting. Ryan's grandparents, David, his work colleague Ms. Maloney, and several of Ryan's schoolmates take part in a restorative "hearing," somewhere between a traditional hearing and the practice of restorative conferencing. This is where defendants, victims, and the community come together to share experiences and ultimately agree on a resolution that is acceptable to all.

In this chapter, we follow Virginia Braun and Victoria Clarke and undertake a reflexive thematic analysis of the episode's transcript.[3] As a product of Shondaland, we would expect *HTGAWM* to give voice to those who have traditionally been systematically "othered"

9. Restorative Versus Retributive Justice   111

and to center the experiences of minority groups. In the context of a criminal justice system otherwise shown to be desperately flawed and discriminatory, it is perhaps unsurprising that RJ is heralded by Annalise as "the future" of criminal justice. RJ's philosophy is to restore ownership of the justice process to those directly involved in the crime, and its practice is precisely about using emotionally and contextually rich dialogue to "un-other" and reach shared understandings and resolutions. This chapter provides an analysis of how the restorative ideal and its practices are represented in *HTGAWM*, highlighting a complex range of intersecting issues including the meaning of "justice," idealized notions of victims and offenders, race, and internalized homophobia.

Background

Restorative Justice

Traditional "retributive" criminal justice is focused on the triad of establishing which state-defined criminal law was broken, by whom, and what punishment or "retribution" they deserve. Such an approach relies on the clear-cut attribution of guilt/innocence and rebalancing the scales of justice by ensuring that without prejudice, the punishment balances out the crime committed. The primary focus is therefore punitive and centered on the offender. Its application is top-down, through the hierarchy of the courts where offenders can be "othered," while victims and those around them can feel forgotten and overlooked. This conception of criminal justice is prevalent in television drama, which in turn reinforces the retributive "ideal."

In contrast, through an RJ lens, crime is seen as relational, resulting from "a breakdown of pre-existing relationships between victims, offenders and the community," "the abuse of pre-existing relationships among offenders and the community," or "the creation, however brief, of a coercive relationship between the offender and the victim, where none existed before."[4] Consequently, justice is about restoring relationships between victims, offenders, and communities. As such, RJ is focused on addressing the "conflict" or "harms" in and around experiences of crime[5] and can be described as primarily concerned with identifying the following: (1) what harms were suffered, (2) by whom, (3) how to prevent and repair them, and (4) who has the obligation/ability to do so.[6] Rather than enforcing retributive hierarchies, the RJ philosophy rests on the empowering values of "agency" and "accountability"[7] and the role of community in understanding and "resolving" crime, rather than "solving" it.

Culture and Crime Drama

Storytelling of crime and criminality is enabled through highly structured narrative functions rooted in the literary traditions of early twentieth-century detective fiction.[8] While the formulaic nature of crime drama offers a sense of linearity and tacitly engages with consequentialism, the diversity of styles present within the genre—such as "cozy," "gritty," "noir"—suggests that their function is perhaps more complex.[9] They allow for the expression of socially constructed ideas such as justice, transgression, retribution, and civic life in a way that speaks to a wide range of audiences.[10]

The enjoyment, and indeed popularity, of crime drama encourages viewers to engage with their own ethical frameworks, giving them a reflexive function whereby audiences allow their own moral attitudes to be reflected and reinforced.[11] However, mediated storytelling can also reflect attitudes that perpetuate stereotypes, where complex social issues are condensed into something that is more easily understandable in order to support a narrative.[12]

The success of crime drama writers in apportioning morality or blame convincingly is linked to gendered and racialized ideas about perpetrators and victims,[13] and the extent to which power, status, and intellectual authority are imbued within a character is dependent upon their function in the drama.[14] However, crime dramas also have the capacity to play an agenda-setting role by focusing attention on a particular issue and capturing public attention.[15] As a consequence, crime drama is both transgressive and conservative, both challenging and reinforcing public ideas in the service of dramatic narrative.[16]

Television Representations of Restorative Justice

Our investigation of scholarly and news media databases revealed that portrayals of RJ in popular culture, including film and television, are few and far between. Possibly for this reason, there is little to no literature examining these portrayals. More broadly, we identified examples of the representation of restorative practices in art,[17] whereby art is seen to "mediate, enhance and make tangible new understandings of the notion and practice of justice."[18] Television portrayals such as the one in *HTGAWM* enable the communication of, and wide public engagement with, the complexity that lies behind the social/relational experience of crime for "victims," "offenders," and their communities. They can help develop better understandings of how these experiences relate to social justice "across social, racial, political and economic boundaries."[19] This episode of *HTGAWM* is thus a vehicle through which to engage the public in the rationale behind a vision of justice that goes beyond simplistic understandings of crime/retribution and is focused on meaningfully repairing harm and relationships in their social settings.

The analysis that follows examines how the restorative ideal and its practices are represented in season 6, episode 7 of *HTGAWM*. It highlights a complex range of intersecting issues including the meaning of "justice," idealized notions of victims and offenders, homophobia, and racism. Direct quotations from the visual text are presented with reference to the approximate time signature.

Themes from How to Get Away with Murder

What Is Restorative Justice?

First, we address the overall purpose and the key features of RJ as portrayed in season 6, episode 7. The purpose of RJ is construed primarily as a process oriented toward healing. It aims to help those affected by the crime, and as Annalise's student Gabriel says, to "move on and heal" (00:05:22) by coming to accept or reconcile themselves with what has happened. The healing and beneficial effects of RJ are further highlighted by contrast effects of the traditional court system. As Annalise describes it to the victim's grandparents, the traditional trial leads to inevitable "secondary victimization," a criminological term meaning the trauma victims experience by engaging with the criminal justice system. As she says, the trial "won't be David's [the defendant], it'll be Ryan's [the victim]," whose "entire life [will be] raked over the coals in court," including "arrests for fighting, drug use" and "rumors that he hurt his mother" (00:11:33).

The traumatizing effects of a traditional trial are further contrasted with the empowering experience of RJ, portrayed as a participatory process where victims, their loved ones, and offenders reconstruct events and the harms suffered. Making one's voice heard is depicted as cathartic for all involved and thus valuable in itself. Urging the victim's grandparents to engage in the process, Annalise's student Asher emphasizes the importance of speaking out by sharing his personal experience of losing his father: "Instead of talking about it, we [the family], we blamed each other, and it spread like cancer, to the point where we still don't talk. Speaking your mind even if it's all anger, grief and rage . . . it can help" (00:10:57). Similarly, Gabriel describes the traditional justice process as a waste of public money, while emphasizing the value of speaking out to the defendant: "[If] you speak about your pain, you can teach people. Take this tragedy and make it mean something" (00:07:09). Through dialogue, both parties are able to reconstruct the meaning of events and begin to learn to cope, even where grief remains. Additionally, all parties contribute to defining the terms of resolution (e.g., sentencing), an empowering exercise even if, as noted below, this differs little from the outcome of a traditional trial.

At the same time, a common perception of RJ as a "soft" option is presented but then challenged throughout the episode. This misconception is presented primarily through Asher's voice, who asks why this defendant should benefit from "a more cushy trial" (00:05:39). However, the challenge of facing the victims and engaging in meaningful conversations about what happened is made clear through David's initial reluctance to take part, Annalise's concern that he will attempt to harm himself, and David's statement that "I would much prefer to go to jail for the rest of my life than to explain how we all got here today" (00:28:15). In addition, at the end of the process, David is sentenced to the same twenty-five years in prison he would have gotten regardless. As such, RJ is shown to be a demanding process that does not necessarily lessen sentences but ultimately aims toward healing. In contrast, the traditional court system may deliver retribution but does so through a process that sidelines both victims and offenders, removing their voice and agency in the resolution of the crime.

The overall portrayal of RJ in this episode is that of a progressive alternative to traditional criminal justice. The RJ process is heralded by Annalise as a much better use of public money than any trial she has ever been involved with. This is unsurprising, as the show portrays Annalise's inability to "heal" from her own victimization (a history of sexual abuse, child loss, intimate partner violence) in the context of a desperately flawed criminal justice system. As the episode progresses, Annalise's team persuades both the defendant and the victim's grandparents of the benefits of engaging in the RJ process, and the audience witnesses the cathartic effects of the restorative encounter between all parties. Finally,

9. Restorative Versus Retributive Justice

the sentencing judge concludes that RJ aims to "help repair the harm done to victims and families" and that if it "brought even a little solace to the Fitzgerald's loss," he considers it "time well spent" (00:30:30). As Annalise says, we are encouraged to see RJ as "the future of the criminal justice system" (00:03:36).

Emotional Expression as Restoration

One of the key aspects of RJ practice portrayed in this episode is the facilitation of dialogue to arrive at a shared understanding of what happened. It is in doing so that all parties learn to cope with and move on from the harms suffered in and around the experience of crime. Central to this practice is the expressing and acknowledging of emotions. This is done in several ways throughout the episode. Emotion is portrayed as both the motivation for the crime (David says, "when Ryan came into the class that day . . . I had hate in my heart for him." 00.28:15) and the practice of RJ (Annalise says, "Expressing grief is a part of this process, now it's time for you to express yours." 00:27:51). Indeed, as the facilitator plainly states: "Emotion is the point of the process" (00:14:26). Emotion is therefore understood as both an enabler of the process of restoration and a catharsis for everyone involved.

The cathartic function of the expression and acknowledgment of emotions plays a wider narrative role that embeds the theme of RJ within the broader story arc of the series. The expression of emotion highlighted by the use of RJ is presented in contrast to the secrecy and restraint that surround the main characters following their own involvement in murder. The courtroom scenes, in which characters' emotional states are clearly and concisely stated, act as a blueprint for the main characters to then express their own tightly held emotions about their part in the murder that serves as catalyst for the entire series. RJ, while presented as a theme to a single episode, serves as a plot device whereby the main characters can explore their own guilt and fear. In doing so, they express the transgressive and conservative qualities of crime drama as a genre, as the transgression of committing murder and not being brought to justice is balanced against the pain and suffering that the characters experience as a result.

Race, Racism, and Insecurity

While this is implicit, it is significant that David is a white male authority figure, and Ryan is a young Black male. The context suggests that Ryan is a vulnerable child, which explains his behavioral problems, but instead of receiving support from David, he was perceived as dangerous. Consequently, while not explicitly acknowledged in the dialogue of this episode, it is implied that Ryan is a victim not just of David's actions but of wider systemic racism, which creates the conditions for a child to be perceived as a threat and shot dead. In contrast, David embodies the power and privilege to which Ryan is "a threat." As noted in other work,[20] while gender and race are not explicitly acknowledged in the dialogue, the storyline and its framing mean that race and the structural aspects of race discrimination and oppression are nonetheless overtly represented. Furthermore, the racialized assumptions about Ryan's dangerous character are exacerbated by a backdrop of fear of crime in the context of gun violence and high school shootings in the United States as his teacher and murderer, David, illegally kept a gun hidden in the classroom "due to his fear of a high school shooting" (00:05:30). In this way, race, racism, and the climate of insecurity created by gun violence all provide context to explain how and why the crime took place.

Sexuality, Shame, and Homophobia

Sexuality, shame, and homophobia play a key role in shaping events and blur the victim–offender dichotomy. It is a fellow staff member at the school, Ms. Moloney, who apologetically and with considerable emotion "outs" David during the restorative "hearing," revealing his sexuality as an open secret in the workplace, known to Ryan and a source of personal shame for David. Ryan's bullying of David thus takes on a new significance. In the scene that immediately follows David's outing, Annalise confronts him with the question of whether he was "sleeping with [the] boy" (00:15:03), drawing the link between homosexuality and pedophilia, a well-established homophobic trope. The same link is made by Ryan's grandmother, who asks David, "did you do this because you're homosexual? Did you think Ryan was too, did you try to . . . ?" (00:25:59), implying he may have shot Ryan to cover up child sexual abuse. It is thus against this background of latent homophobia that David's feelings of shame are articulated—shame for being gay and the shame of being closeted—and that Annalise requests David be put on "suicide watch."

The need for experienced facilitators is thus highlighted vis-à-vis prejudice and situations where shame may be unbearable or used to coerce and intimidate. Nonetheless, RJ enables David to articulate his feelings of shame, reflect on how they influenced his perception of Ryan, as well as feelings and actions toward Ryan, and ultimately apologize for his actions from a place where he himself can better make sense of them. He notes that his hate for Ryan was not due to his behavior in class but because Ryan knew about his homosexuality:

> The thing that I've... most hated about myself... That I'm [gay]... And what character is lacking in me that I didn't have the courage to stand up to a sixteen-year-old boy and say, "Yes, I'm gay"? Instead, I let hate take over and... I'm not sure if it's the reason that I pulled the trigger, but I'm sure that it was a part of it. (00:28:15)

Thus, David admits that this double shame, for being gay and for feeling ashamed, motivated his actions. He is therefore shown to be a "victim" of homophobia, in part internalized, in part perpetrated by Ryan and the wider community around him. In this way, the narrative demonstrates that understanding this crime and healing from its impacts cannot be achieved without acknowledging and understanding the role sexuality, shame, and homophobia played in shaping circumstances and individual actions. It also highlights the importance and value of including the wider community in the RJ process, as well as the necessity that all parties are open to listening and self-reflection as preconditions to arriving at shared understandings of events and harms suffered.

Conclusion

The overall portrayal of RJ in this episode is that of a progressive alternative to traditional criminal justice. Throughout, the healing effects of RJ are highlighted by contrast to the secondary victimization caused by the traditional court system. The aims and contours of RJ practices are explained in the classroom, and thus to the audience, and demonstrated as the narrative unfolds. Throughout, we are invited to reconstruct the meaning of events alongside victims, the wider community, and the perpetrator, who begins the process of healing, even where grief remains. Through this process of reconstruction, the cathartic function of the expression and acknowledgment of emotions embeds the topic of RJ within the broader story arc of *HTGAWM*. The episode both demonstrates the importance of emotional expression in the context of RJ and expresses the transgressive and conservative qualities of crime drama as a genre. At the same time, the themes of racism, insecurity, and homophobia all provide context to explain how and why the crime took place. On one level, the inclusion of these structural themes gives substance to the value of including the wider community in proceedings and reflecting on the community's role in both creating the preconditions for and arriving at a resolution for the harms suffered. At the same time, these themes are key to the exploration of the meaning of justice in this episode and in *HTGAWM* more broadly. Thus, this episode brings the precepts of RJ to a wide audience, demonstrating its potential as an alternative to retributive justice, to enable healing by "un-othering" victims, perpetrators, and their communities.

Notes

1 John Braithwaite, "Restorative Justice and De-Professionalization," *The Good Society* 13, no. 1 (2004): 28–31. See also Howard Zehr, *Changing Lenses: A New Focus for Crime and Justice* (Scottdale: Herald Press, 1990).
2 *How to Get Away with Murder*, season 6, episode 7, "I'm the Murderer," created by Peter Nowalk, written by Laurence Andries, aired November 7, 2019, on ABC.
3 Virginia Braun and Victoria Clarke, "Thematic Analysis," *APA Handbook of Research Methods in Psychology, Vol. 2. Research Designs: Quantitative, Qualitative, Neuropsychological, and Biological*, edited by Harris Cooper (Washington, DC: American Psychological Association, 2012), 57–71. See also Virginia Braun and Victoria Clarke, "Reflecting on Reflexive Thematic Analysis," *Qualitative Research in Sport, Exercise and Health* 11, no. 4 (2019): 589–97, and Virginia Braun and Victoria Clarke, "Can I Use TA? Should I Use TA? Should I *Not* Use TA? Comparing Reflexive Thematic Analysis and Other Pattern-based Qualitative Analytic Approaches," *Counselling and Psychotherapy Research* 21, no. 1 (2021): 37–47.
4 Eugene McLaughlin, Ross Fergusson, Gordon Hughes, and Louise Westmarland, *Restorative Justice: Critical Issues* (London: SAGE, 2003), 5.
5 Braithwaite, "Restorative Justice and De-Professionalization."
6 Zehr, *Changing Lenses*. See also Howard Zehr, *The Little Book of Restorative Justice. The Little Books of Justice and Peacebuilding Series* (New York: Good Books, 2015).
7 David O'Mahony and Jonathan Doak, *Reimagining Restorative Justice* (Oxford, Portland: Hart Publishing, 2017).
8 Mareike Jenner, *American TV Detective Dramas: Serial Investigations* (Houndmills, Basingstoke, Hampshire; New York: Palgrave Macmillan, 2016).

9 Sue Turnbull, *The TV Crime Drama* (Edinburgh: Edinburgh University Press, 2014).
10 Ruth McElroy, *Contemporary British Television Crime Drama: Cops on the Box*, 1st ed. (Oxford; New York: Routledge, 2017).
11 Jeffrey C. Alexander, "On the Social Construction of Moral Universals: The 'Holocaust' from War Crime to Trauma Drama," *European Journal of Social Theory* 5, no. 1 (2002): 5–85. See also Arthur A. Raney and Jennings Bryant, "Moral Judgment and Crime Drama: An Integrated Theory of Enjoyment," *Journal of Communication* 52, no. 2 (2002): 402–15.
12 Scott Parrott and Caroline Titcomb Parrott, "U.S. Television's 'Mean World' for White Women: The Portrayal of Gender and Race on Fictional Crime Dramas," *Sex Roles* 73, no. 1–2 (2015): 70–82.
13 Nobella Indradjaja, Chamdani Chamdani, and Syafi'i Syafi'I, "The Stereotyping Representation of Kensi Blye's Character in Television Crime Drama Series NCIS: Los Angeles," *Lingua Cultura* 16, no. 1 (2022): 1–7. See also Isabel Pinedo, "*The Killing* : The Gender Politics of the Nordic Noir Crime Drama and Its American Remake," *Television & New Media* 22, no. 3 (2021): 299–316; Lisa Coulthard, Tanya Horeck, Barbara Klinger, and Kathleen McHugh, "Broken Bodies/Inquiring Minds: Women in Contemporary Transnational TV Crime Drama," *Television & New Media* 19, no. 6 (2018): 507–14; and Turnbull, *The TV Crime Drama*.
14 Gayle Rhineberger-Dunn and Nicole E. Rader, "Race, Criminal Justice Professionals, and Intellectual Authority in Fictional Crime Dramas," *Journal of Ethnicity in Criminal Justice* 15, no. 2 (2017): 205–25.
15 R. Andrew Holbrook and Timothy G. Hill, "Agenda-Setting and Priming in Prime Time Television: Crime Dramas as Political Cues," *Political Communication* 22, no. 3 (2005): 277–95.
16 McElroy, *Contemporary British Television Crime Drama*.
17 Lindsey Pointer and Brunilda Pali, "Advancing Restorative Justice through Art," *The International Journal of Restorative Justice* 5, no. 3 (2022): 315–22.
18 Brunilda Pali, "Art for Social Change: Exploring Restorative Justice through the New Media Documentary *Inside the Distance*," *Restorative Justice* 2, no. 1 (2014): 85.
19 Ibid., 85.
20 Stephanie L. Gomez and Megan D. McFarlane, "'It's (Not) Handled': Race, Gender, and Refraction in *Scandal*," *Feminist Media Studies* 17, no. 3 (2017): 362–76.

Chapter 10

HIDDEN FANTASTIC MODALITIES OF SHONDA RHIMES'S PROCEDURAL DRAMAS

Ida Yoshinaga

What Makes a Televisual Auteur?

Early researchers of the Third Golden Age of Television, such as journalists Brett Martin and Alan Sepinwall, have pointed to a "revolutionary" narrative inventiveness and content risk-taking in scripted series from the late 1990s through mid-2010s that feature antihero protagonists.[1] Typifying this *quality-TV* form, edgy masculinist dramas (*The Wire, The Sopranos, Breaking Bad, Mad Men*, etc.) are said to uplift stories on the once-derided small screen from lowest-common-denominator fare to increasingly "cinematic" works. What later would get called "peak" or "platinum" television thus became quickly equated with shows about "difficult men" (Martin's term for cops, crooks, con artists, and rebellious others characterizing the new era's protagonists), torn by inner struggles, whose lives play out in classic US film/literary genres such as crime stories and suburban horror[2]—as behind the scenes, a market of newly fragmented audiences allowed veteran series producers the artistic latitude to create televisionary masterpieces, according to Sepinwall.[3]

Needless to say, such media trend-trackers generally failed to recognize female show creators and showrunners of the era; for instance, the few female-protagonist-fronted series included in these laudatory lists of Third Golden Age Television (*Sex and the City, Buffy the Vampire Slayer*) are rarely offered up in pop-culture conversations as exemplar of the new televisual form—perhaps as these shows were for the most part created and run by male executive producers. A scanter few actually made under women's producorial visions, such as feminist Jenji Kohan's *Weeds*, are largely forgotten today, their executive producers rarely if ever common household names.

10. Modalities of Rhimes's Procedural Dramas 121

This chapter proposes network and now streaming mega-producer Shonda Rhimes—whose multiple series are viewed as prototypically mainstream-populist and are thus not considered indicative of such narrowcast televisual-art trends—as a Third Golden Age auteur possessing a remarkably sophisticated range of cinematic techniques. Known in the mass media for her twisty plots, diverse characters, and inclusive casting that power watercooler-chat-worthy iconic moments within several hit series, Rhimes is actually a master of screen tone—and thus of genre hybridization, pulling together an eclectic set of storytelling conventions into a unique audiovisual mix that creates a specific emotional journey for each show's audiences.

In particular, I advance that while they are generic (genre) procedural dramas at the superficial level of televisionary-market labels (e.g., *For the People* was a legal procedural, *Off the Map* a medical procedural, and *Scandal* a political procedural), Rhimesian genre mixes contain hidden speculative and fantastical narrative modes so as to achieve a different onscreen cinematic feel for different series. Within Rhimes's production company Shondaland, veteran creative collaborators praise Rhimes's strength as a tonal artisan of what shows up onscreen. Tom Verica, who played Sam Keating, husband of Annalise (Viola Davis), in *How to Get Away with Murder*, has also directed many episodes for nearly every show coming out of Shondaland. As he said of Rhimes:

> We had tone meetings early on, on specific scripts, and it's hearing her speak about the moments (in specific scenes). And it's not about a precise "this is exactly how it is"; it's about hearing her passion about what this moment is, and the subtlety and the behavior of the characters. There's a specificity, and I think that's where she really shines. It's not just writing things that sound great and a situation that's great; there's a heart and a specificity in what happens between people that she will talk about. And that's exciting as a filmmaker, to be able to find ways to [manifest] that in a visual sense.[4]

Taking Verica's assessment of Rhimes as a distinctly visual screen auteur as my jumping-off point, I will analyze her ability to draw upon the family of fantastic genres—fantasy, science fiction, horror, and fairy-tale cinematic traditions—to enhance her various series' tonal signatures and thus freshen their capacity to electrify and to distinguish Shondaland's screen worlds from that of average scripted shows, series after series.

A Longtime Writer of Imaginative Genre

For anyone familiar with the introvert writer's 2015 coming out as a celebrity figure from *Year of Yes* (wherein Rhimes shares humorous auto-fiction anecdotes on personal risk-taking and public-facing courage)[5] and from *Welcome to Shondaland* (biographer Marc Shapiro's love letter to the showrunner's persistent work ethic),[6] Rhimes's robust childhood exercise of her considerable fantastical imagination is no big secret. "I came into a world of storytellers who were obsessed with reading,"[7] revealed the daughter of academic parents, a self-confessed nerd who often as a young child would secretly carry a tome in her rear pocket or the back of her underpants.[8] Shondaland had in fact existed in Rhimes's eleven-year-old head as an "imaginary place of Shonda. . . . A safe place . . . for my characters to exist until I could get the hell out of being a teenager and run out in the world and be myself."[9] As an even younger child, Rhimes recalls playing in her household pantry for hours, adapting national news of the Watergate break-in and its ensuing political drama into governance tales of Tomatoland, using canned goods as citizen-characters.[10] Imaginative worldbuilding of a whole storyverse, a defining narrative feature of today's most popular cinematic and transmedia works among the fantastic family of genres, seems a skill Rhimes had honed seriously prior to entering high school.

However, it wasn't until 2018, the year after Rhimes had signed her first groundbreaking deal with Netflix—with the summertime announcement that Shondaland would produce eight new series for the streamer including *Sunshine Scouts*, a half-hour postapocalyptic satire about "foul-mouthed teenage girls who are trapped at the end of the world" (both Shondaland's first official speculative-fiction show *and* the team's first comedy series),[11] then with the fall news that the production company partnered with science-fiction auteur Matt Reeves to adapt Blake Crouch's upcoming timeline-jumping spec-fic novel *Recursion* (2019) into not just a streaming series but also a feature film thus constituting an entire storyworld for Netflix[12]—that industry watchers began conjecturing about what Rhimes and Shondaland wielded by way of fantastic/speculative-genre narrative chops. Some media observers scattered sexist, notably misogynoir, reactions online; for instance, in industry news blog *Deadline*'s comments section, one incel snarked, "I guess this means Shonda is going to make this lead female character black even if she wasn't in the book. The lead guy will be white of course."[13] However, those long familiar with Rhimes's showrunning record knew better than to minimize the production team's ambitions

10. Modalities of Rhimes's Procedural Dramas 123

amid Shondaland's growing arsenal of financial resources and creative networks with which to pull off this transmedia adaptation of one of the most anticipated sf novels in recent memory. Within three years, with the 2021 announcements that Rhimes had re-upped her firm's Netflix deal for about $300 to $400 million[14] (a significant raise from the roughly $135 million she and the streamer had originally agreed to[15]) and that the arrangement now included scripted- and interactive-media adaptation into platforms well frequented by speculative-fiction and fantasy fans (traditionally, but not only, cisgender straight white men), including virtual reality and gaming[16] as well as more feature film production, zeitgeist tastemakers began to prepare for the inevitable flood of cross-platform works from Shondaland which would now overtly operate within recognizable sf/f genre traditions.

Despite her much-lauded track record, Rhimes—encountering a glass ceiling faced by other accomplished women producers, successful queer/trans mediamakers, and lauded cinematic artists of color employed in network, cable, and streaming as well as in film media—had not, until Shondaland's Netflix partnership, been given serious opportunities to evolve into a full-blown fantastic-genre auteur, a knighthood-like status typically commanding huge production budgets, as it's been viewed as *the* mainstream commercial-cinematic genre of the past half-century.[17] But not being (previously) contracted to produce such highly profitable, IP-based, explicitly "sf/fantasy"-labeled productions, such as *The Expanse* or *Game of Thrones*, does not mean that Rhimes's team did not already work with televisual fantasy *modes*. For the procedural drama form has not been the sole set of narrative conventions coloring Shondaland series' emotional registers. Most of Rhimes and her team's writing-producing work has also carefully blended in romantic drama and comedy to optimize female viewers' attention and audience loyalty. So rom-dram and comedy have served as *generic modalities* that helped Shondaland add dimension and personality to the procedural, one of the most common, predictable, potentially flat genres within twenty-first-century television.

And to that already heady combination, Rhimes has allowed her series' various producing and writing teams to play with a range of fantastic modalities as well. These hidden genre modes go off unnoticed except when their execution is explicitly marketed to viewers—such as in the 2011 musical-fantasy episode of *Grey's Anatomy*, "Song Beneath the Song" (season 7, episode 18, written by Rhimes), now reevaluated for its innovativeness after initial mixed-to-negative responses from the media.[18]

Defining the Fantastic

But what, in fact, *is* fantasy? Deploying Tzvetan Todorov's well-known definition,[19] I use the term "fantastic" to refer to storytelling that furnishes an audience with a thrilling pause, a curious moment of hesitation, when they encounter a seemingly supernatural event within a fictional story, as witnesses who travel rhetorically alongside fictive characters (such as the protagonist) who directly experience the tale. During this reader/viewer/consumer response of hesitation, the audience feels uncertain as to whether that event is merely *uncanny*—an occurrence explainable by the normal rules of the world (i.e., following the laws of physics or other sciences, known social conventions, acceptable historical facts), however unlikely to occur or bizarre the event seems. Or the audience might wonder whether it is in fact a *marvelous* happening—not explainable by our modern-day science and common-sense secular logic about how the world works, and thus operating in the realm of ghosts, magic spells, imaginary creatures, or other motifs which a contemporary audience might grasp as unreal. That pause between uncanny versus marvelous interpretations of the fantastical event offers the audience what scholars of fantasy distinguish as a structural quality of the genre distinct from that of more naturalistic or realistic narratives. This fantastic moment aesthetically stimulates, sparks, or provokes the imagination. As folklorist Jack Zipes often argued over a lifetime of fairy-tale scholarship, humans crave the fantastic almost "too much."[20] For people do not need fantasy due to its escapist nature, but rather because it helps them to refresh spiritually so as to survive oppressive social structures and dare to imagine alternatives to the political status quo: "More than titillation, we need the fantastic for resistance,"[21] proclaimed Zipes.

Sometimes Shondaland shows pull off this Todorovian moment of hesitation quite well—especially, as I will argue below, in the case of horror modalities, a Gothic-influenced set of darkly fantastic storytelling conventions which is one of Rhimes's longtime generic specialties as a screenwriter. But other times this uncanny-marvelous tension, that critical pause of narrative ambiguity, can feel wrung out. Perhaps the best-known case of fantastic hesitation in which Rhimes and her team narratively stumbled was the *Grey's* storyline of Izzie Stevens (Katherine Heigl) sleeping with what seemed for a half-season to be the ghost of former patient Denny Duquette (Jeffrey Dean Morgan) from 2008 to 2009 in season 5.[22]

When Shondaland's fantastic-genre blending works, their technique often cleaves to well-worn genre-hybridization protocols common to

10. Modalities of Rhimes's Procedural Dramas   125

realism-based storytelling on network, cable, and streaming television. For example, the Todorovian pause is well-utilized in *Station 19*, created by Stacy McKee, within season 3, episode 6 ("Ice Ice Baby," written by Rob Giles), an episode which teases that uncanny-marvelous tension into a tear-producing story arc. Young gay firefighter Travis Montgomery (Jay Hayden) reassuringly speaks to an older woman over the phone from his position in the fire station, trying to pinpoint her location to send out a rescue team but racing time, as she is trapped in an unworking car during a dangerous ice storm. The religious woman, who suffers from either Alzheimer's disease or dementia, becomes a stand-in for Travis's mom, who during their mother–child history had not been accepting of his gender identity/orientation. As the woman speaks to the increasingly stressed-out firefighter about her alienation from her own son and the importance of forgiveness, she references Christian beliefs, framing the narrative potential for a supernatural miracle. Interwoven with flashbacks to Travis's past interactions with his mother, this race-against-time sequence manipulates viewers into hoping that perhaps that Todorovian *deus-ex-machina* convention occasionally practiced in other network/cable/streaming procedurals, where an invisible higher force ambiguously (perhaps) steps in to save the day, will kick in. By the time the narrative heads decidedly in the direction of the uncanny rather than the marvelous near the episode's end, as the woman passes away before she can be found, the whole experience is revealed to have encouraged Travis to rebuild his own parental relationship—this moment of hesitation has produced a powerful, wrenching dramatic tale, getting the audience to pause while pondering issues of faith, higher beings, karma, right/ethical action, and other spiritual-fantastic issues.

Multidimensionality of Genre: The Case of the Horror Mode

Genre hybridization comes easily to innovative writers, because, as theorists Rick Altman and John Frow point out, each genre comprises multiple dimensions: thematic (semantic), formal (syntactic), and rhetorical (pragmatic) structures of meaning and interaction.[23] *Thematic* elements refer to how genres hold expected topics; for instance, one of *Grey's* recurring themes is surgeons' sense of responsibility toward patients, a core issue for medical procedurals. *Formal* elements applied to televisual narrative refer to the genre's common narrative sequences and aesthetic techniques, such as *Scandal*'s original "Olivia Pope and

Associates' (OPA) case of the week" plus "Olivia/Fitz" bifurcated episode structure. In early seasons of *Scandal*, for the former subplot, framed in the audiovisual language of trendy pop music scoring semi-experimental edits suggesting that everyone onscreen might be in the midst of a mysterious surveillance, a client contacts OPA to get help with a political-fixing problem solved through the usual procedural cinema of hunting down clues and vetting possible suspects. The latter subplot develops the ongoing tortured romance between lead antiheroine Olivia (Kerry Washington) and her sometimes secret lover the US president Fitzgerald Grant (Tony Goldwyn), often strung shrilly around high-stakes conflicts. Finally, *rhetorical* elements of genre address audience or participant impacts resulting from a genre story's distribution/exhibition: real-world effects of shows. An example of Rhimes's intentional television rhetoric, of her engagement with loyal fans to share with them not just powerful stories but consequential ones, is *Private Practice*'s 2010–11 season storyline involving a violent sex assault on medical administrator Charlotte King (KaDee Strickland). Strickland put in performance overtime toward Shondaland's collaboration with the Rape, Abuse and Incest National Network (RAINN) on a public-service campaign featuring Strickland that included creative ways that viewers could donate to RAINN.[24]

Riven through with such multiple genre dimensions beyond that of their surface categorization, television and streaming shows made by sought-after showrunners such as Rhimes create small-screen storyworlds marked by constantly surprising narrative blends that exceed simple marketing labels to birth unique *mise-en-scène* made to accentuate unforgettable character interactions and texturize what might otherwise be standard story moments. *Scandal* and *Private Practice* are laced with thematic, formal, and rhetorical elements of the horror genre lurking beyond the surface to foreground villainous character development and punch up iconically climactic scenes. Known among Shondaland for recruiting offbeat scripters and then turning them loose as they come up with inventive not-yet-done ways for the characters to practice murder, torture, deep human betrayal, and other repugnant abuses of political power and militarized espionage,[25] *Scandal* produced many talked-about media moments due to the show's anything-goes ethos—for example as in season 2, episode 21 ("Any Questions?" written by Matt Byrne), when Huck (Guillermo Diaz) tortures his former friend/co-worker Quinn (Katie Lowes) *Marathon-Man*-style with dental extraction. Thematic genre elements of human-violence-driven horror such as killing, kidnapping, hired wetwork, or bloody gun or knife sprees were placed within narrative structures of escalating action-thriller beats as an aesthetic (formal) delivery system for an increasingly stunned but appreciative audience tuning in (rhetorically) week after week. Such heightened scripted moments allowed typically overlooked actors of color and middle-aged female performers to shine in scenes ramped up by a shocking blend of pain administration and heightened drama, such as when versatile Black character actor Khandi Alexander, who plays Olivia Pope's evil spy mother, pretends to chew that character's wrists in a fake suicide attempt to escape imprisonment ("Vermont Is for Lovers, Too," season 3, episode 8, written by Mark Wilding and directed by Black feminist cinematic auteur Ava DuVernay). Executive story editor Ameni Rosza revealed *Scandal*'s generic DNA approximating Grand Guignol as a reason it remained a performer favorite, especially when it came to delivering monologues: "And this whole thing (*Scandal*) has this Gothic, operatic quality to it and the actors embrace it. That just makes it such a joy."[26]

In *Private Practice*, for me the most searingly horrific moment was not the (above-mentioned) sex assault of Charlotte in "Did You Hear What Happened to Charlotte King?" (season 4, episode 7, famously written by Rhimes within just a few hours),[27] a visceral scene that would launch a half-season of plot ramifications. But it was a season 5 arc for neurosurgeon Amelia Shepherd (Caterina Scorsone) where her drug addiction takes her to rock bottom in a whirlwind multiepisode plot in which horror's thematic elements line up to get sucked into a formal narrative tornado of an addict's emotional journey to personal hell, dragging an enraptured audience rhetorically along for the jagged, tragic ride. Unsurprisingly, like the "Did You Hear What Happened to Charlotte King?" episode, Rhimes also scripted the key episodes in Amelia's addiction plotline (episodes 8 and 22).

Historically evolving from the Western European Gothic arts, as well as from regional folklores that crossed over into mass culture including print-literary and audiovisual manifestations of old myths, legends, fables, and cautionary tales, traditional mass-media horror reflects mainstream cultural fears of boundary fluidity, transformation and change, and (body-centered anxieties of) corporeality.[28] This conservative (i.e., classical) approach to the genre has over the decades encountered clapbacks from genealogies of minority communities who have historically been called "monstrous" and framed as villainous in older narrative conventions.

In Rhimes's childhood flights of fancy in her parents' pantry, horror had paired with a natural generic attachment to the slightly surrealistic and starkly aberrant that she has never left. This horror-surrealist penchant generated Rhimes's first produced work to come from her original story idea as well as her first feature-length professional script. While employed as a staffer at McCann Erickson advertising firm in San Francisco, Rhimes told her superiors who'd just landed a new Barbie doll toy account about how "as a kid, I kept all of my Barbie high heels inside the head of my Ken doll. . . . They ended up filming a test commercial based on my suggestion and it was cool to see my words being said out loud."[29] This experience of being produced due to her surrealistic vision got Rhimes to begin to write more and more scripted work in her free time and to apply to the University of Southern California's prestigious MFA program where, again, horror traditions shaped her thesis, *When Willows Touch*, a Midwestern Gothic story about death in a community. "I had written a very dark, very personal thesis script that nobody was ever going to buy because it was about a dead body rotting in a cornfield," she told *TheWrap*.[30] Horror has historically proven for Rhimes to be an organic set of narrative conventions from which to build a story.

Non-Todorovian Fantasy Punch-Ups and Extended Allegories

Outside of Rhimes's beloved horror/Gothic/Grand Guignol modes, Shondaland's main narrative strategy for fantasy-genre mixing is through momentary but trendy pop-cultural references to the unreal, supernatural, or not-yet-achievable. That is: they point the fantastic-needle firmly on the side of the uncanny rather than the marvelous—things that might look, feel, or seem unusual, even borderline non-real, will appear or be heard on the small screen but never those which lack perfectly (or somewhat) good explanations behind them, the reassuring details for which will be furnished right away (no Todorovian hesitation there!). An example of this is the much-talked-about "superhero pose" that Amelia teaches her resident mentee Stephanie Edwards (Jerrika Hinton) so as to boost the latter's self-confidence in their neurosurgery in *Grey's* "The Distance" (season 11, episode 14, written by Austin Guzman).[31] I have often wondered, when viewing scenes where the pose is later repeated, whether this isn't a kind of non-Todorovian feminist fantastic aimed at producing pragmatic genre effects to get female audiences to mentor other women to be spiritually formidable via internalized revisioning of their own strength of character. It's obvious to the fan in me that Amelia power-posing for various residents mirrors the advice that Rhimes herself, in a moment of crippling insecurity as an evanescent public speaker, had received from accomplished female professional peers.[32] In the episodes since "The Distance," the pose has been referred to several times, a seconds-long accent (or in industry jargon, "punch up") hinting toward the fantastic and holding a space for its thrill but never actually attempting to go there.

It's no surprise that this commercial-folkloric genre mode finds its way into Shondaland episodes when a leavening from the plodding, generic demands of narrative realism is called for, a relief that requires the wrenchingly deep suspension of disbelief which the fairy-tale genre can furnish. Rhimes knew the appeal of fairy-tale frameworks for screen stories, especially given the success of *The Princess Diaries 2: Royal Engagement* (2004), her third produced script and the last film she would write before the launch of *Grey's*. This folding-in of cultural folklore in her television series includes momentary character bits, but also sometimes emerges as full narrative themes. For example, in *Grey's* season 5 two-episode opener ("Dream a Little Dream of Me: Parts 1 and 2," both written by Rhimes), supersurgeon Cristina Yang (Sandra Oh) meets her next true love, ex-military trauma specialist Owen Hunt (Kevin McKidd), when he literally sweeps her off her feet, rescuing her from a random icicle impalement outside of the hospital. The fairy-tale reference is made explicit in both episodes from the start with Meredith Grey (Ellen Pompeo), the show's titular heroine, in her voiceover narration drawing an allegory between our expectations based on folkloric stories we're told as children and our adult experiences with lived reality. And to further accentuate the folkloric figuration, guest characters Anna (Kathy Baker), Sarabeth (Bernadette Peters), and Betty (Mariette Hartley), three upper-middle-class female victims of a limousine accident, arrive at the hospital in full-blown ballgowns, a visual costuming detail that remains throughout this pair of episodes mostly set in hospital rooms, as the trio's longtime friendship is revealed as housing betrayal and rivalry. Through the episodes, Anna, Sarabeth, and Betty appear as middle-aged, grown-up princesses whose fairy-tale ending has not worked out; their heightened exchanges of sharp accusations and tearful confessions only underscore Meredith's commentary on the contrast between the fantastic and real life: "The person that invented the phrase 'Happily ever after' should have his ass kicked, so hard!"

A Media Archaeology of Televisual Fantastic-Genre Mixing

In the contemporary mass-media landscape, the fantastic is so dominant that we have come to take for granted its omnipresence, overlooking our assumptions of what actually constitutes that presence. We forget that it is merely part of the larger polyvocal genre language of mass culture,[33] one of several codes or conventions of meaning that we stitch together, often messily, in both producing and interpreting scripted screen stories. In an era of sharpened inequalities as well as resulting calls for social justice, the once-monstrous has re-emerged within that mass culture, newly genre-fying itself as decolonial or as proudly queer or female. There could not be a better time to also conduct close archaeologies of narrative category hybridization to unearth heretofore unmarked, sociopolitical uses of fantastic expression cross-culturally, cross gender, even cross subgenre, in television and post-television. Specifically, I am suggesting a reconsideration/re-read of all Shondaland's work by framing Rhimes as a longtime fantasy-genre practitioner and in particular, a cinematic-horror auteur of small and mobile screens.

Notes

1. Brett Martin, *Difficult Men: Behind the Scenes of a Creative Revolution* (New York: The Penguin Press, 2013); and Alan Sepinwall, *The Revolution Was Televised: The Cops, Crooks, Slingers, and Slayers Who Changed TV Drama Forever* (New York: Simon & Schuster, 2012).
2. Martin, *Difficult Men*, 83–5.
3. Sepinwall, *The Revolution Was Televised*, 4.
4. Tom Verica quoted in Lacey Rose, *Hollywood Reporter*, February 4, 2021.
5. Shonda Rhimes, *Year of Yes: How to Dance It Out, Stand in the Sun and Be Your Own Person* (New York: Simon & Schuster, 2015).
6. Marc Shapiro, *Welcome to Shondaland: An Unauthorized Biography of Shonda Rhimes* (Riverdale: Riverdale Avenue Books, 2015).
7. Rhimes to *Written By*, as quoted in Shapiro, *Welcome to Shondaland*, 11.
8. Rhimes, *Year of Yes* photo spread, notes to pictures #3 and #4, pages unnumbered.
9. Rhimes to *The Hollywood Reporter*, as quoted in Shapiro, *Welcome to Shondaland*, 18.
10. Rhimes, *Year of Yes*, 18–20.
11. Lesley Goldberg, "Shondaland Unveils Slate of Eight Netflix Series," *The Hollywood Reporter*, July 20, 2018.

12 Jerrica Tisdale, "*Recursion* Movie and TV Series: What We Know About the Shonda Rhimes and Matt Reeves Project," *Cinemablend*, January 10, 2020.
13 Anthony D'Alessandro, "Shonda Rhimes & Matt Reeves Team to Develop Blake Crouch's Upcoming Book 'Recursion' for Netflix as Film & TV Series," *Deadline*, October 4, 2018. Quote from the commenter "Barry" is from October 7 of that year.
14 Lesley Goldberg, "Inside Shonda Rhimes' Second Netflix Pact: A 'Significant' Raise and New Revenue Streams," *Deadline*, July 12, 2021.
15 Madeline Berg, "How Shonda Rhimes Became Television's $135 Million Showrunner," *Forbes*, July 11, 2018.
16 Elaine Low, "Netflix, Shonda Rhimes Extend Contract to Include Feature Films, Gaming and Virtual Reality Content," *Variety*, July 8, 2021.
17 I have addressed this issue elsewhere; for example, Ida Yoshinaga, "Seven Inquiries on the Antediluvian Labour Market of Cinematic 'SF Auteurs' and Blade Runner 2049," *Science Fiction Film and Television* 13, no. 1 (2021): 128–34.
18 See Michael Baumann, "Ten Years Later, the 'Grey's Anatomy' Musical Episode Is Still a Ridiculous, Iconic TV Flex," *The Ringer*, March 31, 2021.
19 Tzvetan Todorov, *The Fantastic: A Structural Approach to a Literary Genre* (Ithaca: Cornell University Press, 1975): 25.
20 Jack Zipes, "Why Fantasy Matters Too Much," *CLC Web: Comparative Literature and Culture* 10, no. 4.3 (2008).
21 Ibid.
22 Amy Amatangelo, "It Still Stings: The Worst Storyline *Grey's Anatomy* Ever Told," *Paste*, January 13, 2021.
23 See John Frow, *Genre: The New Critical Idiom* (London: Routledge, 2006): 74–6; and Rick Altman, "Conclusion: A Semantic/Syntactic/Pragmatic Approach to Genre," *Film/Genre* (London: British Film Institute, 1999): 207–15.
24 Rape, Abuse, and Incest National Network, "KaDee Strickland and Gorjana Collaborate to Create RAINN Hope Necklace," *RAINN.org*, 2011.
25 See Alex E. Jung, "7 Years in Scandal-Land," *Vulture*, April 2018. Rhimes has labeled the high-pressure creation of such crazy-dark moments in televisual cinema amid the show's collaborative writers' room, "*Scandal* pace."
26 Jung, "7 Years in Scandal-Land."
27 Rhimes authoring this impressive teleplay in about eight hours comes from an interview with Strickland in Kristin Dos Santos, "Why Didn't Charlotte Report Her Rape on Private Practice? KaDee Strickland Explains," *Today*, May 10, 2010.
28 See Jeffrey Jerome Cohen, "Monster Theory: Seven Theses," *Monster Theory: Reading Culture*, edited by Jeffrey Jerome Cohen (Minneapolis: University of Minnesota Press, 1996), 3–25.

29 Rhimes to *The Hollywood Reporter*, quoted in Shapiro, *Welcome to Shondaland*, 33.
30 Rhimes to *The Wrap*, quoted in Shapiro, *Welcome to Shondaland*, 37.
31 See Ashley Perry, "Power Is in the Pose: The Superhero Pose," *Medium*, April 7, 2015.
32 Inexperienced college-graduation speaker Rhimes received advice from her support group of elite professional women to "Power Pose Like Wonder Woman!" (Rhimes, *Year of Yes*, 62–5).
33 See John Rieder, *Science Fiction and the Mass Cultural Genre System* (Middletown: Wesleyan University Press, 2017), wherein science fiction "is an organic genre of the mass cultural genre system" (9).

Chapter 11

BRIDGERTON

The Progressive Period Pastiche

Shelley Anne Galpin

Dearest Gentle Reader,

Hard as it may be to imagine, the seemingly harmless period drama has incited some most indecorous squabbling among some social circles. . . . Or so might *Bridgerton*'s Lady Whistledown introduce the ideological arena within which debates about the merits or otherwise of the period drama genre have been transacted.[1] Although not confined to the UK, or to any specific "period" in history,[2] the genre is most associated with depictions of British history during the eighteenth, nineteenth, and early twentieth centuries. Consequently, scholars in the UK in particular have found much to debate with regard to the typical representational features of the genre, with class, race, and gender cited as evidence for either a conservative or progressive political stance by various critics. This chapter will give an overview of these debates before exploring the ways that *Bridgerton* (2020–) and its prequel, *Queen Charlotte: A Bridgerton Story* (2023), are situated in response to them. Through this process, I will highlight the ways in which *Bridgerton* operates as a pastiche of the genre, using self-conscious aesthetic and representational choices to both pay homage to and challenge traditional period drama tropes.

The "Heritage Film" Debate

The phrase "heritage film" is most associated with the work of Andrew Higson and his influential article "Re-Presenting the National Past: Nostalgia and Pastiche in the Heritage Film," first published in 1993.[3] This considers the cycle of period dramas, most notably the work of the Merchant Ivory company, who achieved successful cinematic releases throughout the 1980s and early 1990s. Films such as *A Room with a View* (1985) and *Howards End* (1992), both adaptations of E. M. Forster novels by Ruth Prawer Jhabvala, were produced amid a highly divided social and political backdrop, often associated with Margaret Thatcher's tenure as UK prime minister.[4] The production of these films, and many others, coincided with the emergence of what became known as "the heritage industry," in which the UK's past was commodified and, arguably, sanitized for mass consumption. As a result, these seemingly inoffensive films became the subject of criticism from left-leaning commentators keen to point out the ideological foundations upon which much of their presumed appeal was based.

Many period dramas, including those identified above, present an exploration of social relations of various kinds, often including romantic but also generational and class tensions. Higson notes the often progressive tenor of these narratives, acknowledging that "many of the novels and other stories which provide the sources for the heritage films of the 1980s have some edge to them of satire or ironic social critique"[5] and that these films "in various ways propose ... liberal-humanist visions of social relations, at least at the level of dialogue and narrative theme."[6] However, Higson's central argument asserts that the visual splendor and overrepresentation of lifestyles of the privileged few serve to obfuscate the more progressive narrative features:

> Though narrative meaning and narrational clarity are rarely sacrificed, [the] shots, angles and camera movements frequently exceed narrative motivation. The effect is the creation of heritage space, rather than narrative space. . . . The heritage films display their self-conscious artistry, their landscapes, their properties, their actors and their performance qualities, their clothes and their often archaic dialogue. The gaze, therefore, is organised around props and settings—the look of the observer at the tableau image—as much as it is around character point of view.[7]

The apparently pleasing visual style of many period dramas has often been cited as evidence for the genre's inherent conservativeness. Director Alan Parker criticized the approach as "the Laura Ashley school of filmmaking,"[8] and literary scholar Cairns Craig argued that the films represent "film as conspicuous consumption: the country houses, the panelled interiors, the clothes. . . . We are indulged with a perfection of style designed to deny everything beyond the self-contained world the characters inhabit."[9]

Perhaps unsurprisingly, this critical backlash produced its own wave of heritage film defenders keen to rebut the accusation that in watching these films they left their brains at the door as they fell under the spell of the pretty sparkly things on screen. Responses frequently questioned the argument that the visual style of the films resulted in an ideologically conservative text, with several scholars choosing to query Higson's assumption that the progressive narratives were obscured. Julianne Pidduck argued that the picturesque settings served a feminist purpose through their visualizing of the constraints experienced by many female characters within the narratives,[10] and Roberta Garrett has noted the ways in which recent period dramas have used sartorial excess to heighten the viewer's appreciation of the characters' represented experiences.[11] Further interrogating the ideological assumptions at the heart of the heritage film debate, Claire Monk argued that period dramas could be interpreted as progressive through their frequent focus on female characters, including older women, and through their representation of sexual minorities, particularly when "compared to the male-centred and heterosexist norms of mainstream cinema."[12]

From Puddles to Pastels

By the turn of the millennium, stylistic approaches to representing the past were beginning to shift. In a response to accusations of superficially prettifying the past, British period films entered their "muddy" phase. One key example of this is Joe Wright's *Pride and Prejudice* (2005),[13] written by Deborah Moggach and Emma Thompson, which Higson describes as "cross-breeding [Jane Austen's] refined world with the rather different sensibilities of Emily Brontë on the one hand and Henry Fielding on the other. It is more dirty realist than picturesque . . . offering a less safe and less pretty version of the modern English past."[14] In this film, the characters are presented as relatable human beings who get dirty if they go for a walk in the countryside or out of breath if they dance too vigorously.

This insertion of bodily realities into the often demure and cerebral world of the period drama serves to subtly draw attention to the other physical sensations that accompany the romantic relationships central to many period drama storylines. Desire, repulsion, the crushing despair of unrequited love, and the irresistible pull of sexual attraction are all viscerally rendered through the performances of the lead actors, emphasizing the universality of the experiences depicted and thereby avoiding accusations of distracting visual excess through a foregrounding of the humanity of the characters. Sure, they may live in a huge house, wear fine clothes, and get waited on by servants, but what's really important is how they *feel*. This trend was arguably kick-started by another adaptation of *Pride and Prejudice*, the 1995 miniseries written by Andrew Davies,[15] in which the characters' underlying sexuality is alluded to through the famous "wet-shirt" scene starring Colin Firth, a scene referenced in the second series of *Bridgerton* when Jonathan Bailey's Anthony falls into a boating lake while trying to impress Simone Ashley's Kate Sharma. Moving away from the repressed emotions and unspoken feelings that characterized many of the 1980s and early 1990s heritage films, this more earthy approach was dubbed "post-heritage" by Monk and incorporated texts with "aesthetic self-differentiation from the authenticity and 'restraint' of the 1980s heritage film; adjustments to narrative, character or costume to stress resonances with the present; knowing anachronisms of production design or casting; and a generally self-reflexive approach to style, adaptation and/or the treatment of history."[16]

While this mud and realism is all very well, as has been understood in criticism of the genre for years, one of the attractions of the period drama is how they look. In recent years, the visual pleasures of the genre have been embraced anew, with a number of productions opting for a diegesis of heightened femininity in which elaborate costumes and pastel colors are unabashedly prominent. Films such as Autumn de Wilde's *Emma.* (2020, written by Eleanor Catton) and the television series *Sanditon* (2019–23, created by Andrew Davies) immerse their characters—and viewers—in brightly colored interiors and lush green landscapes that recall the genre's previous suspicious critiques.[17] Negative readings of earlier period dramas have been linked to gendered value judgements that, on some level, see the appeal of the genre to female viewers as evidence of its lack of worth.[18] While the movement toward a more realist aesthetic can be read as an attempt to minimize these gendered associations, the most recent trend has been to "own" the genre's supposed feminine appeal through the inclusion of an excess of traditionally feminine colors and settings in which visual spectacle is a significant feature of the drama's brand identity.

These developments coincide with the increased recognition of the importance of the fantasy paradigm when it comes to understanding period drama. Higson alludes to the idea that period dramas operate in some ways at the level of fantasy. Drawing on Craig's criticism (quoted above) of the period drama as "film as conspicuous consumption," Higson argues that "because it is only images being consumed, it is a *fantasy* of conspicuous consumption, a fantasy of Englishness, a fantasy of the national past."[19] While here Higson is using the term in a pejorative sense, with an implicit suggestion that fantasy amounts to a superficial attempt to ignore that which is inconvenient or unattractive in the "real world," more recent assessments of the workings of period drama have used the notion of fantasy in a more exploratory way. Writing in 2012, Belén Vidal notes that "the mannerist aesthetic denotes a productive matrix of fantasy driven by a fetishism of the markers of period reconstruction. It connotes a conventional system of realism that has become figuratively excessive"[20] and argues that "it is on the grounds of fantasy—rather than the plenitude of the realist illusion—that we find the specificity of the period film for the contemporary moment."[21] More recently, Faye Woods has argued that in analyzing period drama "fantasy, affect and emotion should have equal weight alongside the previously dominant frames of heritage, nostalgia and 'quality.'"[22]

Visually attractive production design can, in some cases, still be justified through the utilization of discourses of authenticity, such as with Autumn de Wilde's expressed intention to capture the colorful nature of the Georgian period through her use of pastels in *Emma*.[23] However, recent trends in both scholarship and production indicate a movement away from a (let's face it, completely unrealistic) fixation on realism and toward an embracing of the visually pleasing and escapist nature of the genre. Rather than seeing the presentation of a fantasy version of the past as something to be critiqued, embarrassed by and ultimately avoided, the production design of recent representations of the British past have recognized that escaping to a fantasy version of history is in fact one of the key pleasures of the genre.

"Generic Whiteness"

Before I consider Shondaland's *Bridgerton* in relation to the discourses surrounding period drama, there is one other significant aspect of the genre's visual style that cannot be overlooked. This is the representation of ethnic diversity and its problematic history of reinforcing received perceptions of history through its casting practices. In 2002, Stephen Bourne argued, "the increasing awareness of Britain as a multicultural society in the present has had little impact on British cinema's acknowledgement of our multicultural past . . . there is ample ammunition for regarding 'whiteness' as a specific generic trait of British period films, even if it is one that their audiences unthinkingly take for granted."[24] The repeated representation of a white British past has led to a popular perception that this whiteness is due to historical accuracy rather than being, as Bourne identifies here, a self-perpetuating generic trait that serves to obscure the long-standing nature of racial diversity in Britain. What Bourne describes as the unthinking nature of this taken-for-granted-ness has been especially problematic regarding this trend.

As well as the clear ideological problems this representational practice presents, there are also practical issues. Many British actors have gone on the record about their felt need to relocate to the United States in search of better employment opportunities, often citing the high number of British period productions as a direct cause of this inequality.[25] Since the publication of Bourne's article, there have been notable shifts in casting and narrative practices, with both an increase in production of stories about Britain's multicultural heritage and a more (apparently) conscious effort to consider nonwhite actors for roles in period productions. However, Rachel Carroll notes that the latter trend has generally involved casting nonwhite actors in roles that feel "historically plausible: that is, as figures on the margins of legitimate society."[26] This produces the unfortunate effect of "inadvertently confirm[ing] an impression that the origins of black British subjects must in some way be questionable, if not implicated in transgression or shame."[27]

Bridgerton *as Period Pastiche*

And so, amid the debates regarding the progressiveness or otherwise of period representations of the British past, movements from visual splendor to realism and back again, and the still pertinent debates regarding the situating of nonwhite actors in historical diegeses, we come to *Bridgerton*, created by Chris Van Dusen and executive produced by Shonda Rhimes. Many of the films and series referenced thus far have been UK productions, or co-productions (often with the United States), and therefore it is significant that *Bridgerton* is a Netflix production helmed by Shondaland and hailing from a different production context to many other notable period dramas. While much of Shondaland's previous output has focused on contemporary stories, the female-centric storytelling typical of period drama makes a show such as *Bridgerton* a natural fit for Rhimes and her collaborators.

11. Bridgerton: The Progressive Period Pastiche   139

As Everett notes, the auteur identity of Rhimes is tied up with "her talent [for] crafting complex, driven, powerful and flawed women characters,"[28] and it is this same emphasis on the experiences of well-drawn, relatable female characters that inspired much of the feminist response to initial criticisms of the heritage film. Indeed, with the very notable exception of racial diversity, the diverse representation and casting that Rhimes has been celebrated for throughout her career is reminiscent of the light that defenders of the heritage film argued this genre shone on marginalized members of society.

Referencing *The Crown*, Abbiss notes that "the serial . . . reveals the post-heritage elements encouraged by internet-distributed television, demonstrating that the freedoms offered by the platform are conducive to innovations within period drama."[29] This is no less in evidence in *Bridgerton*, which effectively serves to pastiche the period drama, while using its specific representational and aesthetic choices to shine a light on and challenge genre-based expectations. Described by Richard Dyer as "a kind of imitation you are meant to know is an imitation,"[30] pastiche can effectively interrogate genre tropes and cultural expectations through the use of "discrepancy," or "something inconsistent or inappropriate . . . that makes one see more clearly the style of the rest . . . which is to say, the style that is being pastiched."[31] *Bridgerton* certainly includes many of the typical features of the period drama, including those for which it was initially critiqued. The visual style is consistent with its focus on the wealthiest members of society, with opulence in evidence through the locations and costuming. As well as the simultaneously grand and picturesque Bridgerton family home, complete with pastel purple wisteria, recognizable locations such as Hampton Court Palace feature heavily in the diegesis, adding to both the visual spectacle and (through the use of heritage tourism sites) the show's contribution to the commodification of history. Costumes are ornate and complement the pastel palette, and feminine textures such as feathers, lace, and flowers feature prominently.

As is typical of the period drama genre, the representational style of *Bridgerton* leaves the show open to criticism for its overrepresentation of the privileged, but also allows for nuanced analysis of the ways in which the visual style draws attention to the struggles of its female characters particularly. Prior to the first major falling out between Daphne and key love interest the Duke of Hastings, for instance, the pair attend a ball in which caged birds feature heavily within the mise-en-scène, emphasizing the narrow number of options available to women in Daphne's position. Similarly, the locations and costumes featured throughout the series, while often beautiful, serve to highlight the narrative predicaments of many characters. Contrast the light and airy Bridgerton home and subtly elegant dresses worn by Daphne with the gaudy dresses and oppressive home of the less socially fortunate Featheringtons, and it is clear that the visual splendor is also doing narrative and ideological work, highlighting that although the system works well for some members of society, others are trapped attempting to maintain their lifestyle and reputation in the face of a system that still gives men far too much power and capable women too little of it. In a recent magazine interview, Rhimes discussed her interest in "impossible relationships" as well as the "damsel in distress" archetype:

> I am suggesting that the female characters are the leaders of my stories, and that the pretty ones are the men, and that's okay ... I love the exploration of what happens when you go from the belief in the magical romantic fiction to the realities of what an actual relationship is, can be, and cannot be. Most women have been conditioned from birth to believe that romance and being loved is the most powerful, amazing, special thing that can ever happen to them. I've been writing a deconstruction of that my entire career.[32]

While *Bridgerton* is certainly romantic, its emphasis on female agency—with several significant matriarchal characters, including Violet Bridgerton, Lady Danbury, and Queen Charlotte herself, featured alongside an array of intelligent and strong-minded young women—highlights the importance of women taking ownership over their lives. As Anamarija Šporčič argues,

> Bridgerton simultaneously reinforces and challenges the traditional tropes of the [historical romance] genre, the ... deviations being a clear signal to the viewer that the content they are watching is determined to come across as more progressive than anticipated, yet also (knowingly) failing to fulfil that goal. The viewer is constantly being pulled back into the nineteenth century reality of misogyny, gender and class inequality that continues to flourish in spite of many of the key characters ... being powerful females.[33]

The need for women to be allowed to make significant choices for themselves is humorously underscored in the pilot episode, in which Phoebe Dynevor's Daphne's initial attempts at meeting a suitable husband are derailed by the overzealous interventions of her protective older brother. That this situation is only resolved by the resourcefulness of Daphne and

11. Bridgerton: The Progressive Period Pastiche 141

her mother, and by Daphne's ability to physically defend herself from unwanted advances, immediately cements the show's combination of romance-based plotlines with a celebration of female agency consistent with Rhimes's wish to deconstruct the damsel in distress archetype.

As alluded to by Šporčič, alongside the familiar genre tropes, *Bridgerton* features a range of well-documented anachronisms, evidence of the show's post-heritage approach but far more audacious than most comparable dramas. These serve as the discrepancies identified by Dyer as being central to the workings of pastiche, encouraging us to both pay attention to the production choices made and reflect on our expectations of the genre more generally. As well as the much commented on approach to casting (on which more shortly), the use of classical versions of contemporary popular music, the deliberate inaccuracies in dress and dancing, and the expressed attitudes of many characters all serve to create a diegesis suggestive of "an impossible possibility."[34] This unique amalgamation of the familiar and the new points to *Bridgerton* as a clear example of period drama as fantasy, and the elaborate costumes, locations, and even the melodramatic emphasis on grand gestures of true love all heighten this effect.

"Color-Conscious" Casting in Bridgerton *and* Queen Charlotte

By far the most notable feature of *Bridgerton*'s approach to the period drama genre is the choice to forego the "generic whiteness" identified by Bourne. Avoiding the problem of implicit illegitimacy identified by Carroll, the drama creates a diegesis in which nonwhite members of society are unquestioningly accepted at all levels, presented in the original series with very little explanation and encouraging viewers to accept this phenomenon as natural and unremarkable. As Šporčič observes, "opting for colour-blind casting enabled the creators of the series to highlight the problem of racism by eliminating it from a fictional setting, but consequently also bringing attention to it in reality, as well as enabling actors of colour to take on roles they would not usually be offered to play."[35] The term "color blind" has been questioned, and series creator and showrunner Van Dusen has asserted that the casting is, in fact, "color-conscious."[36] However, as Šporčič's comment makes clear, in addition to the post-heritage reflections on gender inequality familiar from many other examples of the genre, the creation of *Bridgerton*'s fantasy world allows for serious political points to be made regarding both practical and ideological social inequalities.

While many of the characters in *Bridgerton* are entirely fictional, one of the most significant casting choices was the decision to represent the historical figure of Queen Charlotte as biracial, as some historians have speculated may have been the case. An addition to the storyworld of Julia Quinn's series of novels, *Bridgerton*'s Queen Charlotte, played by Golda Rosheuvel, is a clear example of the show's emphasis on strong, capable women, with Charlotte depicted as an effective ruler in the face of the adversity (and personal tragedy) represented by the indisposition of her husband, King George III. Rhimes has stated that she has little interest in the historical realities of Queen Charlotte's ethnicity, with her representation in *Bridgerton* serving as a component of the fantasy diegesis the show constructs.[37] However, as Rhimes's writing of *Queen Charlotte* indicates, the significance of the character both within the *Bridgerton* story world and the period drama genre more generally is not lost on her.

Interviewed in the *New York Times*, Rhimes stated that "Even in historical drama, it was necessary for me to really portray the strength and the elegance of these Black women."[38] While earlier Shondaland productions have been criticized by some for over-reliance on post-racial ideologies,[39] *Queen Charlotte* continues the *Bridgerton*-style exploration of love and romance but also explicitly addresses the struggles of its Black and biracial characters by depicting the early days of what it refers to as "the great experiment." Through a storyline depicting a fictional rebalancing of racial equality through the sudden elevation of various Black members of society to the aristocracy, Rhimes's show effectively demonstrates the challenges of attempting to eliminate inequality in the face of social structures built on an awareness of difference. Storylines exploring the very real anxieties faced by the newly elevated aristocrats—for instance, that they could so quickly lose their newfound wealth and respectability, as well as the microaggressions experienced by young Charlotte upon her initial arrival—provide space for the drama to reflect upon contemporary experiences of social diversity. However, as befits the *Bridgerton* world, *Queen Charlotte*'s position as a prequel allows Rhimes to explore this issue in a relatively optimistic way. Since the majority of viewers will likely have seen the original series, they know that the struggles depicted are not insurmountable and, in fact, will have been resolved so effectively as to have been largely forgotten within one or two generations.

For all its embracing of spectacular visuals, elaborate costumes, and romantic storylines, *Bridgerton* and its prequel *Queen Charlotte* have forced viewers of the period drama to confront all they had taken for granted. Part of a wider trend that has rejected the gendered value-driven

11. Bridgerton: *The Progressive Period Pastiche* 143

suspicion of period drama tropes, the show is unashamedly feminine in style and expressive in design, continuing the Shondaland tradition of centering strong women and celebrating female agency. However, by effectively pastiching the genre, combining the familiar and the strange, *Bridgerton* breaks new ground in its use of anachronism as a tool to illuminate the present in the past (and vice versa), its embracing of the fantasy paradigm to understand the pleasures of historical consumption, and its refusal to allow generic conventions to continue to define how we picture the British past.

Notes

1. *Bridgerton*, showrunner Chris Van Dusen, Netflix, 2020–present.
2. Will Stanford Abbiss, *Post-heritage Perspectives on British Period Drama Television* (London: Routledge, 2023), 1.
3. Andrew Higson, "Re-presenting the National Past: Nostalgia and Pastiche in the Heritage Film," first published in 1993: *Fires Were Started: British Cinema and Thatcherism*, ed. Lester Friedman (University of Minnesota Press), 109–29.
4. *A Room with a View*, dir. James Ivory, Merchant Ivory Productions, 1985; *Howards End*, dir. James Ivory, Merchant Ivory Productions, 1993.
5. Andrew Higson, "Re-presenting the National Past: Nostalgia and Pastiche in the Heritage Film," in *Fires Were Started: British Cinema and Thatcherism* second ed., ed. Lester Friedman (London: Wallflower Press, 2006), 101.
6. Ibid., 93.
7. Ibid., 99.
8. Quoted in Claire Monk, *Heritage Film Audiences: Period Films and Contemporary Audiences in the UK* (Edinburgh: Edinburgh University Press, 2012), 2.
9. Cairns Craig, "Rooms Without a View," *Sight and Sound* 1, no. 2 (June 1991): 10.
10. Julianne Pidduck, *Contemporary Costume Film: Space, Place and the Past* (London: BFI, 2004).
11. Roberta Garrett, *Postmodern Chick Flicks: The Return of the Woman's Film* (Basingstoke: Palgrave Macmillan, 2007), 53.
12. Monk, *Heritage Film Audiences*, 19.
13. *Pride and Prejudice*, dir. Joe Wright, Working Title Films, 2005.
14. Andrew Higson, *Film England: Culturally English Filmmaking Since the 1990s* (London: I.B. Tauris, 2011), 170–1.
15. *Pride and Prejudice*, written by Andrew Davies, BBC, 1995.
16. Monk, *Heritage Film Audiences*, 23.

17 *Emma.*, dir. Autumn de Wilde, Working Title Films, 2020; *Sanditon*, created by Andrew Davies, ITV/PBS, 2019–23.
18 Monk, *Heritage Film Audiences*, 19; Belén Vidal, *Figuring the Past: Period Film and the Mannerist Aesthetic* (Amsterdam: Amsterdam University Press, 2012), 24; Faye Woods, *Period Drama* (Edinburgh: Edinburgh University Press, 2022), 2.
19 Higson, "Re-presenting the National Past," 96.
20 Vidal, *Figuring the Past*, 22.
21 Ibid., 26.
22 Woods, *Period Drama*, 2.
23 Hunter Harris, "*Harold and Maude*, Beck, and 7 Other Things that Influenced *Emma*," *Vulture*, March 3, 2020.
24 Stephen Bourne, "Secrets and Lies: Black Histories and British Historical Films," in *British Historical Cinema*, ed. Claire Monk and Amy Sargeant (Abingdon: Routledge, 2002), 49.
25 See, for example, *BBC News*, "Historical Dramas 'Limit UK Black Actors,'" March 19, 2017; Andrew Pulver, "David Oyelowo: People of Colour Have Been Expunged from British History," *The Guardian*, October 6, 2016.
26 Rachel Carroll, "Black Britain and the Classic Adaptation: Integrated Casting in Television Adaptations of *Oliver Twist* and *Little Dorrit*," *Adaptation* 8, no. 1 (2014): 26.
27 Ibid.
28 Anna Everett, "Scandalicious: *Scandal*, Social Media, and Shonda Rhimes' Auteurist Juggernaut," *The Black Scholar* 45, no. 1 (2015): 38.
29 Abbiss, "Post-heritage Perspectives on British Period Drama Television," 131.
30 Richard Dyer, *Pastiche* (Abingdon: Routledge, 2007), 1.
31 Ibid., 58.
32 Brooke Marine, "Shonda Rhimes Speaks to the Moment," *W*, February 7, 2022.
33 Anamarija Šporčič, "A Metamodernist Utopia: The Neo-Romantic Sense and Sensibility of the Bridgerton Series," Acta Universitatis Sapientiae, *Film and Media Studies* 22, no. 1 (2022): 129.
34 Vermeulen and van den Akker cited in Ibid., 131.
35 Ibid., 135.
36 Chris Van Dusen, "Not Color-Blind but Color-Conscious," *The Hollywood Reporter*, August 18, 2021, 22.
37 Kalia Richardson, "Here's What to Know About 'Queen Charlotte: A Bridgerton Story,'" *The New York Times*, May 11, 2023.
38 Ibid.
39 For discussion of this debate, see, for example, Myra Washington and Tina M. Harris, "Interracial Intimacies: From Shondaland to the Postracial Promised Land," in *Adventures in Shondaland: Identity Politics and the Power of Representation*, ed. Rachel Alicia Griffin and Michaela D. E. Meyer (New Brunswick: Rutgers University Press, 2018), 156–75.

Chapter 12

BRIDGERTON'S QUEER ETHOS

Anthony Guy Patricia

Some nine months or so into the Covid-19 pandemic, on December 25, 2020, Netflix debuted its new Regency-era period drama *Bridgerton* (2020–). The show was brought to life by Shonda Rhimes's Shondaland Productions. It was one of the first tangible results of Rhimes's multiyear, multimillion-dollar deal with the streaming giant, and its success seems to have been written in the stars. Within a month, more than eighty-two million people globally had watched all, or at least part, of *Bridgerton*'s eight-episode first season, making it Netflix's most popular original program ever to that point in time. Indeed, the show was such a massive hit that by January 21, 2021, Netflix had ordered a second season, and by April 13, 2021, just shy of three months later, the streamer had ordered a third and fourth season. Though not unprecedented, a streamer or network committing to four seasons of a series when that series is only in its freshman outing, the move testifies to how much of a phenomenon *Bridgerton* had become for Netflix, Shondaland, and—it is not hyperbole to say—the world in such a short time.

Bridgerton's first season received generally positive reviews from critics and the general public alike, as evidenced by, at the time of this writing, the 87 percent Rotten Tomatoes high score from critics and 71 percent from the public.[1] In particular, *Bridgerton* has been lauded for its welcome depiction of Black characters in a traditionally white-dominated genre, the English Regency romance, as well as its equally welcome frank treatment of women's sexuality. But it is important to be aware that amid the torrents of praise *Bridgerton* has earned, there are some critics who brought up genuine concerns with the series, concerns that deserve to be dealt with on their merits.

Perhaps the most sobering of these critiques is that from E. L. Meszaros, for instance, claims that the "queer content of *Bridgerton* is a let-down, especially given its prominent placement in the trailer."[2] They add:

> While viewers are treated to one queer character and a fleeting glimpse of his lover, neither are central to any storyline or have lasting impact on characters who do matter [in the *Bridgerton* world]. The absence of any meaningful queerness in *Bridgerton* is surprising, and makes the prominent inclusion of Henry [the queer character to whom Meszaros is referring] in the trailer hurt that much more.[3]

What Meszaros is referring to is a *Bridgerton* subplot involving Benedict Bridgerton's (Luke Thompson) platonic friendship with libertine artist Sir Henry Granville (Julian Ovendon), who is in a romantic relationship with another man, one Lord Wetherby (Ned Porteus). Sir Henry keeps up the heteronormative pretense his society demands of him through a marriage of convenience with the equally free-spirited and sexually adventurous Lucy Granville (Sandra Teles). In season 1, which runs for around eight hours, the gay storyline with Sir Henry Granville and Lord Wetherby, and Benedict Bridgerton's nominal association with it, takes up the barest few minutes of time in the whole of the series. As Meszaros says, this hardly qualifies as "meaningful queerness."[4]

That said, looking more closely at the trailer Meszaros mentions proves instructive. It is the first of two teasers Netflix released to promote *Bridgerton* before its Christmas day 2020 premiere. In it, there is a brief snippet (lasting less than a second out of a clip that runs for a total of only seventy seconds or just over a minute) from a scene in which two naked men—one looking out at the audience observing him and the other seen from behind, his back muscles rippling in the artful lighting—embrace and kiss passionately. An art form in its own right, a trailer is meant to pique interest in the film, television program, or streaming series a company like Netflix has (or will have) on offer to its viewers. Quite literally, trailers are specifically designed to "bait" audiences into watching whatever entertainment product it is they are pitching to viewers.

But does a less-than-a-second glimpse of two men engaging in intimate, homoerotic acts truly qualify as "queerbaiting" as Meszaros claims in regard to the first *Bridgerton* promotional video Netflix dropped? The definition of *queerbaiting* in the *Oxford English Dictionary* (*OED*) is: the "practice of incorporating apparently or potentially LGBTQ characters or relationships into a film, television show, etc., as a means of attracting or appealing to LGBTQ audiences, while remaining deliberately coy or ambiguous about the characters' sexuality;" and more generally, the "practice of trying to appeal to and capitalize on LGBTQ audiences or customers in a deceptive or superficial manner."[5] Taking the *OED* definition of queerbaiting at face value, without shading or nuance, means the answer to the question at hand can only be, yes, the-powers-that-be behind *Bridgerton* did, no matter how inadvertently, queerbait its LGBTQIA+ viewers. That is something LGBTQIA+ consumers have a right to be upset about, and it is something for which those responsible should be held accountable.

While I feel Meszaros is right to critique *Bridgerton* in the way that they do about its lack of gay representation in its promos and in season 1 overall—despite whatever was implied by the less-than-a-second glimpse of two men kissing in the show's first trailer—I wonder if Meszaros's view of what counts as queer is not, in this case, too narrow. In the remainder of this chapter, I will argue that *Bridgerton* is, in its entirety, infused with a queer ethos that should not be overlooked. This queer ethos registers on several levels, including behind-the-scenes minutiae, the poetics of genre, and the representation of desire and— even more importantly—sex.

Behind-the-Scenes Minutiae

We can begin by noting that *Bridgerton* is based on Julia Quinn's eight-book series of novels dealing with, respectively, the eight Bridgerton siblings and their adventures in courtship and marriage—all of which are quite thoroughly heteronormative. It so happens that the books came to the attention of none other than television's showrunning and producing powerhouse, Shonda Rhimes. Quinn describes these fortuitous circumstances as follows: "The way I understand it, Shonda ran out of books to read on vacation and somehow stumbled on one of mine."[6] She adds that "[i]t's crazy to think my life is forever changed because Shonda didn't bring enough reading material on vacation, but that's honestly what happened."[7]

There is something wonderfully Dickensian about the happy coincidence Quinn details. But more importantly, as evidenced by shows like *Grey's Anatomy* (2005–), *Scandal* (2012–18), and *How to Get Away with Murder* (2014–20), Rhimes has demonstrated a fearlessness about depicting LGBTQIA+ characters and storylines in the productions for which she and her company, Shondaland, are responsible. One of the more audacious of these is the character Connor

Walsh from *HTGAWM* who, from the first, was a gay "himbo" of epically promiscuous proportions, but who also grew into a far better person by the time the show ended in 2020. From Meszaros's perspective, it can be surmised that they feel Rhimes's involvement alone in *Bridgerton* should have guaranteed more in terms of gay or queer representation. Alas, that did not happen.

We are on somewhat surer ground when it comes to *Bridgerton*'s creator, Chris Van Dusen, who is a gay man himself. Though there is not much information available about his personal life, in one article that appeared touting *Bridgerton*'s twelve Emmy nominations for season 1—including one for outstanding drama series—Van Dusen stated that when he received the news about the accolades, he was in Los Angeles "in the car with my husband and we had just dropped our three-year-old off at nursery school when the texts started coming in. I think we had a good cry for about a minute and then we got it together."[8] Thus, we know he is married to a man and that they have at least one child. In any case, it seems unlikely that he would not bring something of a gay or queer sensibility to an all-encompassing project like *Bridgerton*. On this point, one journalist asked Van Dusen specifically about the Sir Henry Granville and Lord Wetherby story arc: "You kind of also introduced a gay couple through Benedict's storyline.... Was that also important, to show that side of the Regency world that we don't hear about too often?"[9] Van Dusen's response to this question is interesting:

> Absolutely. I think that this is a show about women and men figuring out who they are and who they want to be. Just as much as there is a journey to find a true love match, there's the journey to find yourself. I think that that theme is represented by characters of different sexualities as well. Benedict has a friendship with a gay artist over the course of the season, and what that really is about is it's a story, it's an important story of tolerance in intolerant times.[10]

This statement may well be of little comfort for those like Meszaros who longed for a more substantial and substantive story between Benedict Bridgerton and his gay artist friend. And indeed, there is a strong argument to be made that LGBTQIA+ audiences should not have to settle for less. Still, I for one am not convinced that giving up entirely on *Bridgerton* is the most prudent thing to do from a queer perspective.

As far as behind-the-scenes minutiae are concerned, we cannot move on without commenting on the fact that at least two actors in the season 1 cast are gay. Golda Rosheuvel, who plays Queen Charlotte, was chosen for the role in part because she is Black and in part because of the persistent speculation that the historical Charlotte was of African descent. Hence, Rosheuvel's version of the monarch lives and breathes in an "alternate history where her blackness is not only established but transformative for people of color in Regency Era Britain."[11] Beyond that, Rosheuvel is a gay woman who "introduced herself to her new [Bridgerton] audience by saying she's out and proud of her identity as a Black lesbian."[12] That said, there is no doubt that Rosheuvel plays Queen Charlotte for all she is worth to imperious, self-centered, droll perfection.

Meanwhile, actor Jonathan Bailey, who plays Viscount Anthony Bridgerton, is also gay. In published interviews, Bailey recounts how he was advised by some in the industry—most of whom were, ironically, fellow gay men like himself—to not "come out" publicly because it would only cause him problems in his career and personal life. While mulling such advice, Bailey insists that he never hid his sexuality, nor was he ever not honest about it when the topic arose. While every single *Bridgerton* viewer may not be aware of Bailey's being a gay man, the information is available in all corners of the internet for them to find deliberately or to stumble across accidentally. Furthermore, what makes Bailey's homosexuality even more intriguing in relation to *Bridgerton* is the fact that his character is about as straight as they come. Indeed, Anthony's mile-wide misogynistic streak and his boundless heterosexual libido qualify him to be a figure of toxic masculinity in twenty-first-century terms. Now that is certainly a queer set of circumstances.

Comparatively speaking, we do not have to go very far back in history before we arrive at the time when information about the sexuality of actors and showrunners in entertainment was nowhere near as available as it is today given the reaches of the internet—if it was available at all, especially to the general public. Insiders might have known a great deal about the personal lives of those with whom they worked, but outsiders would not. Since we bring who we are at the deepest levels to all that we do in our lives, it is impossible not to have some understanding that *Bridgerton* can be queered in one tangible way beyond a disappointing male, same-sex storyline that seemed to fizzle precisely because of its queer-allied producer, its gay showrunner, and its gay actors. Indeed, according to scholars Harry M. Benshoff and Sean Griffin, there are "at least five ways one could begin to answer the question 'What is queer film?,'" which can be extended to include television and streaming series.[13] These include productions that feature queer characters; productions that are penned, directed, and/

or produced by queer people or that star queer performers; productions that are viewed by queer spectators; productions such as horror, science fiction, or musicals, all of which have come to be considered, at least in some respects, queer genres; and productions that invite queer identification with their characters on the part of viewers.[14] As detailed above, *Bridgerton* can be considered queer on account of the first three categories identified by Benshoff and Griffin alone. But there is more to be said about *Bridgerton* by building on the work of these scholars.

Poetics of Genre

If we expand Benshoff and Griffin's genre classifications to encompass at least one other, the campy melodrama, then *Bridgerton*'s queer ethos becomes even clearer. Campiness has always had an affiliation with queerness, although it might be a stretch to claim the two are exactly synonymous with each other. Regardless, as an adjective, *camp* describes something so over the top as to be remarkable if not scandalous, something so excessive as to be overwhelming, and something so aware of itself and exactly what it is (and is not) as to be more penetratingly insightful than many people give it credit for in favor of ridiculing it because they simply do not (want to) understand it. *Bridgerton* is nothing if not campy; it is, in fact, an excessively campy delight through and through.

Bridgerton's campiness is obvious from the very beginning of the pilot episode, "Diamond of the First Water," written by Van Dusen and directed by Julie Anne Robinson. It is set in a busily and meticulously realized London that is oversaturated with colors and textures. Much of the so-called "ton" dresses in ways that makes them look like nothing less than peacocks strutting about demanding attention. Very often, the women are befeathered, bejeweled, and robed in swathes of shiny satin and silk and tulle with matching slippers, while the men are smartly dressed in cravats, long-tailed jackets, velvet waistcoats, form-fitting breeches, and polished jackboots that ride up their shapely legs. The music that overlays all of this is at once romantic and contemporary. Many exquisitely choreographed dancing scenes testify to the rituals and demands of Regency courtship for the upper classes. And on occasion, the spectacle of brilliant fireworks and sparklers arrest the attention of characters and audiences alike.

Furthermore, *Bridgerton*'s campiness does not end with what we see as we watch; it also extends to what we hear. There are numerous times when the dialogue is deliciously campy. For example, when Daphne Bridgerton (Phoebe Dynevor) makes her debut before Queen Charlotte and the court, she does so with such grace and unaffected charm that the Queen rises from her throne, reaches out and gently takes Daphne's face in her hand, and then says with great approval: "Flawless, my dear," before kissing her lightly on the forehead. As lovely as these moments are, they are tempered by Lady Whistledown's (Julie Andrews) snarky narration: "But, as we know, the brighter a lady shines, the faster she may burn." This, in particular, is the kind of queer campiness that is aware of itself. And for those of us in on the "joke," as it were, this aspect of *Bridgerton* is wonderfully satisfying.

Bridgerton's campiness also extends to and encompasses its status as a melodrama. Melodrama is all about exaggeration and sensationalism; quite literally everything is at stake, even in the most benign of circumstances. As Lady Whistledown tells us in the first episode, no matter how brightly she appeared in the beginning, that only makes it more likely that Daphne will all too quickly burn out as the favorite of Queen Charlotte and, by extension, the ton. And that is exactly what happens once Marina Thompson (Ruby Barker), a distant but outrageously beautiful cousin of the Featheringtons, makes her first appearance before the court and quickly catches the eye of the queen and every possible male suitor. Daphne's star plummets so far that, in true melodramatic fashion, she is virtually dismissed by society and courted only by the weasel-faced buffoon Lord Berbrooke (Jamie Beamish). It is enough to make a debutante angry, frustrated, and sad. That is until, again in true melodramatic fashion, Simon Basset, the Duke of Hastings (Regé-Jean Page), in order to prevent Daphne from being ruined by being in the wrong place at the wrong time, suggests they form an alliance that makes it seem like they have fallen madly in love, though the reality is they do not fancy each other very much at all. This is campy melodrama writ large, especially with its built-in enemies-to-lovers trope possibilities. This brief poetics of genre shows in another way *Bridgerton*'s queer ethos.

Representation of Desire and Sex

Finally, we can consider *Bridgerton*'s treatment of desire and sexuality. The show has been widely praised for using, specifically, the "female gaze" in its scenes involving erotic intimacy. In other words, instead of showing things from a man's point of view, as might be expected,

Bridgerton shows them from a woman's point of view. Put in slightly different terms, *Bridgerton* presents sex as women might like to see it rather than as men would like to see it. This is also something that is part of the show's larger queer ethos, and not just because it turns the camera completely around and upends the normative masculine representation of desire and sexuality but also because, in so doing, at least some gay men—if they are interested in doing so—are invited to participate in the "female gazing" at men that is encouraged by this aspect of the series.

Perhaps the season 1 storyline, such as it is, involving Sir Henry Granville and Lord Wetherby, could have been more fully developed if not presented as an integral part of the overall narrative with a corresponding increase in airtime. Regardless, I do not think that what was shown of Granville and Wetherby's relationship in the initial *Bridgerton* trailer versus what was shown in the drama itself rises to the level of queerbaiting in any sense of the word. The queer ethos that surrounds all of *Bridgerton*, inclusive of behind-the-scenes aspects such as the queerness of series creator Chris Van Dusen and actors like Jonathan Bailey and Golda Rosheuvel, as well as the richly decadent lavishness of the costumes and settings, and perhaps most of all, the series' penchant for camp make charges of queerbaiting seem petty and mean-spirited. Instead, we should be celebrating all the additional queerness that *Bridgerton* does offer rather than bemoaning its perceived lack of queerness as far as Sir Henry Granville and Lord Wetherby as a semi-closeted couple in Regency-era London is concerned.

Notes

1 "Bridgerton Season 1 (2020)," *Rotten Tomatoes*, November 3, 2023, https://www.rottentomatoes.com/tv/bridgerton/s01.
2 E. L. Meszaros, "Bridgerton's Queerbaiting Lets Down Its Audience—and Fails Its Characters," *CBR* (*Comic Book Resources*), January 2, 2021, https://www.cbr.com/bridgerton-queerbaiting-benedict/.
3 Ibid.
4 Ibid.
5 See *Oxford English Dictionary Online*, s.v. "queerbaiting," November 2023, https://www.oed.com/dictionary/queerbaiting_n?tab=meaning_and_use #1316606660.
6 Christopher Rosa, "How Shonda Rhimes Found the Bridgerton Book Series Is So Funny," *Glamour*, January 26, 2021, https://www.glamour.com/story/how-shonda-rhimes-found-the-bridgerton-book-series-is-so-funny.

7 Ibid.
8 Chris Murphy, "*Bridgerton*'s Creator Had a 'Good Cry' on His Big Emmy Morning," *Vanity Fair*, July 13, 2021, https://www.vanityfair.com/hollywood/2021/07/awards-insider-bridgertons-creator-had-a-good-cry-on-his-big-emmy-morning#.
9 Meghan O'Keefe, "'Bridgerton' Creator Chris Van Dusen Takes Us Inside the Easter Eggs (and Sex Scenes) of the Shondaland Show," *DECIDER*, December 25, 2020, https://decider.com/2020/12/25/bridgerton-showrunner-chris-van-dusen-interview/.
10 Ibid.
11 Britni De La Cretaz, "*Bridgerton* Star Golda Rosheuvel Is Proud to Be 'Gay, Female, and Black,'" *them*, February 11, 2021, https://www.them.us/story/bridgerton-golda-rosheuvel-proud-to-be-gay-female-black#.
12 Ibid.
13 Harry M. Benshoff and Sean Griffin, *Queer Images: A History of Gay and Lesbian Film in America* (Lanham: Rowman and Littlefield, 2006), 9.
14 Ibid., 9–11.

Part III

RECENT WORKS
Building Shondaland

Chapter 13

ENSEMBLE STORYTELLING IN *HOW TO GET AWAY WITH MURDER*

E. Deidre Pribram

From about the year 2000, scripted dramatic television programming has taken shape, most prominently, as "ensemble storytelling," a phrase I borrow from Michael Newman.[1] Attributes of ensemble storytelling involve the following. First, a reliance exists on multiple, temporally simultaneous plotlines that regularly alternate but also frequently intersect.[2] Second, instead of focusing on a primary individual, ensemble storytelling features a collective of characters who interact as "a counterpoint of narrative voices" by rotating among their many perspectives but whose combined presence creates a larger, complex social world.[3] Finally, ensemble storytelling supports a plurality of themes creating the potential for "thematic parallelism," in which comparison generates ideational similarities, differences, ironies, and so on, by aligning separate story threads in inventive juxtapositions.[4]

The dominance of ensemble storytelling in the twenty-first century has been enabled by the advent of widespread, prestigious serialization. Once seen on television almost exclusively in the often-denigrated daytime serials known as "soap operas," serialized storytelling now spreads across the broadcast, subscription, and streaming spectrums. Identified as an ongoing or long-form manner of conveying content, serial storylines continue across episodes and seasons, in contrast to episodic series in which a weekly controversy is normally resolved within the hour. Popular serialization constitutes a narrative mode highly conducive to, and since the nineteenth century founded upon, the attributes of ensemble storytelling as defined above. In this chapter, I augment the notion of ensemble storytelling beyond its association with narrative *content* by expanding it to also incorporate contemporary practices in television *production*. I do so by means of the Shondaland representative case, *How to Get Away with Murder*, a scripted, dramatic serial that aired on ABC from 2014 to 2020.

The Showrunner

Also coalescing around the beginning of the twenty-first century, the term "showrunner" has come to designate the creator, head writer, and executive producer of a television program.[5] Although showrunner is not a title that appears in a program's credits, she or he is widely understood to be the primary creative and managerial force behind a series, whether episodic or serial. Indicating the "executive-creative producer having the greatest responsibility during the creative and production process in most contemporary TV series," showrunners are in charge of scripts and oversee the "writers' room," the collaborative working space utilized by a show's head writer and ensemble of staff writers.[6] Additionally, showrunners supervise the entire on-set production sequence as well as subsequent postproduction and are tasked with the making of a television episode and season from beginning to end.[7] Showrunners have become much admired for their prodigious skills and creative talent; indeed, they are "among the most powerful and well-paid individuals in the television industry."[8]

The origin of the term "showrunner" dates back to the mid-1990s, initially used sporadically but solidifying in the 2000s.[9] But the functions of showrunners, beginning with the role of the hyphenate writer-producer, rose early in the history of American television. Miranda Banks attributes the onset of the hyphenate to Gertrude Berg, who wrote, produced, and starred in *The Goldbergs* (1949–51), and to the now infrequently cited Jess Oppenheimer, creator, head writer, and principal producer for *I Love Lucy* (1951–7).[10] In part, the concept of showrunner grew out of an effort to identify and promote a single individual who could be distinguished as the "vision" or "voice" for a series, thereby helping elevate dramatic television programming to fine art status. Among many others, Michaela Meyer and Rachel Alicia Griffin describe the contemporary showrunner as "counterpart to the film auteur," the cinematic figure most identified with a film's artistic signature.[11]

Cinematic auteurism developed as a means of assessing certain Hollywood films as genuine works of art that, traditionally, have derived from the efforts of singular visionaries, as in the cases of literature and painting. Although a highly questionable maneuver, as mainstream feature films have always been collective endeavors, the notion of a sole filmic "author" (e.g., John Ford, Alfred Hitchcock, or Douglas Sirk) contributed toward cinema's recognition as the seventh art. However, while the auteur was established as a film's director, the televisual situation developed quite differently. For scripted programming, writers became regarded as the principal creative source. Long considered a writer's medium because television series rely on the abundant, regular production of scripted content, the writer-producer—and later, the showrunner—rose to the dominant creative and executive position.

In the broadcast era, a dramatic series season consisted of twenty-two to twenty-six episodes.[12] More recently, as subscription and streaming services like HBO and Netflix have gained greater prominence, scripted drama series customarily generate between ten and thirteen episodes per season. *HTGAWM*, distributed in the United States by the broadcast network ABC, straddles the two figures at fifteen episodes per season. Over the course of its six seasons, *HTGAWM* ran for a total of ninety episodes, constituting approximately 3,870 minutes of onscreen story time (at forty-three minutes per episode). While this represents a prolific amount of scripted material, it is not atypical. The demand for continuous content provides television writers with status, enabling some to move from their initial positions into high-level producing roles. Beginning in the early years, when Jess Oppenheimer served as "creator, head writer, and producer of *I Love Lucy*," the combination of writer-producer roles transported individuals who began by scripting television shows to "a position of power and authority previously unseen within the industry."[13] Integration of the creator-writer-producer functions led, ultimately, to today's showrunners who, at the core of their position, remain responsible for the generation of uninterrupted, high-quality scripts.

The attribution of auteur status to showrunners, as well as the prestige associated with the position, allows Meyer and Griffin to speak of "showrunners' specific, stylized creative visions" and, more particularly, of Shonda Rhimes's "signature showrunning style."[14] Rhimes is renowned as the creator, head writer, and showrunner for series such as *Grey's Anatomy* (2005–), *Private Practice* (2007–13), *Scandal* (2012–18), and *Inventing Anna* (2022).[15] Her pervasive television presence, the popularity and success of her shows, as well as the significant cultural influence that Rhimes exerts easily place her among the select group who can be considered, in the words of Michael Newman and Elana Levine, a "celebrity showrunner."[16] However, while *HTGAWM* is unquestionably a creation of the producing entity, Shondaland, Rhimes did not serve as its showrunner. The credit for creator, head writer, and showrunner of that series belongs to Peter Nowalk.

Massive Collaboration

Akin to *I Love Lucy*'s often overshadowed Jess Oppenheimer, Nowalk is far less frequently mentioned in connection with *HTGAWM* than Rhimes. Her cultural pervasiveness and celebrity showrunner status have led to including *HTGAWM* in the Rhimes repertoire that showcases her signature style, with often only passing references to Nowalk's imprint. Such attribution occurs not only in the popular press but also arises, for instance, in several contributions to the scholarly volume, *Adventures in Shondaland: Identity Politics and the Power of Representation*.[17] In one example evaluating the musical soundtracks for *Grey's*, *Scandal*, and *HTGAWM*, Jennifer Billinson and Michaela Meyer explain that the three shows discussed "span Rhimes's primetime career [and] demonstrate her evolution as an auteur."[18]

My intention here is not to quibble about insufficient acknowledgment of Nowalk's contributions or, inversely, to argue why *HTGAWM* merits inclusion as part of Rhimes's stylistic vision. Both arguments hold substantial validity. Rather, I want to reflect on the implications of a medium that so thoroughly represents behind-the-scenes, as well as onscreen, ensemble storytelling. As Newman and Levine observe: "Like film production, series television is a massively collaborative endeavor."[19] Television production is not only massively collaborative but also messily so in terms of trying to sort out the specific contributions of any particular individual. I want to suggest that serial television's thoroughly collective process and resulting mosaic-like end product, contributed to by so many, needs to be comprehensively analyzed—and, moreover, embraced—for what it manages to achieve as a massive, messy collaboration.

Part of the difficulty in assessing television series as the work of a single person, or even a handful of individuals, lies in the enormity and range of tasks involved in producing a scripted television show, as indicated by the dizzying array of executive producers, co-executive producers, supervising producers, producers, co-producers, and associate producers most shows credit.[20] Practical constraints alone demand high levels of "delegation, specialization, and close collaboration."[21] But even at the top of the hierarchy, determining who has made which decisions remains murky. On the one hand, Nowalk has been clearly designated as *HTGAWM*'s showrunner throughout its duration.²² And inevitably, as Shondaland offerings grew in number, the attention Rhimes could devote to any single production correspondingly decreased. On the other hand, *HTGAWM* fits so appositely within the Rhimes compendium, among other characteristics, because it is fully serialized, features a diverse ensemble cast of flawed characters, and presents what is frequently regarded as sensational material.

Nowalk describes the working relationship between him and fellow executive producers, Rhimes and Betsy Beers, as one in which he spent much of his time with the show's writers "breaking the stories and writing the scripts," tasks I discuss further in this chapter's next section.²³ However, he also indicates that Rhimes and Beers read and responded to the outline and script for each episode. Nowalk stresses that one of the benefits of working with Rhimes is the freedom she accords him to make the story decisions he believes are best.²⁴ At the same time, just as it seems impossible to imagine Oppenheimer ignoring the wishes of either Lucille Ball as incontestable star or Desi Arnaz as head of the studio Desilu, which produced *I Love Lucy*, Rhimes is undoubtedly the major force steering Shondaland productions.

Complicating the matter further is that Nowalk himself is so thoroughly a product of Shondaland that it becomes difficult to differentiate him from its overall output. Between 2008 and 2012, Nowalk wrote eleven *Grey's* episodes, as well as serving as a story editor for the series. From 2010 to 2013, he is credited as a co-producer, producer, then supervising producer on *Grey's*, as well as writing an episode of *Scandal*. From 2012 to 2013, he is named co-executive producer for *Scandal*. By the time Nowalk arrives at *HTGAWM* as showrunner, he is already deeply immersed in the Shondaland universe, helping to account for *HTGAWM*'s comfortable fit within the Shondaland Media collection.

However, rather than asking how an additional contribution like *HTGAWM* "fits" into the notion of a pre-existing, creative style belonging to the entity called "Shondaland," or to the person of Shonda Rhimes, perhaps the better question to pose is how does the new addition expand the parameters and possibilities of Shondaland as a producing enterprise of significant cultural influence? Shondaland itself is something of a serial production, each new contribution broadening our understanding of what might constitute a Shondaland endeavor. As the company grows and accumulates series, it also gathers casts, producing personnel, crew, and other people affiliated with its work. In other words, "Shondaland Media" does not arrive with an inherent, already established or fixed identity. It is formulated by the ongoing accrual of all the practices, participants, and television programs involved. Shondaland represents an active, evolving concept more than it signals a particular individual.

Suggesting that Shondaland and Rhimes are different entities is not intended to minimize Rhimes's talents as a writer and showrunner or detract from her remarkable career. She is clearly the steering force behind Shondaland. On the contrary, my intention is to augment the scope of talents for which she is already recognized. Navigating the production of multiple, complex series in the highly collaborative art (and business) of television requires its own skillset and creative talent. Rhimes and Shondaland offer an example of ensemble producing, not limited to fashioning a single individual's style but enabling the presentation of a collective of stories, people, ideas, and visions.

Collective Authorship

Normally, we regard tasks undertaken by committees as invariably leading to mediocrity, forged by the continual compromises necessary to achieve some form of consensus. Yet, in significant ways, contemporary television scripts are produced as the outcome of committee work. Felicia Henderson describes this mode of creation as "collective authorship," even if such collectivity fails to be officially indicated in a program's writing credits.[25]

As quoted above, Nowalk describes spending much of his time on *HTGAWM* with the show's writers "breaking the stories and writing the scripts." The phrase "breaking story" applies to the process of determining a season's story arcs and character development, a task carried out collaboratively by the head writer/showrunner and staff writers.[26] Once the contours of the entire season have been worked out, the next step involves "breaking" each episode into "beats" of more specific plot and character events, a project also carried out collectively by the show's ensemble of writers. Thought of as "scenes" in film, "beats" are approximately one to two minutes of screen time that follow a specific story thread or character before cutting, back and forth, among others. Conceiving of contemporary dramatic television as "a shaped collection of pieces," beats are story fragments of relatively brief duration that, accumulated over the course of the episode, constitute a coherent story strand.[27] Seasonal and episodic breakdowns may well take up the largest portion of time involved in the scripting process, the entire extent of which is conducted "in the committee-like setting of a writers' room."[28]

Although each series develops its own balance between team and individual activities, generally it is only once the season and episodes have been carefully choreographed by the whole group that specific episodes are turned over to one or two staff writers for completion. A knowledge of "what the episode has to accomplish" is collaboratively secured prior to the detailed minutiae of composing an actual draft.[29] One advantage of this procedure rests in the substantial flexibility engendered because every member of the writing team is versed in what is required and, therefore, equally qualified to write, revise, or otherwise contribute to the detailed episodic draft. However, only those who carry out this last stage of fleshing out a full script receive the credit of "written by," meaning that much of the process of collective authorship remains obscured because it is typically unattributed.

Like showrunner, the position of head writer remains uncredited. As originator of a series and (often) author of its pilot script, the showrunner receives "created by" for each episode over the course of the program's duration. Although as head writer the showrunner holds ultimate decision-making power over each episode's script, she or he only receives a "written by" credit for the ones they themselves draft. Accordingly, Nowalk is credited as *HTGAWM*'s creator on all ninety installments, but he is acknowledged for writing just eleven of those ninety episodes. While no other individual is named for as many as Nowalk, a number of others make sizable contributions (Sarah Thompson and Joe Fazzio at eight each; Erika Harrison and Michael Foley at seven apiece). Writers credited for *HTGAWM* over its six seasons come to a total of thirty, in addition to Nowalk.

Similarly, Rhimes is recognized as creator of *Grey's* and *Scandal* for every episode. However, in the case of *Scandal*, she is recorded as having drafted 15 of its 124 episodes. Again, this amounts to more than any other *Scandal* writer, but five others each delivered an extensive ten or more scripts.[30] *Scandal*'s six seasons arrive at a combined total of twenty-six writers, including Rhimes. The constant demand for new material, combined with the limited number of scripts any individual can reasonably produce, prompts the proliferation of writers assembled over the life of a series. Along with the teamwork involved in designing seasons and episodes, the sheer number of writers who participate affords an additional meaning to the notion of collective authorship, in which tens of writers possess a hand in scripting a television series.

The use of multiple writers is not new in television. Returning to the early example of *I Love Lucy*, an episodic series, Banks describes how Oppenheimer worked with four other writers. All five conceived of an episode's story together. Oppenheimer then split them into pairs, with one duo assigned to write a first draft and the other twosome tasked with the second draft. Oppenheimer reserved the final draft for himself, ensuring he had ultimate approval of the finished script.[31] Consequently, each writer had input into every script, with all of them receiving a writing credit for the episodes to which they contributed.[32]

Still, the impetus toward collective authorship has greatly intensified in the current era of extensive serialization, causing considerable impact on and commensurate changes to television writing practices. Serialization calls for writers who are versed in the intricate entirety of shows. A serial's continuity and coherence rely upon authorship that must continually refer to past events, sustain interweaving story threads and character arcs over lengthy periods while also introducing and situating elements that will only come to fruition in future episodes or seasons. Juggling a profusion of storylines and an often prodigious cast of characters demands intimacy with a narrative world beyond that required for episodic series. In the earlier episodic context, series drew on freelance writers who could script "stand-alone episodes more autonomously than is today's norm."[33] The template now entails a permanent staff of writers who spend much of their time engaged in teamwork. Ensemble storytelling onscreen has meant a corresponding proliferation of behind-the-scenes ensemble storytelling.

Considerable attention is now being paid to the onscreen qualities and impact of the currently flourishing television serial drama. Attending to behind-the-scenes dynamics may prove equally revelatory. Rather than seeking out singular inspired authorship, television could be more valuably evaluated for what it actually is: a thoroughly collective aesthetic form. Intensely collaborative working methods demand their own set of skills and creative talent. Producing environments that facilitate creative collaboration, like Shondaland, provides insight into the complexities and nuances of effective ensemble storytelling.

Notes

1 Michael Newman, "From Beats to Arcs: Towards a Poetics of Television Narrative," *The Velvet Light Trap* 58 (Fall 2006): 18.
2 Ibid., 16, 17.

3 Ibid., 22. For more on ensemble characterization in *How to Get Away with Murder*, see E. Deidre Pribram, *Emotional Expressionism: Television Serialization, the Melodramatic Mode, and Socioemotionality* (Lanham: Lexington, 2024), chapter 4.
4 Newman, "From Beats to Arcs," 22.
5 The senior-most position in the production hierarchy, executive producers are normally multiple in number, one of whom is the showrunner. For *How to Get Away with Murder*, three executive producers were credited for the entire run of the show: Peter Nowalk, Shonda Rhimes, and Betsy Beers. Additionally, Bill D'Elia served as executive producer for forty-four of the serial's ninety episodes (2014–17) and Stephen Cragg for thirty episodes (2018–20). Internet Movie Database (IMDb), https://www.imdb.com.
6 María-José Higueras-Ruiz, Francisco-Javier Gómez-Pérez, and Jordi Alberich-Pascual, "Historical Review and Contemporary Characterization of Showrunner as Professional Profile in TV Series Production: Traits, Skills, Competences, and Style," *Communication & Society* 31, no. 1 (2018): 92.
7 Denise Mann, "It's Not TV, It's Brand Management TV: The Collective Author(s) of the *Lost* Franchise," in *Production Studies: Cultural Studies of Media Industries*, ed. Vicki Mayer, Miranda Banks, and John Caldwell (New York: Routledge, 2009), 100.
8 Ibid., 105.
9 Higueras-Ruiz, Gómez-Pérez, and Alberich-Pascual, "Historical Review," 93.
10 Miranda Banks, "*I Love Lucy*: The Writer-Producer," in *How to Watch Television*, ed. Ethan Thompson and Jason Mittell (New York: New York University Press, 2013), 249–50; 247.
11 Michaela Meyer and Rachel Alicia Griffin, "Introduction: Riding Shondaland's Rollercoasters: Critical Cultural Television Studies in the 21st Century," in *Adventures in Shondaland: Identity Politics and the Power of Representation*, ed. Rachel Alicia Griffin and Michaela Meyer (New Brunswick: Rutgers University Press, 2018), 5.
12 Trisha Dunleavy, *Complex Serial Drama and Multiplatform Television* (New York: Routledge, 2018), 71.
13 Banks, "*I Love Lucy*," 248–9; 250.
14 Meyer and Griffin, "Introduction," 6, 5.
15 Rhimes was the original showrunner for *Grey's Anatomy*. As Shondaland productions increased in number, she relocated with them, turning the showrunner position for *Grey's* over to Krista Vernoff.
16 Michael Newman and Elana Levine, *Legitimating Television: Media Convergence and Cultural Status* (New York: Routledge, 2012), 55.
17 Griffin and Meyer, *Adventures in Shondaland*.
18 Jennifer Billinson and Michaela Meyer, "Soundtracking Shondaland: Televisual Identity Mapped through Music," in *Adventures in Shondaland:*

Identity Politics and the Power of Representation, ed. Rachel Alicia Griffin and Michaela Meyer (New Brunswick: Rutgers University Press, 2018), 80. To be clear, later in their chapter Billinson and Meyer outline a number of ways that *HTGAWM*'s soundtrack differs from the other two shows because of Nowalk's role and input (92–3). My interest here is precisely in the difficulty of making such determinations, resulting in shifting attributions of authorship.

19 Newman and Levine, *Legitimating Television*, 53.
20 An extensive list of producing personnel involved in all Shondaland programs can be found on the website, Internet Movie Database.
21 Dunleavy, *Complex Serial Drama*, 71.
22 Shondaland Media. https://www.shondaland.com.
23 Nowalk quoted in Laura Prudom, "*How to Get Away with Murder* Creator Peter Nowalk on Working with Shonda Rhimes, Diversity on TV," *Variety*, September 25, 2014, n.p., accessed June 24, 2023, https://variety.com/2014/tv/news/how-to-get-away-with-murder-creator-peter-nowalk-shonda-rhimes-viola-davis-diversity-1201313779/.
24 Ibid.
25 Felicia Henderson, "The Writer's Room," in *Production Studies: Cultural Studies of Media Industries*, ed. Vicki Mayer, Miranda Banks, and John Caldwell (New York: Routledge, 2009), 227. Henderson was the creator of and an executive producer on *Soul Food* (2000–2004). She also worked as a writer and co-executive producer for shows such as *Sister, Sister* (1994–9), *Gossip Girl* (2007–12), and *Fringe* (2008–13). Internet Movie Database.
26 Dunleavy, *Complex Serial Drama*, 84–5.
27 Sean O'Sullivan, "Broken on Purpose: Poetry, Serial Television, and the Season," *Storyworlds: A Journal of Narrative Studies* 2 (January 2010): 61–2. See also Newman, "From Beats to Arcs," 17–18.
28 Dunleavy, *Complex Serial Drama*, 83.
29 Newman, "From Beats to Arcs," 18.
30 These five *Scandal* contributors are Matt Byrne, Mark Fish, Heather Mitchell, Raamla Mohamed, and Chris Van Dusen. All figures are from Internet Movie Database. IMDb does not differentiate between episodes that are drafted by an individual or a pair as they all receive "written by" attribution. While Nowalk describes considerable input from Rhimes on *HTGAWM* story outlines and scripts, she earns no writing credits throughout *HTGAWM*'s history. Prudom, "*How to Get Away*," n.p.
31 Banks, "*I Love Lucy*," 248.
32 According to data on IMDb, the situation appears to have been more complicated. *I Love Lucy* ran for six seasons, from 1951 to 1957, producing a total of 181 episodes. Madelyn Davis and Bob Carroll

stayed as writers for all six seasons, accumulating 181 writing credits each. Bob Schiller and Bob Weiskopf joined for the last two seasons, both receiving credit for fifty-three episodes. Jess Oppenheimer was not involved during the last season, having left in 1956 to become an NBC executive, by which time his writing credits totaled 154. Internet Movie Database.

33 Newman and Levine, *Legitimating Television*, 41.

Chapter 14

STREAMING SHONDALAND

Shonda Rhimes and Netflix—From *Bridgerton* and Beyond

Sheri Chinen Biesen

Shonda Rhimes supported writers across the industry just hours before her new long-form limited series *Queen Charlotte: A Bridgerton Story* (2023) premiered to stream on Netflix. It was early May 2023 and the film, television, and streaming media entertainment industry had just been thrown into turmoil as the scribes and creative talent of Hollywood supported the Writers Guild of America (WGA) and went on strike after failing to reach an agreement with the studios and production companies of the Alliance of Motion Picture and Television Producers by a May 1st deadline,[1] thus shutting down the majority of Hollywood productions.

Receiving a BAFTA tribute in New York, Rhimes voiced her support: "I am a writer on strike right now," the influential hyphenate media writer-producer-creator declared. "I really wish that we didn't have to be on strike, and I feel the pain of the people who are dealing with the strike, but for me, for writers to get paid for what they do in a fair way is far more important."[2]

For decades, Rhimes has been highly regarded as a trailblazing prolific talent and powerfully savvy media auteur and woman of color in a white male-dominated industry. Creator of hit network shows like *Grey's Anatomy* (2005–) and *Scandal* (2012–18), Rhimes has most recently moved into long-form streaming media productions with the enormously successful Regency romance franchise series, *Bridgerton* (2020–), including its prequel spin-off, *Queen Charlotte*, which earned blockbuster viewership ratings as audiences around the world binged the series on Netflix.[3]

With this in mind, it was all the more significant that Rhimes admitted, "To have somebody devalue art, it's bad enough as it is right now. That's happening everywhere. But for writers to not be able to make a living wage while making a television show or making a movie is a problem."[4]

Shondaland's Move to Netflix

As CEO of her media company Shondaland, the *Hollywood Reporter* called Rhimes a "megaproducer,"[5] and the *New York Times* (NYT) referred to her as a "mogul,"[6] especially after inking her successful partnership in production deals and distinctive programming with Netflix. Hollywood trade papers heralded Rhimes's $100 million Shondaland production deal with Netflix in 2017, which industry analysts reported to include a base salary of $150 million,[7] with incentives that could make it much higher. "In a huge blow to ABC and Disney, the prolific television hitmaker Shonda Rhimes has signed an exclusive overall [multiyear] deal with Netflix," the *NYT* proclaimed on August 14, 2017.[8]

Netflix chief executive Ted Sarandos noted, "I've gotten the chance to know Shonda and she's a true Netflixer at heart—she loves TV and films, she cares passionately about her work, and she delivers for her audience."[9] Rhimes explained Shondaland's move to Netflix, stating:

> [it is] the result of a shared plan Ted Sarandos and I built based on my vision for myself as a storyteller and for the evolution of my company. Ted provides a clear, fearless space for creators at Netflix. He understood what I was looking for—the opportunity to build a vibrant new storytelling home for writers with the unique creative freedom and instantaneous global reach provided by Netflix's singular sense of innovation. The future of Shondaland at Netflix has limitless possibilities.[10]

The *NYT* also noted that Rhimes's move from ABC (and parent corporation, the Walt Disney Company) to Netflix was a "major counterpunch" to Disney, which previously had streaming and co-production deals with Netflix, and then announced that it was starting its own streaming service, Disney+, in an arrangement that would "force the removal of Disney and Pixar movies from Netflix."[11]

With Rhimes's move to Netflix, she wanted to broaden the conception of what television series could be beyond the conventional constraints of broadcast network programming, which air once a week at a certain time and run for an hour, interrupted by commercials. In 2018, Rhimes and her collaborators at Shondaland began developing and producing eight new streaming media projects for Netflix, including, in addition to *Bridgerton*, the Debbie Allen ballet documentary *Dance Dreams: Hot Chocolate Nutcracker* (2020), the White House murder mystery thriller *The Residence* (currently in production at the time of this writing), and the Manhattan con artist drama *Inventing Anna* (2022). Rhimes is credited as creator of *Inventing Anna*—the first series she created and penned herself since *Scandal*—and she spoke candidly about why the story of Anna Sorokin drew her back to writing, particularly the notion of critiquing society's

> value [of] the image over the actual event . . . how we look or what the picture is over what the actual happenings were . . . that's what makes an Anna . . . image is everything, the cover of the magazine is far more important than the person on the cover of the magazine. I hope we start a discussion about the fact that having a real relationship and being connected to other people is much more important than faking it.[12]

John Koblin of the *NYT* reported that after signing her multiyear deal with Netflix, Rhimes would "try to match or top her network success in the wide-open expanse of streaming, free of time slots, commercial interruptions, and restrictions on language and content,"[13] especially for the global market. Rhimes noted that her main goals for Shondaland's productions at Netflix were to create long-form series that were more expansive (i.e., than her broadcast network shows at ABC), and to make Shondaland an "enduring company" with longevity that would "live within Netflix in the same way that Marvel exists inside the Walt Disney Company."[14] In other words, Rhimes aspired to create her own Shondaland streaming franchise "story world" universe at Netflix.

The Bridgerton *Franchise*

This soon became a reality in late 2020 with the lavish, stylish period Regency romance *Bridgerton*, created by Chris Van Dusen and adapted from Julia Quinn's novels. The series cost $7 million per episode to produce, and in the wake of the Covid-19 lockdown and the surge in streaming viewership, it was the most popular title on Netflix up to that date.[15] By 2021, Rhimes expanded her lucrative deal with Netflix, which industry trade reports estimated to be worth as high as $300 to $400 million.[16]

Shondaland's hip, inclusive, multiracial Regency saga *Bridgerton* empowers women, ethnicity, and diversity and boasted an impressive eighty-two million viewers in the first four weeks,[17] outpacing an array of grittier, more masculine programming, brooding macho neo-noir fare and grisly graphic Gothic horror content. "I have nothing but excitement for *Bridgerton* continuing to steam train off and conquer the globe," noted British Zimbabwean star Regé-Jean Page, who portrays Simon Basset the Duke of Hastings in season 1.[18] Premiering on December 25, 2020, *Bridgerton* was streaming comfort food for viewers during the pandemic as the series highlighted refined, savvy women (and gentlemen) of color, Black aristocracy and royalty, and multiracial romance, love, courtship, dance, and classical music. As Page explained, "One of the things that is different . . . is that the audience knows" that things will work out in the end "because they have that reassurance that we're going to come out and we're going to have the marriage and the baby."[19]

Indeed, Rhimes's Netflix–Shondaland partnership deal spawned multiple seasons of *Bridgerton,* including the spin-off *Queen Charlotte* prequel, which Sarandos's late mother-in-law, Jacqueline Avant, encouraged Rhimes to create as an addition to the franchise.[20] Shondaland also announced live events, such as an extravagant touring *Bridgerton* ball, video games, novelization, and ancillary merchandise such as *Bridgerton* Monopoly and Clue board games—and even a screenwriting training fellowship with Netflix UK.[21] Thus, it was clear that the megahit long-form streaming series would be an ongoing Shondaland franchise for Netflix.

Of course, Rhimes is considered a media innovator in terms of greater inclusion in her productions, especially in elevating women-centered genres and narratives and including marginalized texts and programming content that is typically dismissed or censored entirely. In particular, *Bridgerton* and *Queen Charlotte* heighten a broader, more respected audience for the historical romance genre, as well as portraying multiethnic images and racial representation. (Page won the prestigious NAACP Image Award as Outstanding Actor in a Drama Series for his portrayal of Simon Basset the Duke of Hastings.) Rhimes is also notable for championing the greater creative "freedom" of working in streaming media formats (free from conventional broadcast television strictures, time constraints, and censorship), advocating for and advancing media representation of gender, gay romance and sexuality, and racy sex scenes with an abundance of nudity. These innovations are distinctive in *Bridgerton*, particularly in that the genre of historical romance is typically marginalized, neutered, and censored, often relegated to considerably tamer and sanitized "low brow," "whitewashed" palatable narratives. So, it is notable that Shondaland updated, elevated, and celebrated that generic form as a distinctive genre that appeals to women, featuring women's points of view in a serial long-form franchise in lieu of the typical "blockbuster" film, usually a decidedly masculine (action or superhero narrative) domain targeting adolescent males.

The distinctive voice of Julie Andrews opens the pilot as Lady Whistledown narrates the story from a decidedly female point of view, an aural reminder that Rhimes had, of course, scripted the royal romance film, *The Princess Diaries II: The Royal Engagement* (2004), starring Andrews. Moreover, there are eight novels in Quinn's book series in which to adapt for the women-centered *Bridgerton* franchise streaming series. Van Dusen is credited as creator of *Bridgerton*, but Rhimes and her longtime collaborator, executive producer Betsy Beers, have been heavily involved in the show's development, as well as other new streaming series under Shondaland's umbrella.[22]

The second season of *Bridgerton* premiered on March 25, 2022, and boasted a huge streaming audience viewership, which Nielsen clocked at 2.5 billion viewing minutes in its first week, and in its fourth week, it was the number one English language show on Netflix, even surpassing season 1.[23] *Queen Charlotte*, which premiered on May 4, 2023, soared to the top of Netflix ratings as the company's most-watched series. Nielsen reported that *Queen Charlotte* had an impressive 1.9 billion viewing minutes streamed in the first four days of its premiere, and it was the most-watched Netflix series globally, as well as in North America, for weeks after its premiere. By May 27, 2023, *Queen Charlotte* had been watched for over 390 million viewing hours.[24] As *Queen Charlotte* premiered, *Bridgerton* also re-entered the Netflix top ten most-watched titles again in May 2023, at one point being the second highest viewed series after *Queen Charlotte*, which remained one of Netflix's most-watched series into June.

Bridgerton and *Queen Charlotte* were both filmed in England, including at historic locations around London and Bath. Season 1 of *Bridgerton* was shot from July 2019 through February 2020, just before the pandemic and emergency lockdown. Season 2 was shot from March through November 2021,[25] during the pandemic, and as such, experienced filming challenges that delayed and even shut down production when cast and crew got ill with the virus. In fact, hair and makeup artist Marc Pilcher, who won an Emmy for seasons 1 and 2, died of Covid while shooting the second season.[26] As a result, season 2 was significantly tamer, with milder and fewer intimate scenes and less nudity and sexual bodily contact as close physical proximity became more dangerous to shoot. *Queen Charlotte*, however, was shot from February through August of 2022,[27] allowing for racier sex scenes, including multiethnic, interracial, and gay couples.

Rhimes's infusion of multiethnic, interracial couples and characters of color into positions of nobility and royalty is especially significant, as seen in Page's Simon Basset the Duke of Hastings, Golda Rosheuvel and India Amarteifio's Queen Charlotte, Adjoa Andoh's Lady Agatha Danbury (and Arsenal Thomas as her younger incarnation), and Tunji Kasim's Adolphus. Simone Ashley and Charithra Chandran's casting as the sisters from India, Kate and Edwina Sharma, is also notable in that these characters in the book are fair-skinned and blonde-haired. Some critics insist that the inclusion of the Sharma sisters from India is a narrative commentary on British colonialism.[28]

Bridgerton and *Queen Charlotte* ingeniously reimagine a more idealized historical notion of a multiracial English nobility. This representation is achieved despite the disclaimer that the series portray the Queen Charlotte of *Bridgerton* rather than of history. The multiracial world of *Bridgerton* with a biracial queen of color and Black nobility is explained in the prequel spin-off, *Queen Charlotte*. Rhimes, working with Beers, provocatively considers the fascinating possibility that the real Queen Charlotte, who came as a princess from Germany to the British royal court to marry King George and become Queen of England, may have indeed been biracial. Rhimes creates an alternate history in which she imagines the beginning of a "great experiment" whereby the British Royal Family and House of Lords concoct a plan and invite, bestow titles upon, and include multiethnic, multiracial people of color in English nobility, desegregating the upper-class ton in British society.

This contemporary reinvention and reimagining of race and ethnicity allows Rhimes to create and tell new iterations of stories that include interracial romances in an historical period setting with a new updated twenty-first-century sensibility. Thus, Lady Danbury is given a title (which she retains after her husband dies) in *Queen Charlotte*, and nobility is also bestowed on Simon's family, which leads to him being the titled Duke of Hastings in *Bridgerton*. In *Queen Charlotte*, Rhimes also makes a point of explaining that Lady Danbury is a descendant of a royal family in Sierra Leone. Nevertheless, Agatha Danbury (Arsenal Thomas) endures rough, misogynistic sexual violence in bed until her husband actually dies in the act.

Rhimes's innovative overall approach to diverse casting in the *Bridgerton* franchise is noteworthy, as in *Queen Charlotte* where Charlotte is presented as being of African and European heritage. "'The love of Queen Charlotte and King George united the nation'—that's one sentence in *Bridgerton*, and to me that told a whole [story] world," Rhimes noted in describing the series.[29] "We are telling the story of how their love united the world in a very small way. . . . It was permission to really fantasize about telling the story of the character I was most fascinated by, and that was an easy jumping off point for me," Rhimes explained. "It's not a history lesson. It's really the story of the Queen Charlotte as we know her from *Bridgerton*."[30]

Moreover, Rhimes tells the story in *Queen Charlotte* from Charlotte's and multiple points of view, including that of her husband George (Corey Mylchreest), to convey the same narrative events from different perspectives and provide new meaning that transforms viewers' understanding of what transpired. For instance, at first, we see a teenage Charlotte (India Amarteifio) forced into a royal marriage from her viewpoint where her new husband George immediately abandons her in lieu of a wedding night and honeymoon, leaving her alone and entrapped in a royal mansion, evocative of a female Gothic thriller. We later see George's version of events where he is bullied and manipulated by his mother and a sadistic doctor, who violently abuses and tortures the young king; George tries to hide the fact that he is having psychotic episodes from his new wife, the queen, who finally saves him. As a *Bridgerton* story, however, *Queen Charlotte* ultimately revolves around love and compassion despite the characters' mental illness and human frailty.

In describing *Queen Charlotte* set in the Georgian era, Rhimes emphasized her intention to empower the women of the story. "If you really look at the show, all of the moves are made by these women," from Queen Charlotte and Lady Danbury to King George's mother, the Dowager princess Augusta (Michelle Fairley). "They're all basically shaping society and culture from the posts that they have. I just wanted to really show that kind of soft power—how a woman rises to power that way."[31]

It is notable that in a male-dominated society, the female characters transcend their historical gender norms, restrictions, misogyny, and even sexual violence in the marital bedroom, to instead "use their positions to advance their motives despite the constraints they live with as women."[32] From *Bridgerton* to its spin-off prequel, *Queen Charlotte: A Bridgerton Story*, the empowerment of women shows how Rhimes's innovative cinematic storytelling universe conveys the advancement of women, particularly women of color, in a man's world. Moreover, in streaming Shondaland, the empowered women in these productions certainly parallel Rhimes's ascent as a rising, talented, and powerful hyphenate writer-creator-producer and woman of color, transcending limits in a white male-dominated entertainment media industry.

Notes

1. Abbey White, "Shonda Rhimes Shows Support for WGA Strike, Says Writers Being Unable to Make a Livable Wage 'Is a Problem,'" *Hollywood Reporter*, May 3, 2023.
2. Ibid.
3. Katie Campione, "'Queen Charlotte: A Bridgerton Story,' Enters Netflix's All-Time Most Popular List at No. 10," *Deadline*, July 2023.
4. White, "Shonda Rhimes Shows Support for WGA Strike, Says Writers Being Unable to Make a Livable Wage 'Is a Problem.'"
5. Rick Porter, "Shonda Rhimes Expands Netflix Deal," *Hollywood Reporter*, July 8, 2021.
6. John Koblin, "Shonda Rhimes Describes Her Grand Netflix Ambitions," *New York Times*, July 20, 2018.
7. Ibid.
8. John Koblin, "Netflix Signs Shonda Rhimes in Counterpunch to ABC and Disney," *New York Times*, August 14, 2017.
9. Ibid.
10. Ibid.
11. Ibid.
12. Netflix, "Shonda Rhimes Reveals What Drew Her Back to Writing for 'Inventing Anna,'" *Netflix.com*, February 9, 2022.
13. Koblin, "Shonda Rhimes Describes Her Grand Netflix Ambitions."
14. Ibid.
15. Nellie Andreeva, "'Bridgerton' Smashes Netflix Viewership Records to Become Streamer's Biggest Series Ever," *Deadline*, January 27, 2021.
16. Lesley Goldberg, "Inside Shonda Rhimes' Second Netflix Pact: A 'Significant' Raise and New Revenue Streams," *Hollywood Reporter*, July 12, 2021.
17. Ibid.
18. Angelique Jackson, "'Bridgerton' Breakout Regé-Jean Page Will Not Appear in Season 2," *Variety*, April 2, 2021.

19 Ibid.
20 Maureen Lee Lenker, "Why *Queen Charlotte* Is Dedicated to Jacqueline Avant," *Entertainment Weekly*, May 4, 2023.
21 Shondaland. https://www.shondaland.com/inspire/shondaland-bridgerton-behind-the-scenes/a37531132/get-ready-for-the-queens-ball-a-bridgerton-experience/.
22 Joy Press, "EXCLUSIVE: Shonda Rhimes and Betsy Beers Reign Supreme as Netflix Greenlights Bridgerton Seasons 3 and 4," *Vanity Fair*, April 13, 2021.
23 Jennifer Mass, "Nielsen Streaming Top 10: 'Bridgerton' Watched for More Than 2.5 Billion Minutes Over Season 2 Premiere Week," *Variety*, April 21, 2022.
24 Rick Porter, "'Queen Charlotte' Opens at No. 1 on Nielsen Streaming Chart," *Hollywood Reporter*, June 1, 2023.
25 IMDb. https://www.imdb.com/title/tt8740790/locations/.
26 Alex Ritman, "Marc Pilcher, Emmy-Winning 'Bridgerton' Makeup Designer, Dies of COVID-19 at 53," *Hollywood Reporter*, October 4, 2021.
27 Kasey Moore, "'Queen Charlotte: A Bridgerton Story': Everything You Need to Know," *What's on Netflix*, May 3, 2023.
28 Desiree Ibekwe, "How 'Bridgerton' Touches on Colonialism in India," *New York Times*, March 28, 2022.
29 Kalia Richardson, "Here's What to Know About 'Queen Charlotte: A Bridgerton Story,'" *New York Times*, May 11, 2023.
30 Ibid.
31 Malcolm Venable, "Shonda Rhimes Breaks Down How the Best Moments of 'Queen Charlotte' Came to Be—and What's Next for the Bridgerverse," *Shondaland.com*, May 5, 2023.
32 Ibid.

Chapter 15

HEY, PELOTON! SAY YES!

Stephanie O'Brien

In 2015, Shonda Rhimes published her book, *Year of Yes: How to Dance It Out, Stand in the Sun, and Be Your Own Person*. She followed this up with a wildly successful 2016 TED Talk "My Year of Saying Yes to Everything."[1] The *Year of Yes Journal* was published in 2016 as an "aspirational companion journal"[2] to the book. As of this writing, the TED Talk had been viewed 5.4 million times,[3] and the original book is described in promotional material as "an instant *New York Times* bestseller."[4]

In early December 2020, Rhimes announced on Instagram the *Year of Yes: A Peloton X Shonda Rhimes Collaboration*. Peloton promoted the joint venture with Rhimes as allowing users to "join (Rhimes) in experiencing the power of showing up for yourself consistently, in order to bring forth that energy in all areas of your life."[5] Peloton's synergistic approach to marketing includes many class collections featuring musical artists, but this was its first alliance with a mega creative force who was directly involved in the programming.[6]

When the Covid-19 pandemic forced nationwide shutdowns, social distancing, and required many to work from home, the at-home fitness and sports equipment industries saw their revenues surge to 2.3 billion dollars with demand for treadmills, stationary bikes, and outdoor equipment outpacing supply, often resulting in months-long waits for products to arrive at consumer homes.[7] One of the beneficiaries of this boom was the at-home fitness company, Peloton.

Peloton joined the fitness market in 2012 with a mission to "(use) technology and design to connect the world through fitness, empowering people to be the best version of themselves anywhere, anytime."[8] Or as their promotional video states, provide "high quality, boutique fitness for anyone."[9] The first stationary bikes were sold in 2013, followed by treadmills in 2018, and rowers in 2022.[10] By September 2020, Peloton reported a quarterly profit for the first time in the company's history with "a 172% surge in sales and more than one million people subscribing to its streaming classes."[11]

I was one of those consumers who waited three months for a Peloton bike to arrive and am an avid streaming class subscriber. In this chapter, I share what I gleaned from my participation in the Rhimes–Peloton collaboration, particularly as it pertains to Rhimes's marketing (and community-building) strategy for the release of Shondaland's streaming series, *Bridgerton* (2020–), created by Chris Van Dusen.

My bike arrived in October 2020, and I immediately fell for the basic premise of the bike and app—a virtual connection to thousands of others while confined at home. It was during a ride in December 2020 when a large banner appeared across the top of the bike tablet advertising the *Shonda Rhimes X Peloton* collaboration. I took a few classes out of curiosity but did not stick with the eight-week program. Eventually, my academic curiosity was engaged as I questioned the symbiotic benefits for Rhimes and Peloton in the collaboration. I decided to take a scholarly dive into the collaboration as a marketing tool and at the same time, work on my physical and mental fitness. Win-win!

Critical Discourse Analysis (CDA)

The following research questions guided my eight-week *Year of Yes* journey: (1) What are the synergistic aspects of this clearly promotional partnership? And (2) What contextually is happening in each company during this time—what values or products is the public relations campaign promoting?

Critical discourse analysis provides the methodological foundation for this study. CDA has many forms but is most often associated with Norman Fairclough and Ruth Wodak who individually examined the use of language in socially specific contexts to show how words and phrases can be discursively employed in social relations.[12] While analyzing the various aspects of this specific collaboration, I relied on a branch of CDA that Gunther Kress terms "multi-modal, social semiotic discourse" where "language is only one resource or mode for making-meaning. Others include images, gestures, body language, proxemics, color, movement, space, and time."[13] Sean Phelan adds to this multimodal approach by highlighting where CDA and media studies intersect, paying particular attention to how identities, social belonging, and cultural and institutional values are presented.[14]

When interacting with the classes, I made note of language used by the instructors, music choices, hashtags associated with the classes, and numbers of participants. Because I took the classes "on demand" a year after they were presented live, the numbers are skewed in terms of who interacted with the classes during the initial eight weeks and those who have taken the classes since. I then analyzed cross-promotion aspects of the collaboration by examining the Shondaland website, Peloton's news, and Instagram sites for both companies. Peloton instructors regularly encourage users to interact with them on Instagram, giving their social media handles at the end of each class. Many also encourage users to join them live before or after classes on social media. The Rhimes collaboration is still accessible on the Peloton app under a heading of "Collections." Readers with the app can find the classes to follow along with the information presented below.

Eight Weeks/Eight Themes

Rhimes announced the partnership in an Instagram post on December 10, 2020: "This is happening. I asked and @onepeloton said YES. We're giving you 8 weeks to say yes to your own self-care with special classes, different instructors, round table discussions. Just say YES. Yes to your body. Yes to beginning again. Yes to athleticism in every form."[15]

The first week of classes began on December 14, 2020. The eight weeks focused on eight themes, all based on inspirational ideas from Rhimes's journey through her *Year of Yes*:

Week One: The Power of You
Week Two: Self-Care: Resistance and Activism
Week Three: CEO Mission Statement
Week Four: Regal Resistance
Week Five: The Power of Saying No
Week Six: Gratitude Roll Call
Week Seven: Protecting Your Peace
Week Eight: Unlocking Your Unknown

Each week's fitness program consists of six to nine classes intermixing cycling, treadmill, strength, yoga, stretching, and meditation. Only the classes labeled "Year of Yes" are specifically produced for the collaboration. Other classes have been curated from single class offerings to round out the program. Each class is twenty minutes or less, seemingly made to fit into the busy working lives of participants or make the classes more desirable and perhaps less daunting for those who may just be starting out on a workout journey. Five Peloton instructors lead all the various classes. All instructors are people of color, and four of the five are female identifying.

Music and Language

For the Year of Yes collaboration, songs, words, and phrases emphasize empowerment through personal improvement and growth. BIPOC female-identifying artists dominate the musical choices of the instructors throughout the eight-week program for Year of Yes classes. The artist whose songs we hear most often across the classes in singular and collaborative performances is Beyoncé. Whitney Houston, Lizzo, Janet Jackson, and Alicia Keys are other artists who appear multiple times in each week's programming. The theme of each week influences the underlying foundation of the music and the instructors' inspirational language during the classes. One example of a playlist comes from the first bike class offered. It includes two Beyoncé songs, one from Lizzo, the powerful "Fight Song" from Rachel Patton, and it begins with "Royals" from Lorde. (This last song foreshadows a reason for the collaboration.) The most on the nose song example appears in Week Three during a treadmill class: "Say Yes" from the British R&B female duo, Floetry.

Each Year of Yes class begins with a shout-out to Rhimes, often using words like "our queen," "the icon," "the amazing," or "the one and only Shonda Rhimes." In many of the classes, the instructors impart inspirational phrases, then look in the camera to say, "Right, Shonda?" or "Like my girl Shonda would say" or "How are you doing, Shonda?" This served two purposes: first, to remind the participants that Rhimes is most likely taking the class with them. An aspect of the collaboration, when it ran live, was that Rhimes would join the social media audience post-workout. Second, these phrases reminded participants of the spectacle and community of the collaboration. The immediacy and intimacy of virtual contact through a mediated source continued the overall themes of self-care and supportive alliances.

Language use for each week included encouraging words and phrases that served to empower the participant not only in their fitness lives but more importantly in their Covid-19-induced isolation. Words such as "regal," "resilient," and "self-care" are continually emphasized. Phrases such as "Say yes to you," "Say yes to self-care," and "Say yes to saying no" are repeated throughout classes for each corresponding week. Peloton users are told that they can be better "partners, parents, and community members" by unlocking their "yes potential." Participants are called "queens, kings, and non-binary royalty," terms which appear appropriate for the beneficial marketing partnership, as will become apparent as one moves through the fitness program.

What is never mentioned is Covid-19. It is inferred but never mentioned. In fact, I've never heard the pandemic mentioned by name in any of the hundreds of classes I've taken on Peloton. In the Rhimes collaboration classes, we hear phrases like "We've heard no a lot this year" or "We've been told no a lot lately." During one class in the week of "Saying Yes to Your Regal Resilience," one instructor recounts a time when she lost both her brother and parents within a year's time frame. This moving story reminds participants of the lives lost daily during the pandemic and struck a chord with many making the rounds on social media. Even in the news coverage of the collaboration, Peloton is careful to never connect the program to the pandemic.

Audience Participation

Along with language and music, another feature I examined is the use of hashtags associated with participants taking the Year of Yes classes. Research on hashtags and social media reveals a connection between motivation and the use of hashtags. Users of hashtags on Peloton exhibit all six of the motivations that Erz, Marder, and Osadchaya identified in a 2018 study: self-presentation (e.g., branding), inventiveness (e.g., humor), chronicling (e.g., documenting experiences), information seeking (e.g., communal inspiration), venting (e.g., negative emotions), and etiquette (e.g., it is what other users do).[16] Pelton members' hashtags also align with motivational use when interacting with branded content: two-way engagement with the brand, entertainment and fun, mentioning the brand in the hashtag, and personalization.[17]

As part of a user's personal profile on Peloton, they can add hashtags. There is no limit to the number of hashtags one can associate with their profile. When a user logs on, a hashtag icon appears on the bottom of the interactive touch screen attached to the equipment. If one clicks on the hashtag, they can see how many members are working out at that moment using one of the associated hashtags. They can also track which classes and instructors are most often connected to certain hashtags.

Before tracking and coding the hashtag use on the Year of Yes classes, I expected the most popular tags associated with the program to be some of the top tags in the Peloton community: #Pelomoms, #WorkingmomsofPeloton, and #Pelotondads. It seemed to me that the target audience of this collaboration would be female and family-centric. Based on the maximum twenty-minute time frames of the main classes, the mostly female-identifying instructors in the program, the heavily female-centric casts of Rhimes's shows, and Rhimes's target audience for her programming, I felt rather certain that those hashtags would be the ones most associated with the fitness program.

When I conducted the data collection on the hashtag association, the top three for the fitness program were #Pelo4wine, #BlackGirlMagic, and #NoLimitLegion. Of course, there could very well be overlap between these hashtags and the top hashtags in the Peloton community, particularly in the #Pelo4wine tag, which is the sixth most popular tag on Peloton. What we can discern, based on motivational use, is that those who identify with Rhimes, the instructors, and the resilience and power of yes rhetoric are logging on to take classes in the program. All three of these hashtags exhibit self-presentation and personalization, inventiveness and fun, chronicling experiences, and etiquette. #Pelo4wine adds the two-way engagement motivation by mentioning the brand in the tag.

Connections to the collaboration do not end during the classes or associating your hashtag with the fitness program. Social media interaction was an integral part of the synergism of the partnership. In many of the classes, particularly those that vice president of Fitness Programming Robin Arzón teaches, participants are encouraged to head over to Instagram to comment and join in on the post-class discussions. This continues the collaborative experience in the virtual world. There are many instances of support and encouragement in the comments on the #OnePeloton Instagram posts. One example is highlighted on a Peloton post on January 5, 2021, touting the "Year of Yes classes" as being "way more than a workout" and asking "(w)ho's been joining @shondarhimes in this challenge?" One Peloton user replies, "I just finished my Year of Yes full body strength workout with Jess Simms and I almost cried . . . it was that good." This post is met with clapping emojis and other users' comments on their experiences in classes they had taken.

Marketing as Renewal

By January 2021, the main reason behind the collaboration is revealed through an instructor's inspirational words to the fitness audience.

The synergistic marketing campaign not only highlights a past Rhimes creative project, reviving interest in her highly successful book; it also serves as a push for her new Netflix series. A carefully choreographed timeline of announcements, fitness classes, and social media combines promotion with encouragement and inspiration for participants. Rhimes's announcement about the partnership arrives via Instagram on December 10, 2020; the first class of the eight-week collection drops on December 14, 2020; and Shondaland's first project under Rhimes's new Netflix deal, *Bridgerton*, debuts on December 25, 2020. The series earns the highest streaming numbers in Netflix history, until it is dethroned by *Squid Game*.[18]

On January 8, 2021, in a twenty-minute bike ride class during the "Gratitude Roll Call" week, Arzón mentions *Bridgerton*, asking participants if they have seen the show and then stating that she is going to "put on her crown and join the *Bridgerton* world." She also wears a T-shirt with a large crown image. This is the most obvious example of promotion for the series in all the Year of Yes classes.

On the Shondaland website and on Rhimes's Instagram, posts from before, during, and after the collaboration foreshadow and highlight the synergistic partnership. On the website in September 2020, a story on the growth of at-home fitness showcases a Peloton bike in the thumbnail. Although the story covers several fitness companies, Peloton is most prominent. During the collaboration, profiles of Peloton's Year of Yes instructors Chelsea Jackson-Roberts and Adrian Williams appear detailing their resilience through life-affirming obstacles. A story featuring Rhimes focuses on what she is grateful for, coinciding with the "Gratitude Roll Call" week of the Year of Yes program. In March 2021, another Year of Yes instructor, Tunde Oyeneyin, is featured in a web story. Rhimes's Instagram posts about Peloton start as early as 2019 and run through November 2021. Peloton, as well, produced web content during the collaboration. Several news releases and links to #OnePeloton Instagram posts are available on the website. An article toward the end of the collaboration, "How the Year of Yes Series Changed Our Members' Lives," focuses on user experiences and serves as a wrap-up.

What is interesting when looking through @onepeloton Instagram comments is that many used the space to complain about the fact that their bike had not yet arrived even though they ordered it months ago. This is a second, never acknowledged function of the collaboration: to distract from the bad press Peloton was receiving for being underprepared for the demand for their bikes and treads. Each week of the Year of Yes classes included workouts on the bike and tread. While you can take the classes on your phone or computer with the Peloton app and use it outside for a bike ride or walk/run, the Year of Yes program occurred during the winter months. Thus, not having the bike or tread in order to enjoy most of the classes indoors appeared to be frustrating for many customers.

Peloton battled the perception of being underprepared for most of 2020, finally putting out a news release from CEO John Foley on November 25 about what the company was doing to meet demand. Foley stated:

> This unprecedented year has accelerated an inevitable permanent shift of fitness to the home. Many of our new Members are discovering that Peloton has made the home the most convenient and motivating place to work out.... While we're working to bring you your Bike and/or Tread, we hope you will begin your Peloton journey by downloading the Peloton App and joining our #OnePeloton community. Included in your purchase is complimentary pre-delivery access to every Peloton class from your phone, tablet, TV, and web browser. We have thousands of classes that don't require equipment, such as yoga, strength, cardio, barre, outdoor running/walking, stretching, and meditation.[19]

Rhimes, in her own attempt to tamp down the distraction, made a point to stress that the weekly classes could be taken without the equipment. A quote to the *Hollywood Reporter* echoes Foley's press release as Rhimes states:

> It's been quite a year, 2020 put a halt on many areas of our lives, and it continues to be quite a challenging time for so many. For me, working out has been a practice to help build resilience and strength, so I am excited to partner with Peloton and join others in saying *yes* to embracing athleticism in every form. I wanted to make sure this program was accessible whether you owned a bike or not and no matter where you were in your fitness journey. All you need to do is download the app and to start the journey with me.[20]

Challenges are expected when a brand tries to promote a new venture or collaboration. In the case of *Shonda Rhimes X Peloton*, the marketing campaign unfortunately launched during a global pandemic. On the one hand, the pandemic expanded the at-home fitness craze and kept most people at home watching Netflix. On the other, supply chain issues meant many who might have liked to join the eight-week program when it happened in real time were not able to do so. Even with these issues, participation by Peloton users in the program has been successful, with some classes surpassing 100,000 total workouts.

The inspirational aspects of the *Shonda Rhimes X Peloton* collaboration arrived at a time when many needed motivations and a sense of community. The synergistic marketing promotion melded with the isolation we experienced from a global pandemic to provide an outlet for our collective angst. We were told that "Yes!" we can get through these challenging times with resilience and self-care. We were empowered as royalty with Rhimes, the Year of Yes instructors, and Peloton joining us on our journey. We spent our days at home working out, interacting with Rhimes and others via social media outlets. Our evenings were spent with the Bridgerton family, getting lost in the escapism of the Regency-era nobility of London, making the new series at the time the most-viewed program in Netflix history. Even for users who missed the live fitness experience due to delayed equipment, with the on-demand feature, this collaborative marketing campaign provides an ongoing promotion for Rhimes's book and series. Across fifty-six classes and eight weeks, hundreds of thousands of users joined in and said, "Yes, Peloton!" and "Yes, *Bridgerton!*"

Notes

1 "Peloton X Shonda Rhimes Collaboration: Year of Yes," *Peloton x Shonda Rhimes Partnership: Year of Yes*, December 10, 2020, https://www.onepeloton.com/blog/shonda-rhimes-partnership/.
2 Peloton followed up the Rhimes collaboration with a partnership in 2022 with actor and producer Ashton Kutcher. "Our Future Selves Series with Ashton Kutcher," *Peloton Support*, August 29, 2022, https://support.onepeloton.com/hc/en-us/articles/8916700726804-Our-Future-Selves-Series-with-Ashton-Kutcher-.
3 Shonda Rhimes, "My Year of Saying Yes to Everything," *TED Talk*, February 16, 2016, https://www.ted.com/talks/shonda_rhimes_my_year_of_saying_yes_to_everything.
4 Shonda Rhimes, "Year of Yes by Shonda Rhimes," *Year of Yes*, September 13, 2016, http://theyearofyesbook.com/.
5 Ibid.
6 "Year of Yes," Book by Shonda Rhimes | Official Publisher Page | Simon & Schuster, accessed July 14, 2023, https://www.simonandschuster.com/books/Year-of-Yes/Shonda-Rhimes/9781476777122.

7   Hamza Shaban, "The Pandemic's Home-Workout Revolution May Be Here to Stay," *The Washington Post*, January 8, 2021, https://www.washingtonpost.com/road-to-recovery/2021/01/07/home-fitness-boom/.
8   "Exercise Bike with Indoor Cycling Classes Streamed Live & On-Demand," *Peloton*®, accessed July 17, 2022, https://www.onepeloton.com/company.
9   Ibid.
10 Ibid.
11 Ibid.
12 Jan Blommaert and Chris Bulcaen, "Critical Discourse Analysis," *Annual Review of Anthropology* 29 (2000).
13 Gunther Kress, "Discourse Analysis and Education: A Multi-modal Social Semiotic Approach," in *An Introduction to Critical Discourse Analysis in Education*, ed. Rebecca Rogers (New York: Routledge, 2004).
14 Sean Phelan, "Critical Discourse Analysis and Media Studies," *The Routledge Handbook of Critical Discourse Studies*, August 3, 2017, https://www.academia.edu/34124822/Critical.
15 Shonda Rhimes (@shondarhimes), "This Is Happening. I Asked and @Onepeloton said YES!" *Instagram Post*, December 10, 2020, https://www.instagram.com/p/CInxxrAJWCP/?hl=en.
16 Antonia Erz, Ben Marder, and Eleana Osadchaya, "Hashtags: Motivational Drivers, Their Use, and Differences Between Influencers and Followers," *Computers in Human Behavior* 89 (2018), https://doi.org/10.1016/j.chb.2018.07.03.
17 Mitchell Hamilton, Velitchka Kaltcheva, and Andrew J. Rohm, "Hashtags and Handshakes: Consumer Motives and Platform Use in Brand-Consumer Interactions," *Journal of Consumer Marketing* 33, no. 2 (2016), https://doi.org/10.1108/JCM-04-2015-1398.
18 Todd Spangler, "Netflix Releases New Data on Most Popular TV Shows and Movies," *Variety*, October 1, 2021, https://variety.com/2021/digital/news/netflix-most-popular-tv-shows-movies-1235075301/.
19 Peloton, "A Note of Thanks from Our Cofounder and CEO John Foley," *Peloton News*, November 25, 2020, https://www.onepeloton.com/blog/peloton-thanksgiving-2020.
20 Chris Gardner, "Shonda Rhimes on Her Peloton Deal and How She's 'Embracing Athleticism in Every Form,'" *The Hollywood Reporter*, December 17, 2020, https://www.hollywoodreporter.com/news/general-news/shonda-rhimes-on-her-peloton-deal-and-how-shes-embracing-athleticism-in-every-form-4105449/.

CONTRIBUTORS

Sheri Chinen Biesen is Professor of Cinema/Media Studies at Rowan University and author of *Through a Noir Lens: Adapting Film Noir Visual Style* (2024), *Blackout: World War II and the Origins of Film Noir* (2005), *Music in the Shadows: Noir Musical Films* (2014), and *Film Censorship: Regulating America's Screen* (2018). She received her PhD at UT Austin, and her MA and BA at USC and has contributed to *The Netflix Effect*, *Historical Journal of Film, Radio and Television*, *Netflix Nostalgia*, *Literature/Film Quarterly*, *Historian*, *Television and Television History*, the BBC documentary *Rules of Film Noir*, and serves on the editorial board of *Film Criticism*.

Louise Coopey obtained her PhD in film and television from the University of Birmingham. Her research focuses on reading representation in complex television, exploring how identity manifests within character development arcs through the layered complexity of HBO's *Game of Thrones* (2011–19). Additionally, she is interested in seriality, adaptation, and on and offscreen diversity. Louise has contributed to *The Forgotten Victims of Sexual Violence in Film, Television and New Media*, edited by Stephanie Patrick and Mythili Rajiva (2022), and has also written on *Game of Thrones*' Epic 9s episodes for the *Moments of Television* series.

Cate Correia-Hopkins is completing a PhD at Cardiff University's School of Journalism, Media and Culture (Wales, UK), where her research focuses on data justice and its applications for political activism.

Sara Correia-Hopkins is Lecturer at Swansea University's School of Law (Wales, UK). Sara is a trained Restorative Justice (RJ) facilitator and has explored how RJ principles and practices may develop in modern digital societies.

Rani Deighe Crowe is Associate Professor at Ball State University and a practicing independent filmmaker and screenwriter. Her short films include *Beautiful Eyes, Texting: A Love Story, Heather Has Four Moms, Quiet on Set,* and *Safety State*. She has an MFA in film from Ohio University.

Shelley Anne Galpin is Lecturer at King's College London. She has published in *The Journal of British Cinema and Television, Studies in European Cinema,* and *Feminist Media Studies*, as well as the edited collections *Intercultural Screen Adaptation* (2020) and *The Edinburgh Companion to the Brontës and the Arts* (forthcoming). Her work focuses on the period drama genre and the representation and use of the British past.

Zsuzsanna Lénárt-Muszka teaches at the Institute of English and American Studies, University of Debrecen, Hungary. She has published in journals such as *Critique* (2023), *Short Fiction in Theory and Practice* (2022), and *Gender Studies* (2021), and has contributed chapters to edited collections such as *Jesmyn Ward: New Critical Essays* (2023), *Normative Motherhood: Regulations, Representations, and Reclamations* (2023), *Critical Insights: The Color Purple* (2022), and *Identity, Violence and Resilience in 21st-Century Black British and American Women's Fiction* (forthcoming). Her research interests include the representations of violence and embodiment in contemporary North American short fiction.

Sébastien Mignot is Associate Professor at the University of Caen Normandy. He specializes in cultural studies and queer studies, with a focus on US television. His work has thus far dealt with the representation of nonheterosexual sexualities in US TV series and the evolution of paradigms of representation. His doctoral dissertation centered on the notion of post-closet representation.

Stephanie O'Brien is Lecturer in Mass Communication at the University of North Carolina Asheville. Her research interests reside at the intersection of cultural studies and media studies. She is currently engaged in research on the history of film and television production in North Carolina. Prior to becoming an educator, Dr. O'Brien worked in the film and television industry as an assistant director. While working on the TV series *The Shield*, her neighbors in an adjacent studio soundstage just happened to be a new series titled *Grey's Anatomy*. She is a member of the Director's Guild of America.

Anthony Guy Patricia is Associate Professor of English at Concord University. His book *Queering the Shakespeare Film: Gender Trouble, Gay

Spectatorship and Male Homoeroticism was published by Bloomsbury Arden Shakespeare in 2017. His essays have appeared in *Presentism, Gender, and Sexuality in Shakespeare* (2009), *Shakespeare and Emotions: Inheritances, Enactments, Legacies* (2015), *Adoring Outlander: Essays on Fandom, Genre and the Female Audience* (2016), and *Exploring Downton Abbey: Critical Essays* (2018), as well as in the undergraduate textbook, *Literature for the Masses* (2015).

E. Deidre Pribram is Professor Emerita in the Communications Department, Molloy University, on Long Island, New York. Her most recent book is *Emotional Expressionism: Television Serialization, The Melodramatic Mode, and Socioemotionality* (2024). She writes on cultural emotion studies, film and television studies, gender, and popular culture.

William Rabkin teaches at the University of California, Riverside-Palm Desert's Low Residency MFA in Creative Writing and Writing for the Performing Arts. He has written and/or produced hundreds of hours of dramatic television, serving as showrunner on *Diagnosis Murder* and *Martial Law* and co-creator and writer on HBOAsia's *Dream Raider*. His writing and producing credits include *Monk*, *Psych*, *Nero Wolfe*, and *Baywatch*. More recently, he co-wrote the Swedish miniseries *Estonia*. He is also the author of three best-selling books on writing for television, *Writing the Pilot*, *Writing the Pilot: Creating the Series*, and *Writing the Pilot: The Streaming Series*.

Kara Raphaeli is Assistant Professor at Simpson College. They received their PhD in theater and drama with a specialization in critical gender studies from the joint program between UC San Diego and UC Irvine. Their dissertation, "The Clothes Make the Man: Theatrical Crossdressing as Expression of Gender Fluidity in Seventeenth- through Nineteenth-Century Performance," explores cross-dressing and male impersonation through a transmasculine lens. They are also a community organizer, director, producer, and performer.

Rosanne Welch is Executive Director of Stephens College MFA in TV and Screenwriting. She wrote for *Beverly Hills 90210*, *Picket Fences*, *ABCNEWS: Nightline*, and *Touched by an Angel*. Welch edited *When Women Wrote Hollywood* (2018), runner-up for the Susan Koppelman feminist studies award; and co-edited *Women in American History* (2018), named to the Outstanding References Sources List and Best

Historical Materials. She wrote *Why the Monkees Matter: Teenagers, Television and American Popular Culture* (2016). Welch serves as book reviews editor for the *Journal of Screenwriting* and is on the editorial boards of *Written By* magazine and *California History Journal*.

Anna Weinstein is Assistant Professor of Screenwriting at Kennesaw State University. She is the editor of the Screen Storytellers book series and PERFORM: Succeeding as a Creative Professional book series. Her most recent book is *Writing Women for Film & Television: A Guide to Creating Complex Female Characters* (2023). She serves as co-chair of the Film area for the Popular Culture Association (PCA) and secretary of the Screenwriting Research Network (SRN). She publishes on screenwriting, women in film/television, and industry studies.

Chriss Williams is Professor at William Paterson University in New Jersey. He teaches film production, screenwriting, visual effects, and film theory courses. A graduate of New York University's graduate film program, Chriss served as assistant to Director Spike Lee on his film, *Crooklyn*. Chriss's first feature film, *Asbury Park*, premiered at Lincoln Center's "Independent's Night" series. Chriss's second film, *Bellclair Times*, won the prestigious Newark Black Film Festival. Chriss holds a Law degree from Rutgers University and serves as a pro bono attorney for Partners, a nonprofit public interest law firm serving victims of domestic violence and sexual assault.

Ida Yoshinaga is a Sansei filmmaker and Assistant Professor of Literature, Media, and Communication at Georgia Tech, where she researches science-fiction/fantasy/horror/fairy-tale genre expression by BIPOC, female, immigrant, disabled, working-class, and LGBTQIA+ writer-producers of cinematic and televisual narratives; and where she teaches cultural and community-oriented screenwriting to her fellow skiffy nerds. Co-editor of *Uneven Futures: Strategies for Community Survival from Speculative Fiction* (2022), she serves as an editor of *Science Fiction Film and Television*, as vice president of the Science Fiction Research Association, and as a member of speculative/fantastic studies editorial boards for two other journals and a book series.

BIBLIOGRAPHY

Abbiss, Will Stanford. *Post-heritage Perspectives on British Period Drama Television*. London: Routledge, 2023.

Alexander, Jeffrey C. "On the Social Construction of Moral Universals: The 'Holocaust' from War Crime to Trauma Drama." *European Journal of Social Theory* 5, no. 1 (2002): 5–85.

Altman, Rick. *Film/Genre*. London: British Film Institute, 1999.

Banks, Miranda. "I Love Lucy: The Writer-Producer." In *How to Watch Television*, edited by Ethan Thompson and Jason Mittell, 244–52. New York: New York University Press, 2013.

Basinger, Jeanine. *A Woman's View*. New York: Alfred A. Knopf, 1993.

Benshoff, Harry M., and Sean Griffin. *Queer Images: A History of Gay and Lesbian Film in America*. Lanham: Rowman and Littlefield, 2006.

Berke, Annie. *Their Own Best Creations: Women Writers in Postwar Television*. Oakland: University of California Press, 2022.

Bielby, Denise D. "Gender Inequity in Culture Industries: Women and Men Writers in Film and Television." *Sociologie du Travail* 51, no. 2 (2009): 237–52.

Billinson, Jennifer, and Michaela Meyer. "Soundtracking Shondaland: Televisual Identity Mapped through Music." In *Adventures in Shondaland: Identity Politics and the Power of Representation*, edited by Rachel Alicia Griffin and Michaela Meyer, 79–97. New Brunswick: Rutgers University Press, 2018.

Blommaert, Jan, and Chris Bulcaen. "Critical Discourse Analysis." *Annual Review of Anthropology*, no. 29 (2000): 447–66.

Bogle, Donald. *Primetime Blues: African Americans on Network Television*. New York: Farrar, Straus and Giroux, 2002.

Bourne, Stephen. "Secrets and Lies: Black Histories and British Historical Films." In *British Historical Cinema*, edited by Claire Monk and Amy Sargeant, 47–65. Abingdon: Routledge, 2002.

Braithwaite, John. "Restorative Justice and De-Professionalization." *The Good Society* 13, no. 1 (2004): 28–31.

Braun, Virginia, and Victoria Clarke. "Thematic Analysis." In *APA Handbook of Research Methods in Psychology*, edited by Harris Cooper. Vol. 2. Research Designs: Quantitative, Qualitative, Neuropsychological, and Biological. Washington, DC: American Psychological Association, 2012.

Braun, Virginia, and Victoria Clarke. "Reflecting on Reflexive Thematic Analysis." *Qualitative Research in Sport, Exercise and Health* 11, no. 4 (2019): 589–97.

Braun, Virginia, and Victoria Clarke. "Can I Use TA? Should I Use TA? Should I *Not* Use TA? Comparing Reflexive Thematic Analysis and Other Pattern-based Qualitative Analytic Approaches." *Counselling and Psychotherapy Research* 21, no. 1 (2021): 37–47.

Bridgerton. Created by Chris Van Dusen. 2020–: USA: Netflix/Shondaland. Television.

Campbell, Joseph. *The Hero with a Thousand Faces*, 3rd ed. 1949. Reprint, Novato: New World Library, 2008.

Carroll, Rachel. "Black Britain and the Classic Adaptation: Integrated Casting in Television Adaptations of *Oliver Twist* and *Little Dorrit*." *Adaptation* 8, no. 1 (2014): 16–30.

Cheers, Imani M. *The Evolution of Black Women in Television: Mammies, Matriarchs, and Mistresses*. New York: Routledge, 2018.

Cohen, Jeffrey Jerome. "Monster Culture: Seven Theses." In *Monster Theory: Reading Culture*, edited by Jeffrey Jerome Cohen, 3–24. Minneapolis: University of Minnesota Press, 1996.

Coulthard, Lisa, Tanya Horeck, Barbara Klinger, and Kathleen McHugh. "Broken Bodies/Inquiring Minds: Women in Contemporary Transnational TV Crime Drama." *Television & New Media* 19, no. 6 (2018): 507–14.

Craig, Cairns. "Rooms Without a View." *Sight and Sound* 1, no. 2 (1991): 10–13.

Crane, Jonathan. "Exploding the Myth of Scientific Support for the Theory of Black Intellectual Inferiority." *Journal of Black Psychology* 20, no. 2 (1994): 189–209.

Creed, Barbara. "Horror and the Monstrous-Feminine: An Imaginary Abjection." *Screen* 27, no. 1 (1986): 44–71.

Crossroads. Directed by Tamra Davis; written by Shonda Rhimes. 2002: USA: Paramount. Film.

Dance Dreams: Hot Chocolate Nutcracker. Directed by Oliver Bokelberg; Executive Produced by Debbie Allen. 2020: USA: Netflix. Documentary.

Davis, Angela Y. *Women, Race and Class*. New York: Vintage, 1983.

Dunleavy, Trisha. *Complex Serial Drama and Multiplatform Television*. New York: Routledge, 2018.

Dyer, Richard, *Pastiche*. Abingdon: Routledge, 2007.

Edelman, Lee. *No Future: Queer Theory and the Death Drive*. Durham: Duke University Press, 2004.

Edwards, Kelly. *The Executive Chair: A Writer's Guide to TV Series Development*. Studio City: Michael Wiese Productions, 2021.

Epstein, Greg M. *Good Without God: What a Billion Nonreligious People Do Believe*. New York: HarperCollins, 2009.

Erz, Antonia, Ben Marder, and Eleana Osadchaya. "Hashtags: Motivational Drivers, Their Use, and Differences Between Influencers and Followers." *Computers in Human Behavior*, no. 89 (2018): 48–60.

Everett, Anna. "Scandalicious: *Scandal*, Social Media, and Shonda Rhimes' Auteurist Juggernaut." *The Black Scholar* 45, no. 1 (2015): 34–43.

Feasey, Rebecca. *From Happy Homemaker to Desperate Housewives: Motherhood and Popular Television*. London: Anthem Press, 2012.

Fehl, Andrea, Shannon Ferrari, Zoe Wecht, and Margaret Rosenzweig. "Breast Cancer in the Transgender Population." *Journal of the Advanced Practitioner in Oncology* 10, no. 4 (2019): 387–94.

Fisher, Deborah A, Douglas L. Hill, Joel W. Grube, and Enid L. Gruber. "Gay, Lesbian, and Bisexual Content on Television: A Quantitative Analysis Across Two Seasons." *Journal of Homosexuality* 52, no. 3–4 (2007): 167–88.

For the People. Created by Paul William Davies. 2018–19: USA: ABC/Shondaland. Television.

Francus, Marilyn. *Monstrous Motherhood: Eighteenth Century Culture and the Ideology of Domesticity*. Baltimore: Johns Hopkins University Press, 2013.

Frow, John. *Genre: The New Critical Idiom*. London: Routledge, 2006.

Garland-Thomason, Rosemarie. *Extraordinary Bodies: Figuring Physical Disability in American Culture and Literature*. New York: Columbia University Press, 2017.

Garrett, Roberta. *Postmodern Chick Flicks: The Return of the Woman's Film*. Basingstoke: Palgrave Macmillan, 2007.

Geena Davis Institute on Gender in Media. "Portrayals of Female STEM Characters in TV and Film Haven't Improved in 10 Years." *Geena Davis Institute*, September 25, 2018, https://seejane.org/gender-in-media-news-release/portrayals-of-female-stem-characters-in-tv-and-film-havent-improved-in-10-years/.

Geena Davis Institute on Gender in Media. "Representations of Black Women in Hollywood." *Geena Davis Institute*, 2021, https://seejane.org/wp-content/uploads/rep-of-black-women-in-hollywood-report.pdf.

Gomez, Stephanie L., and Megan D. McFarlane. "'It's (Not) Handled': Race, Gender, and Refraction in *Scandal*." *Feminist Media Studies* 17, no. 3 (2017): 362–76.

Greimas, Algirdas Julien. *On Meaning: Selected Writings in Semiotic Theory. Theory and History of Literature*, vol. 38. Minneapolis: University of Minnesota Press, 1987.

Grey's Anatomy. Created by Shonda Rhimes. 2005–: USA: ABC/Shondaland. Television.

Gross, Larry. *Up From Invisibility: Lesbians, Gay Men, and the Media in America*. New York: Columbia University Press, 2002.

Hamilton, Mitchell, Velitchka Kaltcheva, and Andrew J. Rohm. "Hashtags and Handshakes: Consumer Motives and Platform Use in Brand-consumer Interactions." *Journal of Consumer Marketing* 33, no. 2 (2016): 135–44.

Henderson, Felicia. "The Writer's Room." In *Production Studies: Cultural Studies of Media Industries*, edited by Vicki Mayer, Miranda Banks, and John Caldwell, 224–9. New York: Routledge, 2009.

Higson, Andrew. "Re-presenting the National Past: Nostalgia and Pastiche in the Heritage Film." In *Fires Were Started: British Cinema and Thatcherism*

2nd ed., edited by Lester D. Friedman, 91–109. London: Wallflower Press, 2006.

Higson, Andrew. *Film England: Culturally English Filmmaking Since the 1990s.* London: I B Tauris, 2011.

Higueras-Ruiz, María-José, Francisco-Javier Gómez-Pérez, and Jordi Alberich-Pascual. "Historical Review and Contemporary Characterization of Showrunner as Professional Profile in TV Series Production: Traits, Skills, Competences, and Style." *Communication & Society* 31, no.1 (2018): 91–106.

Hobson, Janell. "The 'Batty' Politic: Toward an Aesthetic of the Black Female Body." *Hypatia* 18, no. 4 (2003): 87–105.

Holbrook, R. Andrew, and Timothy G. Hill. "Agenda-Setting and Priming in Prime Time Television: Crime Dramas as Political Cues." *Political Communication* 22, no. 3 (2005): 277–95.

How to Get Away with Murder. Created by Peter Nowalk. 2014–20: USA: ABC/Shondaland. Television.

Hudson, Kim. *The Virgin's Promise: Writing Stories of Feminine Creative, Spiritual, and Sexual Awakening.* Los Angeles: Michael Wiese Productions, 2009.

Hunter, Latham. "Motherhood, Prime-time TV, and *Grey's Anatomy*." In *Mediating Moms: Mothers in Popular Culture,* edited by Elizabeth Podnieks, 320–38. Montreal: McGill-Queens University Press, 2012.

I Love Lucy. Created by Jess Oppenheimer. 1951–7: USA: CBS. Television.

Indradjaja, Nobella, Chamdani Chamdani, and Syafi'i Syafi'i. "The Stereotyping Representation of Kensi Blye's Character in Television Crime Drama Series NCIS: Los Angeles." *Lingua Cultura* 16, no. 1 (2022): 1–7.

Introducing Dorothy Dandridge. Directed by Martha Coolidge; Written by Shonda Rhimes and Scott Abbott. 1999: USA: HBO. Television Movie.

Inventing Anna. Created by Shonda Rhimes. 2022: USA: Netflix/Shondaland. Television.

Jenner, Mareike. *American TV Detective Dramas: Serial Investigations.* Crime Files. Houndmills, Basingstoke, Hampshire, New York: Palgrave Macmillan, 2016.

Jordan-Zachery, Julia S. "Mythical Illusions: Cultural Images and Black Womanhood." In *Black Women, Cultural Images, and Social Policy,* 26–48. New York: Routledge, 2009.

Kaplan, E. Ann. "The Case of the Missing Mother." *Heresies* 16 (1983): 81–95.

Karlyn, Kathleen Rowe. *Unruly Girls, Unrepentant Mothers: Redefining Feminism on Screen.* Austin: University of Texas Press, 2011.

Keishin Armstrong, Jennifer. *When Women Invented Television: The Untold Story of the Female Powerhouses Who Pioneered the Way We Watch Today.* New York: HarperCollins, 2021.

Kinnick, Katherine. "Media Morality Tales and the Politics of Motherhood." In *Mommy Angst: Motherhood in American Popular Culture,* edited by Ann C. Hall and Mardia J. Bishop, 1–28. Santa Barbara: ABC-CLIO, 2009.

Kress, Gunther. "Discourse Analysis and Education: A Multi-modal Social Semiotic Approach." In *An Introduction to Critical Discourse Analysis in Education*, edited by Rebecca Rogers, 205–26. New York: Routledge, 2004.

Lauzen, Martha. "Boxed In: Women on Screen and Behind the Scenes on Broadcast and Streaming Television in 2022–23." *Center for Study of Women in Television and Film*, 2023.

Levine, Elana. "Grey's Anatomy: Feminism." In *How to Watch Television*, edited by Ethan Thompson and Jason Mittell, 139–47. New York: New York University Press, 2013.

Levine, Elana. *Her Stories: Daytime Soap Opera & US Television History*. Durham: Duke University Press, 2020.

Mann, Denise. "It's Not TV, It's Brand Management TV: The Collective Author(s) of the *Lost* Franchise." In *Production Studies: Cultural Studies of Media Industries*, edited by Vicki Mayer, Miranda Banks, and John Caldwell, 99–114. New York: Routledge, 2009.

Martin, Brett. *Difficult Men: Behind the Scenes of a Creative Revolution*. New York: Penguin Press, 2013.

McElroy, Ruth. *Contemporary British Television Crime Drama: Cops on the Box*. Oxford, New York: Routledge, 2017.

McLaughlin, Eugene, Ross Fergusson, Gordon Hughes, and Louise Westmarland. *Restorative Justice: Critical Issues*. Crime, Order and Social Control. London: SAGE, 2003.

McLemore, Elisabeth C., Sonia Ramamoorthy, Carrie Y Peterson, and Barbara L Bass. "Women in Surgery: Bright, Sharp, Brave, and Temperate." *The Permanente Journal*, 54–9, https://www.ncbi.nlm.nih.gov/pmc/articles/PMC3442763/.

Meyer, Michaela, and Rachel Alicia Griffin. "Introduction: Riding Shondaland's Rollercoasters: Critical Cultural Television Studies in the 21st Century." In *Adventures in Shondaland: Identity Politics and the Power of Representation*, edited by Rachel Alicia Griffin and Michaela Meyer, 1–19. New Brunswick, NJ: Rutgers University Press, 2018.

Mittell, Jason. *Complex TV: The Poetics of Contemporary Television Storytelling*. New York: New York University Press, 2015.

Monk, Claire. *Heritage Film Audiences: Period Films and Contemporary Audiences in the UK*. Edinburgh: Edinburgh University Press, 2012.

Morgan, Jennifer L. *Laboring Women: Reproduction and Gender in New World Slavery*. Philadelphia: UPenn Press, 2004.

Morgan, Jennifer L. "Partus Sequitur Ventrem: Law, Race, and Reproduction in Colonial Slavery." *Small Axe* 22, no. 1 (2018): 1–17.

Murdock, Maureen. *The Heroine's Journey: Woman's Quest for Wholeness*. Boulder: Shambhala Publications, 1990.

Nash, Jennifer C. *Birthing Black Mothers*. Durham: Duke University Press, 2021.

Newman, Michael. "From Beats to Arcs: Towards a Poetics of Television Narrative." *The Velvet Light Trap* 58 (2006): 16–28.

Newman, Michael, and Elana Levine. *Legitimating Television: Media Convergence and Cultural Status*. New York: Routledge, 2012.

Off the Map. Created by Jenna Bans. 2011: USA: ABC/Shondaland. Television.

Ojanuga, Durrenda. "The Medical Ethics of the 'Father of Gynaecology,' Dr. J. Marion Sims." *Journal of Medical Ethics* 19, no. 1 (1993): 28–31.

O'Mahony, David, and Jonathan Doak. *Reimagining Restorative Justice*. Oxford, Portland: Hart Publishing, 2017.

O'Sullivan, Sean. "Broken on Purpose: Poetry, Serial Television, and the Season." *Storyworlds: A Journal of Narrative Studies* 2 (2010): 59–77.

Oxford English Dictionary Online. Oxford: Oxford University Press, 2023.

Pali, Brunilda. "Art for Social Change: Exploring Restorative Justice Through the New Media Documentary *Inside the Distance*." *Restorative Justice* 2, no. 1 (2014): 85–94.

Parrott, Scott, and Caroline Titcomb Parrott. "U.S. Television's 'Mean World' for White Women: The Portrayal of Gender and Race on Fictional Crime Dramas." *Sex Roles* 73, no. 1–2 (2015): 70–82.

Parsemain, Ava Laure. *The Pedagogy of Queer TV*. Palgrave Entertainment Industries. Cham: Palgrave Macmillan, 2019.

Patton, Venetria K. *Women in Chains: The Legacy of Slavery in Black Women's Fiction*. New York: State University of New York, 2000.

Phelan, Sean. "Critical Discourse Analysis and Media Studies." In *The Routledge Handbook of Critical Discourse Studies*, edited by John Flowerdew and John E. Richardson, 285–97. Abingdon: Routledge, 2017.

Phillips, Irna. *All My Worlds*. (unpublished) Washington, DC: Library of Congress, 1973.

Pidduck, Julianne. *Contemporary Costume Film: Space, Place and the Past*. London: BFI, 2004.

Pinedo, Isabel. "The Killing: The Gender Politics of the Nordic Noir Crime Drama and Its American Remake." *Television & New Media* 22, no. 3 (2021): 299–316.

Pointer, Lindsey, and Brunilda Pali. "Advancing Restorative Justice Through Art." *The International Journal of Restorative Justice* 5, no. 3 (2022): 315–22.

Press, Andrea. *Women Watching Television: Gender, Class, and Generation in the American Television Experience*. Philadelphia: University of Pennsylvania Press, 1991.

Press, Joy. *Stealing the Show: How Women Are Revolutionizing Television*. New York: Atria Books, 2018.

Pribram, E. Deidre. *Emotional Expressionism: Television Serialization, the Melodramatic Mode, and Socioemotionality*. Lanham: Lexington, 2024.

Priggé, Steven. *Created By . . . Inside the Minds of TV's Top Show Creators*. Los Angeles: Silman-James Press, 2005.

Private Practice. Created by Shonda Rhimes. 2007–13: USA: ABC/Shondaland. Television.

Queen Charlotte: A Bridgerton Story. Created by Shonda Rhimes. 2023: USA: Netflix/Shondaland. Television.

Raney, Arthur A., and Jennings Bryant. "Moral Judgment and Crime Drama: An Integrated Theory of Enjoyment." *Journal of Communication* 52, no. 2 (2002): 402–15.

Rhimes, Shonda. "My Year of Saying Yes to Everything." February 16, 2016. TED Talk. Video, 18:35. https://www.ted.com/talks/shonda_rhimes_my_year_of_saying_yes_to_everything.

Rhimes, Shonda. *Year of Yes: How to Dance It Out, Stand In the Sun and Be Your Own Person*. New York: Simon & Schuster, 2016.

Rhimes, Shonda. "Shonda Rhimes: Writing for Television." *MasterClass*. Video, 6 hrs. https://www.masterclass.com/classes/shonda-rhimes-teaches-writing-for-television.

Rhineberger-Dunn, Gayle, and Nicole E. Rader. "Race, Criminal Justice Professionals, and Intellectual Authority in Fictional Crime Dramas." *Journal of Ethnicity in Criminal Justice* 15, no. 2 (2017): 205–25.

Rich, Adrienne. *Of Woman Born*. New York: W. W. Norton & Co, 1976.

Rieder, John. *Science Fiction and the Mass Cultural Genre System*. Middletown: Wesleyan University Press, 2017.

Riley, Wayne J. "Health Disparities: Gaps in Access, Quality and Affordability of Medical Care." *Transactions of the American Clinical and Climatological Association* 12, no. 3 (2012): 167–72.

Roberts, Dorothy E. *Killing the Black Body: Race, Reproduction, and the Meaning of Liberty*. New York: Pantheon Books, 1997.

Rodham Clinton, Hillary. "Women's Rights Are Human Rights." In *Remarks to the U.N. 4th World Conference on Women Plenary Session*. September 5, 1995. Beijing, China. Video, 19:41. https://www.americanrhetoric.com/speeches/hillaryclintonbeijingspeech.htm.

Russo, Vito. *The Celluloid Closet: Homosexuality in the Movies*. New York: Harper & Row, 1981.

Scandal. Created by Shonda Rhimes. 2012–18: USA: ABC/Shondaland. Television.

Scanlan, Laura Wolff. "Joe Papp and the Transformation of American Theater." *Humanities, NEA* 43, no. 2 (2022). https://www.neh.gov/article/joe-papp-and-transformation-american-theater.

Sepinwall, Alan. *The Revolution Was Televised: The Cops, Crooks, Slingers, and Slayers Who Changed TV Drama Forever*. New York: Simon and Schuster, 2012.

Shapiro, Marc. *Welcome to Shondaland: An Unauthorized Biography of Shonda Rhimes*. Riverdale: Riverdale Avenue Books, 2015.

Signorielli, Nancy. "Race and Sex in Prime Time: A Look at Occupations and Occupational Prestige." *Mass Communication and Society* 12 (2009): 332–52.

Smith-Shomade, Beretta E. *Shaded Lives: African-American Women and Television*. New Brunswick: Rutgers, 2002.

Šporčič, Anamarija. "A Metamodernist Utopia: The Neo-Romantic Sense and Sensibility of the *Bridgerton* Series." *Acta Universitatis Sapientiae, Film and Media Studies* 22, no.1 (2022): 122–38.

Station 19. Created by Stacy McKee. 2018–23: USA: ABC/Shondaland. Television.
Strolovitch, Dara Z., and Chaya Y. Crowder. "Respectability, Anti-Respectability, and Intersectionally Responsible Representation." *PS: Political Science & Politics* 51, no. 2 (2018): 340–1.
The Goldbergs. Created by Gertrude Berg. 1949–51: USA: CBS. Television.
The Princess Diaries 2: The Royal Engagement. Directed by Garry Marshall; Written by Shonda Rhimes. 2004: USA: Disney. Film.
The Residence. Created by Paul William Davies. (In Production): USA: Netflix/Shondaland. Television.
Todorov, Tzvetan. *The Fantastic: A Structural Approach to a Literary Genre*. Ithaca: Cornell University Press, 1975.
Trawalter, Sophie, Kelly M. Hoffman, and Adam Waytz. "Racial Bias in Perceptions of Others' Pain." *PLOS ONE* 7, no. 11 (2012): 1–8.
Tropiano, Stephen. *The Prime-Time Closet: A History of Gays and Lesbians on TV*. New York: Applause Theatre Book Publishers, 2002.
Turnbull, Sue. *The TV Crime Drama*. Edinburgh: Edinburgh University Press, 2014.
UCLA Entertainment & Media Research Initiative. "Hollywood Diversity Report 2023." 2023.
Ussher, Jane. *Managing the Monstrous Feminine: Regulating the Reproductive Body*. London: Routledge, 2006.
Vidal, Belén, *Figuring the Past: Period Film and the Mannerist Aesthetic*. Amsterdam: Amsterdam University Press, 2012.
Vogler, Christopher. *The Writer's Journey: Mythic Structure for Writers*. Los Angeles: Michael Wiese Productions, 1992.
Walters, Suzanna Danuta. *All the Rage: The Story of Gay Visibility in America*. Chicago: University of Chicago Press, 2001.
Washington, Harriet A. *Medical Apartheid: The Dark History of Medical Experimentation on Black Americans from Colonial Times to the Present*. New York: Doubleday, 2006.
Washington, Myra, and Tina M. Harris. "Interracial Intimacies: From Shondaland to the Postracial Promised Land." In *Adventures in Shondaland: Identity Politics and the Power of Representation*, edited by Rachel Alicia Griffin and Michaela D. E. Meyer, 156–75. New Brunswick: Rutgers University Press, 2018.
Wegner, Gesine. "Relocating the Freakshow: Disability in the Medical Drama." *Zeitschrift für Anglistik und Amerikanistik* 67, no. 1 (2019): 19–36.
Weinstein, Anna. *Writing for the Screen*. Abingdon: Routledge, 2017.
Weinstein, Anna. *Writing Women for Film & Television: A Guide to Creating Complex Female Characters*. Abingdon: Routledge, 2023.
West, Emily, and R. J. Knight. "Mothers' Milk: Slavery, Wetnursing, and Black and White Women in the Antebellum South." *Journal of Southern History* 83, no. 1 (2017): 37–68.

Wilks, Lauren. "Is Grey's Anatomy on the Wave? A Feminist Textual Analysis of Meredith Grey and Cristina Yang." Thesis, Trinity University, 2012.

Woods, Faye. *Period Drama*. Edinburgh: Edinburgh University Press, 2022.

Wu, Ellen D. *The Color of Success: Asian Americans and the Origins of the Model Minority*. Princeton: Princeton University Press, 2014.

Yoshinaga, Ida. "Seven Inquiries on the Antediluvian Labour Market of Cinematic 'SF Auteurs' and *Blade Runner 2049*." *Science Fiction Film and Television* 13, no. 1 (2021): 128–34.

Zehr, Howard. *Changing Lenses: A New Focus for Crime and Justice*. Scottdale: Herald Press, 1990.

Zehr, Howard. *The Little Book of Restorative Justice*. The Little Books of Justice and Peacebuilding Series. New York: Good Books, 2015.

Zipes, Jack. "Why Fantasy Matters Too Much." *CLC Web: Comparative Literature and Culture* 10, no. 4.3 (2008): 2.

INDEX

Note: Page numbers followed by "n" refer to notes.

24 27

ABC 2, 3, 35, 38, 59, 108 n.22, 158, 159, 169, 170
abortion, representations of 36, 65–8, 71
Actors' Equity Association 54–5
Adelstein, Paul 47
Ader, Tammy 9
AFI, *see* American Film Institute (AFI)
Alexander, Erika 8
Alexander, Khandi 127
All My Worlds 10
Altman, Rick 125
Amazon Studios 104
American Film Institute (AFI) 38
Andoh, Adjoa 173
Andrews, Julie 3, 151
Andries, Laurence 110
The Andy Griffith Show 60
Another World 9–10
antinormativity 87
Arnaz, Desi 59, 60, 161
The Artist 31
Arzón, Robin 182
Ashley, Simone 173
As the World Turns 9
audience, Shondaland shows 13, 34, 57, 68, 123, 168, 169, 171, 172, 181–2
Aurthur, Kate 7
Austen, Jane 135
awards, Shondaland shows 3, 34, 65, 86

Bailey, Jonathan 149

Baker, Kathy 129
Barker, Ruby 151
Barron, Fred 11
Beamish, Jamie 151
Beers, Betsy 3, 6, 15 n.30, 161, 165 n.5, 172, 173, 176 n.22
Bell, William J. 10
Benshoff, Harry M. 149, 150
Benson 8, 11
Berg, Gertrude 10, 158
Berry, Halle 2
Better Call Saul 92
Billings, Alexandra 99–100
Billinson, Jennifer 160
A Black Lady Sketch Show 4
Black mistress, representations of 68
Black motherhood, representations of 65–72
 abortion 66–8
 breastfeeding 69–70
 childbirth 68–9
 miscarriage 66–8
 postpartum conditions 69–70
 pregnancy 66–8
Black women characters, representations of ix, 66, 68, 71
Black women television creators, early
 Akil, Mara Brock 8, 16 n.45
 Boone, Eunetta T. 8, 9
 Bowser, Yvette Lee 8
 DeLoatch, Meg 8–9
 Finney-Johnson, Sara 8
 Goldberg, Whoopi 9
 Henderson, Felicia D. 8, 162, 166 n.25

Hervey, Winifred 8
Spears, Vida 8
Black women television creators, recent
   Barrois, Janine Sherman 4
   Brunson, Quinta 4
   Carroll, Nkechi Okoro 4
   DuVernay, Ava 4, 127
   Kemp, Courtney A. 4
   Oliver, Tracy 4, 89, 90, 92
   Rae, Issa 4
   Thede, Robin 4
   Waithe, Lena 4
Blige, Mary J. 58
Bogle, Donald, *Primetime Blues: African Americans on Network Television* 59
Borowitz, Andy 11
Bourne, Stephen 137-8
Boy Meets World 11
Brand, Joshua 43
Brandt, Michael 26
Braun, Virginia 110
Breaking Bad 26, 92, 120
breastfeeding, representations of 69-70
Brenneman, Amy 47
Bridgerton 3, 145, 146, 168, 170-5, 183
   behind-the-scenes 147-50
   color-aware casting 54, 60-1
   color-conscious casting 141-3
   desire and sex, representation of 151-2
   "Diamond of the First Water" 150
   franchise 170-5
   generic whiteness 137-8
   as melodrama 151
   poetics of genre 150-1
   progressive period pastiche 133-43
   queer ethos 145-52
Brontë, Emily 135

Buffy the Vampire Slayer 25, 26, 120
Burton, Kate 77
Byrne, Matt 126

Cabot, Meg 35
Cagney & Lacey 11
Cahn, Debora 6, 15 n.26, 23, 31 n.4, 40 n.14
Cannel, Stephen J. 31 n.6
Caroline in the City 11
Carroll, Diahann 59
Carroll, Rachel 138, 141
Carter, Chris 31-2 n.6
Catton, Eleanor 136
Cayne, Candis 98
CBS 60
CDA, *see* critical discourse analysis (CDA)
Chambers, Justin 5, 102
Chandran, Charitha 173
character flaws 38, 43, 84, 139, 161
Chase, Allan 10
Chase, Debra Martin 9
Chicago Fire 26
childbirth, representations of 68-9
cinematic auteurism 158
Clarke, Victoria 110
CNM, *see* consensual nonmonogamy (CNM)
Cochran, Robert 27
collective authorship 162-4
color-aware casting 10, 53-61
color-blind casting, *see* color-aware casting
consensual nonmonogamy (CNM) 89
contraception 66
Coolidge, Martha 2
Corday, Ted 10
Cosby, Bill 59
The Cosby Show 8, 72
The Count of Monte Cristo 26
Craig, Cairns 134-5

Crane, David   11
Crichton, Michael   43
Crime Story   31 n.6
critical discourse analysis (CDA)   178–9
Crossroads   2
Crouch, Blake   122
CROWN Act   57, 58
Cruz, Matthew   89
cultural impact, Shondaland shows   66, 71, 87, 174, 178
Cusick, Henry Ian   48
Cuts   8

Daly, Tim   47
Dance Dreams: Hot Chocolate Nutcracker   170
Dane, Eric   100
Davies, Andrew   136
Davis, Alex Blue   105
Davis, Tamra   2
Davis, Viola   38, 57, 58, 62 n.14, 63 nn.15–16, 89, 110, 121
Days of Our Lives   10
Deggans, Eric   61
Dempsey, Patrick   1, 47, 69
Designing Women   11
Desilu Productions   60
de Wilde, Autumn   136
Dexter   92
Dharma & Greg   11
Diagnosis Murder   25
Diaz, Guillermo   29, 126
The Dick Van Dyke Show   60
A Different World   9
Diggs, Taye   45
The Diplomat   23–4, 30
Disney+   169
Drew, Sarah   37
Dr. Quinn, Medicine Woman   11
Dyer, Richard   139
Dynasty   11
Dynevor, Phoebe   151

early women television creators and writers
   Ball, Lucille   10, 59, 60, 161
   Berg, Gertrude   10, 158
   Davis, Madelyn Pugh   10, 166 n.32
   Nixon, Agnes   9
   Phillips, Irna   9, 10
Edelman, Lee   90
Edwards, Kelly   8
Elliot, Jaicy   106
Emma   136, 137
Empty Nest   11
ensemble storytelling, *HTGAWM*   10, 157–64
   collective authorship   162–4
   showrunner, Peter Nowalk   158–60
Epstein, Greg M.   33
ER   43, 101
Eve   8–9
Everett, Anna   139
The Expanse   123

The Facts of Life   11
Fairley, Michelle   174
fairytale, representations of   121, 124
Falahee, Jack   87
Falsey, John   43
Family   11
fantastic, as genre   124–5
Farquhar, Ralph   8
Fellowes, Julian   31
female characters, *see* women characters, representations of
feminism   33
   in *Grey's Anatomy*   35–7
   second-wave   78
   in Shondaland's later series   37–9
Ficarra, Glenn   24
Fightmaster, E. R.   106
"Fight Song"   180

Firth, Colin 136
Foley, John 184
Foley, Scott 38
Ford, John 159
Forster, E. M. 134
For the People 14 n.16, 121
The Fosters 108 n.22
franchise, *Bridgerton* 170–5
The Fresh Prince of Bel-Air 8, 11, 65
Friends 11
Frow, John 125

The Gallery of Madame Liu-Tsong 59
Game of Thrones 123
Garrett, Roberta 135
Gay and Lesbian Association Against Defamation (GLAAD) 86, 87, 94 n.1
Gay Media Task Force 87
Gellar, Sarah Michelle 25
generic whiteness 137–8, 141
genre 9, 11, 12, 22, 23, 43, 49, 112, 115, 117, 120, 129, 133, 134, 139, 141–3, 145, 171–2
  fantasy 121, 123, 124, 128, 130, 137
  formal (syntactic) dimension of 125–6
  hybridization 121, 124
  imaginative 122–3
  multidimensionality of 125–8
  poetics of 147, 150–1
  rhetorical (pragmatic) dimension of 126, 127
  thematic (semantic) dimension of 125–7
  visual pleasures of 136
George, Jason 104
Get Christie Love! 21
The Gilded Age 31
Giles, Rob 125

Gilligan, Vince 26
Girlfriends 8
GLAAD, *see* Gay and Lesbian Association Against Defamation (GLAAD)
The Goldbergs 10, 158
The Golden Girls 11
Goldwyn, Tony 29, 47, 55, 126
Grammy Awards 65
Grey's Anatomy 1, 13, 34, 42, 60, 98–107, 147, 159, 168
  "1-800-799-7233" 105
  "Bad Reputation" 37
  breastfeeding 69–70
  childbirth 68, 69
  color-aware casting 53
  cultural folklore 129
  "The Distance" 128, 129
  "Elevator Love Letter" 36
  "Every Day Is a Holiday (with You)" 66–7
  "The Face of Change" 102
  family shame 98–9
  "Fear (of the Unknown)" 37
  feminism in 35–7
  "Fight the Power" 68
  "The Great Pretender" 104
  "A Hard Day's Night" 77, 79
  humanism in 35–7
  miscarriage 68
  motherhood 66, 77–84
  "The Name of the Game" 70
  "Out of Nowhere" 105
  pathologizing gaze 99
  plots 46–8
  postpartum conditions 70–1
  pregnancy 66–7
  setups 44–6
  "Sledgehammer" 36
  "Song Beneath the Song" 123
  "Sorry Doesn't Always Make It Right" 70
  "This Is Why We Fight" 37
  "The Time Warp" 82

"Today Was a Fairytale"   106
    trans characters   99–103
    trans narratives,
        shifting   98–107
    "What Have I Done to Deserve
        This?"   69
    "Where the Boys Are"   99–100
    "Wishin' and Hopin'"   81–3
    women in   4–7
    world of   43
Griffin, Rachel Alicia   158, 159
Griffin, Sean   149, 150
Gross, Terry   54
Guiding Light   9

Haas, Derek   26
Haley, Alex   59
Hanalis, Blanche   11
Harrington, Ellen   61
Hartley, Mariette   129
Hathaway, Anne   2–3
Hayden, Jay   125
HBO   159
    A Black Lady Sketch Show   4
    The White Lotus   4
Heigl, Katherine   5, 36, 46–7,
    79, 124
Henry, Gregg   29
heritage film   133–6, 139
Hickey, Andrew   31 n.6
Higson, Andrew   136–7
    "Re-Presenting the National
        Past: Nostalgia and
        Pastiche in the Heritage
        Film,"   133–4
Hill Street Blues   25
Hinds, Carolyn   61
Hinton, Jerrika   128
*A History of Rock Music in 500
    Songs*   31 n.6
Hitchcock, Alfred   159
HIV   89
homophobia   116–17
    internalized   111

hormone replacement therapy
    (HRT)   99, 104
horror, representations in
    Shondaland shows   121,
    124–8, 130, 171
House of Cards   95 n.16
Howards End   134
How to Get Away with Murder
    (*HTGAWM*)   2, 3, 9, 12,
    57, 58, 60, 121, 147, 148,
    166 nn.18, 30
    ensemble storytelling
        in   10, 157–64
    feminism in   38–9
    humanism in   38–9
    "I Hate the World"   89
    "I Love Her"   39
    "I'm the Murderer"   110
    "Lahey v. Commonwealth of
        Pennsylvania"   94 n.11
    marriage   90
    "Nobody Else Is Dying"   39
    queer character representation,
        respectability
        politics   87, 89, 90, 92,
        93, 94 nn.10, 11
    restorative justice   110–18
    retributive justice   110–18
    villains   92, 93
HRC, *see* Human Rights
    Campaign (HRC)
HRT, *see* hormone replacement
    therapy (HRT)
HTGAWM, *see How to Get Away
    with Murder* (*HTGAWM*)
humanism   33–5, 107 n.6
    in *Grey's Anatomy*   35–7
    in Shondaland's later
        series   37–9
humanistic female characters   33–9
Human Rights Campaign
    (HRC)   86, 94 n.2
Human Rights Law, New York
    City   54

Index

hysterectomy, representation of 67, 68

I Love Lucy 10, 158–61, 164, 166 n.32
 color-aware casting 59–60
In the House 8
Introducing Dorothy Dandridge 2
Inventing Anna 3, 159, 170
I Spy 59
It's a Living 11

Jacobs, Michael 11
The Jazz Singer 21
Jhabvala, Ruth Prawer 134
Julia 59

Kaplan, E. Ann 78–9
Karlyn, Kathleen Rowe 80–1
Kasim, Tunji 173
Kate & Allie 11
Kelley, Mike 26
Keyser, Christopher 11
The Kings of Napa 4
Kinnear, Rory 23
Knight, T. R. 46, 79
Kohan, Jenji 103, 120

L.A. Law 11
Latifah, Queen 8
Lavender Scare 95 n.17
Laverne & Shirley 8
LGBTQ+ characters
 representation of 12, 86, 87, 91, 92, 99, 117, 149
 as villains 94
Little House on the Prairie 11
Living Single 8
Lois & Clark 11
Lorre, Chuck 11
Lowes, Katie 126
Lupo, Frank 31 n.6

McDonald, Audra 37, 45

McKidd, Kevin 6, 129
Mad Men 120
Malina, Joshua 38
Mama's Family 11
Mann, Michael 31 n.6
Marinis, Meg 66
marriage, representations of 6, 36, 39, 59–61, 95 n.16, 146, 147, 171, 174
 same-sex marriage 90
Marshall, Garry 2
Martin, Brett 120
The Mary Tyler Moore Show 10
maternal rights disparities 66
Meszaros, E. L. 145–6
Meyer, Michaela 158–60
miscarriage, representations of 66–8
Mission Impossible 60
Moesha 8
Moggach, Deborah 135
Monk, Claire 135
Mooney, Debra 29
Moore, Demi 72
Mork & Mindy 8
Morrisett, Lloyd 10
mothers, representations of 65–72
 monstrous mother 77–84
MTM Enterprises 10
Murphy Brown 11
Mylchreest, Corey 174
My So-Called Life 11
My Three Sons 60

NAACP Image Award for Outstanding Drama Series 38
Nardini, Nicholas 91
narrative arcs 47–9, 88
narrative pace of television series, tracking 24–6
narrative pacing, of *Scandal* 24–31
National Broadcast Association 2
The Nat "King" Cole Show 59

NBC 9
Netflix 2, 122, 123, 159
    Bridgerton 3, 54, 60-1, 133-52,
        168, 170-5, 183
    Dance Dreams: Hot Chocolate
        Nutcracker 170
    Inventing Anna 3, 159, 170
    Orange Is the New Black 103
    Queen Charlotte: A Bridgerton
        Story 3, 133, 159,
        171, 172
    The Residence 170
    Sense8 104
    Shondaland's move to 169-70
    Shonda Rhimes X
        Peloton 184-5
    Squid Game 183
New Amsterdam 71
Newman, Michael 157, 160
non-Todorovian fantasy 128-9
Nowalk, Peter 9, 38, 39, 57, 89,
    110, 160-3, 166 nn.18,
    30
Nurses 11

Off the Map 14 n.16, 121
Oh, Sandra 1, 3, 6, 36, 47, 79, 129
One on One 9
Oppenheimer, Jess 10, 158-61,
    164, 167 n.32
Orange Is the New Black 103
Ovendon, Julian 146

Page, Regé-Jean 151, 171, 173
parenthood, representations
    of 37, 83
Parker, Alan 134
The Parkers 8
Party of Five 11
Pascua, Matt 102
Patterson, Benjamin 104
Patton, Rachel 180
Peabody Award for Excellence in
    Television 38

Peloton, collaboration with
    Shondaland 177-85
Pennette, Marco 11
period drama 133-9, 141-3, 145
Perry, Jeff 28, 48, 87
Peters, Bernadette 129
Phelan, Tony 74 n.17, 75 n.40, 81,
    85 n.15, 104, 106, 108 n.22
Pickens, James, Jr. 5, 83
Pidduck, Julianne 135
Pilcher, Marc 173
pilot episodes, crafting of 1, 5, 13,
    38, 42, 77, 140, 150
plots, in Shondaland series
    episodes 22-4, 28, 35,
    43, 44, 46-7, 104, 115,
    121, 127, 162
Pompeo, Ellen 1, 36, 43, 53, 77,
    100, 129
Porteus, Ned 146
postpartum conditions,
    representations of 70-1
pregnancy, representations of 66-8
Pride and Prejudice 74, 135
The Princess Diaries 2: Royal
    Engagement 2, 9,
    129, 172
    cultural folklore 129
    feminism in 35, 37
    humanism in 35, 37
Private Practice 3, 12, 34, 42-8, 159
    abortion, representation of 68
    "Another Second Chance" 68
    childbirth, representation of 68
    "Did You Hear What Happened
        to Charlotte King?" 127
    "A Family Thing" 37
    feminism in 37, 39
    horror 126, 127
    humanism in 37, 39
    motherhood, representation
        of 66
    plots 47-9
    setups 45, 46

"Vermont Is for Lovers,
  Too" 127
  world of 43
procedural dramas, hidden fantastic
  modalities of 120–30

*Queen Charlotte: A Bridgerton
  Story* 3, 133, 142, 143,
  159, 168, 171–5
queerbaiting 152
  definition of 146–7
Quinn, Julia 147, 170

Rabbit Hole 24, 30
race and racism 4, 26, 29, 53–5,
  59, 61, 67–9, 111, 112,
  115–16, 118, 125, 133,
  141, 173
  medical 69, 71
  systemic 116
radio stories 9
Rae, Issa 4
RAINN, *see* Rape, Abuse and
  Incest National
  Network (RAINN)
Rape, Abuse and Incest National
  Network (RAINN) 126
Rater, Joan 74 n.17, 75 n.40, 81, 85
  n.15, 104, 106, 108 n.22
Raver, Kim 6, 106
Recursion 122
reproductive labor 66
reproductive rights violations 66
Requa, John 24
The Residence 170
The Resident 71
respectability politics 86–94
  definition of 86
  dehumanizing 94
  mechanical adoption of 94
restorative justice (RJ)
  background of 111–12
  in crime cinema 112
  culture and 112

definition of 113–15
emotional expression and 115
homophobia and 116–17
race/racism and 115–16
representations of, in
  HTGAWM 110–18
sexuality and 116–17
shame and 116–17
television representations
  of 112–13
retributive justice 110–18
Revenge 26
Rhimes, Shonda, films
  Crossroads 2
  *Introducing Dorothy
    Dandridge* 2
  *The Princess Diaries 2: Royal
    Engagement* 2, 9, 35,
    37, 129
Ricamora, Conrad 87
Richards, J. August 80
RJ, *see* restorative justice (RJ)
Robe, Blythe 70
Robinson, Julie Anne 150
Rodham Clinton, Hillary 34
A Room with a View 134
Roots 59
Rosheuvel, Golda 142, 148–9, 173
Russell, Keri 23

St. Elsewhere 43
same-sex marriage 90
Sanditon 136
Sandoval, Miguel 23
Sarandos, Ted 169
Scandal 2, 3, 12, 13 n.7, 21–31,
  42–9, 60, 121, 125–7, 147,
  159–61, 163, 166 n.30,
  168, 170
  "Allow Me to Reintroduce
    Myself" 94 n.11
  "Any Questions?" 126
  "Baby, It's Cold Outside" 67
  children 91

color-aware casting 55–7
feminism in 38, 39
"Happy Birthday Mr. President" 55
horror 126
humanism in 38, 39
marriage 90
motherhood 66
narrative pacing 26–31
"Nobody Likes Babies" 91
"People Like Me" 91
plots 47–9
"Put a Ring on It" 90
respectability 86–93, 94 nn.10, 11
setups 45–6
villains 91–3
world of 43
Scarecrow and Mrs. King 11
Scorsone, Caterina 127
Scrubs 43
second-wave feminism 78
Sense8 104
Sepinwall, Alan 120
serialization 31 n.6, 157, 164
Sesame Street 10–11
setups, in Shondaland pilot scripts 44–6, 48
sex, representations of 89, 147, 151–2
Sex and the City 120
sexuality 8, 89, 110, 115–16, 136, 145, 147, 151, 152, 172
sexual trauma, representation of 71
Shapiro, Marc 122
Sharma, Edwina 173
Sheen, Martin 22
Shondaland, *see also* individual entries
audience 13, 34, 57, 68, 123, 168, 169, 171, 172
awards 3, 34, 65, 86
business practices 12
cultural impact 66, 71, 87, 174, 178

horror representations 121, 124, 126, 128, 130, 171
humanism and feminism, representations of 37–9
Shondaland, series writers and creators
Andries, Laurence 110
Bans, Jenna 14 n.16
Burgess, Bridgette 74 n.25
Byrne, Matt 126
Cahn, Debora 6, 15 n.26, 23, 31 n.4, 40 n.14
Carr, Patricia 74 n.20
Clack, Zoanne viii, 68, 74 n.15, 74 n.24, 75 n.40, 82
Cruz, Matthew 89
Culver, Emily 109 n.37
Donovan, Kiley 74 n.22, 107 n.1, 109 n.37
Driscoll, Mark 37, 104
Garrity, Bronwyn 75 n.34
Giles, Rob 125
Guzman, Austin 37, 128
Harper, William 37, 105
Heinberg, Allan 34
Hope, Mariana 109 n.32
Klaviter, Elizabeth 73 n.12
Lee, J. C. 58
McCormick, Kathy 68
McKee, Stacy 9, 13, 36, 69, 102, 125
Manugian, Alex 106
Marinis, Meg 66
Nardini, Nicholas 91
Nowalk, Peter 9, 38, 39, 57, 89, 110, 160–3, 166 nn.18, 30
Noxon, Marti 37
Olsen, Lara 74 n.20
Phelan, Tony 81, 104, 106, 108 n.22
Rater, Joan 81, 104, 106
Reaser, Andy 105
Renshaw, Jeannine 74 n.26
Robe, Blythe 70

Swafford, Erika Green 57
Thompson, Sarah L. 39, 163
Van Dusen, Chris 9, 13 n.7, 54,
    60, 61, 90, 91, 138, 141,
    148, 150, 152, 166 n.30,
    170, 172, 178
Vernoff, Krista 68, 106
Wilding, Mark 67, 91, 99, 127
Wong, Julie 70, 106
Shondaland, television characters
    Addison Montgomery 37,
        43, 125
    Alex Karev 5, 102, 103
    Annalise Keating 38–9, 57,
        89, 110
    Catherine Avery Fox 9, 37
    Cristina Yang 1, 36, 79, 129
    Derek Shepherd 1, 5, 6, 13, 47,
        48, 69
    Izzie Stevens 36, 79, 107 n.5, 124
    Meredith Grey viii, xiv, 1, 5–8,
        13, 15 n.25, 33, 36, 39 n.2,
        43–8, 53, 77–84, 100, 101,
        106, 107, 107 n.5, 129
    Miranda Bailey viii, 5, 7, 36,
        67–72, 104, 105
    Olivia Pope 27, 28, 30, 33, 38,
        43, 46, 47, 49, 55, 67, 91,
        94 n.11, 125, 127
    Owen Hunt 6, 129
    Richard Webber 5, 45, 47, 69,
        80, 83, 105, 106, 107 nn.6, 7
    Teddy Altman 6, 106
Shondaland, television series
    For the People 14 n.16, 121
    Grey's Anatomy 1, 4–7, 34–7,
        42, 53, 60, 66, 77, 98–107,
        123, 147, 159, 168
    How to Get Away with
        Murder 2, 3, 9, 10, 12,
        38, 39, 57, 58, 60, 87, 89,
        90, 92, 93, 94 nn.10, 11,
        110–18, 121, 147, 148,
        157–64, 166 nn.18, 30

Inventing Anna 3, 159, 170
Off the Map 14 n.16, 121
Private Practice 3, 12, 34, 37,
    39, 42–8, 66, 68, 126,
    127, 159
Queen Charlotte: A Bridgerton
    Story 3, 133, 159, 171, 172
Scandal 2, 3, 12, 13 n.7, 21–31,
    38, 39, 42–9, 55, 57, 60,
    66, 67, 86, 87, 90–3, 94
    nn.10, 11, 121, 125–7, 147,
    159–61, 163, 166 n.30,
    168, 170
Station 19 3, 9, 125
Short, Columbus 27, 47
showrunner 6, 10, 25, 33, 61, 84, 86,
    98, 106, 120, 122, 126, 141,
    149, 158–63, 165 nn.5, 15
Sirk, Douglas 159
Smith, Murray 93
Soap 11
soap operas 157
Soloway, Joey 103–4
The Sopranos 120
Soul Food 8
Spears, Britney 2, 14 n.10
Spencer, John 22
Šporčič, Anamarija 140, 141
Squid Game 183
Stanchfield, Darby 48
Star Trek 60
Station 19 3, 9
    "Ice Ice Baby" 125
Steinmetz, Katy, "The Transgender
    Tipping Point" 103
The Steve Harvey Show 8
Strickland, KaDee 126
Strong Medicine 9
structure 12, 124–7, 142
    pilot scripts 44–7
Sunshine Scouts 122
Surnow, Joel 27

teaser, in pilot episodes 44

Teles, Sandra 146
televisual fantastic-genre mixing, media archaeology of 130
Thatcher, Margaret 134
That Girl 10
themes 42, 43, 18, 125, 129
  in Shondaland shows 157, 179–80
These Are My Children 9
Thomas, Arsenal 174
Thomas, Rosemary Garland 99
Thompson, Emma 135
Thompson, Luke 146
Tinker, Grant 10
Today's Children 10
Todorov, Tzvetan 124, 125
Trachtenberg, Michelle 26
trans characters, in *Grey's Anatomy*
  deadnaming 100, 101, 103
  representation of 99–103
Transparent 103–4

vaginoplasty 98, 101
Vann, Amirah 39
VBAC (vaginal birth after C-section) 71
Verica, Tom 121
Vidal, Belén 137
visibility, history of 59–60
voiceovers, use of 43–5, 77, 103, 129

Walsh, Kate viii, 37, 43, 68
Walt Disney Company 169
Washington, Kerry viii, 27, 38, 40 n.23, 43, 53, 55, 67, 72, 91, 126
Waters, Ethel 59
Weeds 120
Weil, Liza 28
Wendkos, Gina 35
The West Wing 22–4, 29, 30, 43–4, 95 n.16
WGA, *see* Writers Guild of America (WGA)

When Willows Touch 128
Wilder, Laura Ingalls 11
Williams, Jesse 98
Williams, Vanessa 65
Wilson, Chandra viii, 5, 7, 36, 67, 104
The Wire 92, 120
Wiseguy 31 n.6
women characters, representations of ix, 5, 6, 33, 39, 66, 139
women of color on television, early representations 3, 4, 8, 33, 37, 38, 57, 58, 69, 175
Waters, Ethel 59
Wong, Anna May 59
women television creators and producers, early 7–11
  Akil, Mara Brock 8, 16 n.45
  Allen, Debbie 9, 37, 98, 170
  Allen, Jay Presson 11
  Avedon, Barbara 11, 17 n.58
  Black, Carol 11
  Bloodworth-Thomason, Linda 11
  Boone, Eunetta T. 8, 9
  Borowitz, Susan 11
  Bowser, Yvette Lee 8
  Coben, Sherry 11
  Cooney, Joan Ganz 10
  Corday, Barbara 11
  DeLoatch, Meg 8–9
  English, Diane 11
  Finney-Johnson, Sara 8
  Fisher, Terry Louise 11
  Goldberg, Whoopi 9
  Hanalis, Blanche 11
  Harris, Susan 11
  Henderson, Felicia D. 8, 162, 166 n.25
  Hervey, Winifred 8
  Holzman, Winnie 11
  Kauffman, Marta x, 11
  Kelly, April 11
  LeVine, Deborah Joy 11

Lippman, Amy 11
McMahon, Jenna 11
Ross-Leming, Eugenie 11
Shapiro, Esther 11
Spears, Vida 8
Sullivan, Beth 11
Thomas, Marlo 10
Zicklin, Dottie Dartland 11
The Wonder Years 11
Wong, Anna May 59
Wong, Julie 70
Woods, Faye 137
Wright, Joe 135

Writers Guild of America (WGA) xii n.4, 3, 168, 175 nn.1, 4

The X-Files 32 n.6

Year of Yes: How to Dance It Out, Stand in the Sun, and Be Your Own Person 2, 6, 122, 177–85
Young, Bellamy 29

Zipes, Jack 124

www.ingramcontent.com/pod-product-compliance
Lightning Source LLC
Chambersburg PA
CBHW060340170426
43202CB00014B/2829